SSN 14

Submarine Leadership

Greg, Thanks for the opportunity

Ryan.

Ryan Ramsey

To order additional copies of this book, contact:
Xlibris
800-056-3182
www.Xlibrispublishing.co.uk
Orders@Xlibrispublishing.co.uk
726143

SSN 14

CONTENTS

INTRODUCTION

'Half ahead, revolutions three-zero, starboard five steer one-eight-one.'

HMS *Turbulent* surged forward in complete silence. I could feel the shudder as the propulsor caught the water and whipped it into frenzy behind the submarine. I looked over towards the jetty. Everyone there was standing to attention, alert and staring at the submarine. I caught the eye of Captain SM, or to give him his full title, Devonport Flotilla Captain Submarines, who was responsible for the management of six Trafalgar class submarines. This man ran our support organisation, taking in administration, maintenance, and personnel at the waterfront. I saluted him, and after returning the salute, he then took off his hat and waved it.

It was time to get going, to leave Devonport and go and defend our country in our own covert and unique way. As speed built up, the chill of the cold February morning bit into my body, and for a brief moment, I wished I was in my cold weather kit. Mind you, I wouldn't need it where we were going.

'Navigator, steering one eight one at half ahead revolutions three-zero, ready to take the submarine,' I instructed.

He repeated the course and speed back to me.

'I have the submarine,' he said, as I sat on the top of the bridge and looked behind me at the retreating figures.

'Gareth, all good?' I said, turning to my XO (second in command).

'Yes, sir,' he said. His voice sounded serious, but I could tell by his facial expression he was as enthused as I was.

I looked to the left at the frigates and destroyers alongside in Devonport.

I bet they soon sail to the fight too, I thought.

I looked over to my right, towards Torpoint, where life continued as normal. Cars were moving, children were scampering off to school, and adults were hurrying about their business, heads hunched low against the winter chill. Occasionally, someone close to the water's edge would stop and look at us. We must have been quite a sight. I wondered what they were thinking. Everyone on the bridge was silent, drinking it all in. We all knew it was our last glimpse of normality for a while.

As we altered course towards Ocean Court, Devils Point, and Vanguard Bank, I stopped looking around me and concentrated on the job in hand. This was the point where there was the most risk to the submarine during the exit. I knew from experience that dozens of families would have made their way to Devils Point to say goodbye and get a final glimpse of *Turbulent*, but I wouldn't see them today. As the commander of this vessel, with ultimate responsibility, I would be watching to check that the navigator turned when he was supposed to, to get us round this tight corner out of Plymouth.

Tidal stream looks fine, the wind isn't having much effect, and both tugs are close by, I said to myself, mentally ticking off all the points I needed to check. *The pilot knows what to do with the tugs if we lose control. If there's a failure in the rudder, I've got a couple of seconds to react. I'm going to bring in the one tug, go full astern, and regain control.*

'Navigator, position looks good,' I said out loud.

'Port thirty-five,' the navigator ordered. We started this crucial turn.

The rudder moved, but the mighty *Turbulent* stayed where she was. I could feel my heart rate start to quicken. *I've got thirty seconds.* Out of the corner of my eye, I glimpsed the families jostling for position to wave us off. They'd be battling with their own emotions, torn between loving seeing those closest to them and hating waving them goodbye. Thank God, none of them could see the concern that the navigator and I were hiding. Then magnificently, the vessel 'bit' and started moving in the right direction. We could relax.

The wind was behind us now, and it felt quite nice, not like February at all. We passed Smeaton's Tower, Plymouth's prominent landmark that has provided guidance and comfort to so many seafarers throughout history, and next Mountbatten Pier. Then, in the distance, beside Mountbatten Pier, I saw them, my family, my wife, Corrinne, and children Olivia and Theo—three small figures on the horizon. They were waving. I looked around me, working through my mental checklist rapidly. We were in a good position and safe. I took my cap off and waved back at them with it. As soon as they knew I'd spotted them, they began waving back even more. The emotions flooding through me at that moment were so intense. I was so sad to leave my life at home behind but also excited and ready for the challenges ahead. My job is an emotional roller-coaster ride.

I'm going to miss them, I thought. I went through this every time I left on deployments.

And then it was back to it.

'Navigator, slow down here,' I said. 'XO, let's bring the boat in and disembark the pilot. Pilot, thanks very much. We'll see you at the end of the year.'

I shook the pilot's hand.

We'll see you at the end of the year? It's only February!

SSN (submerged ship nuclear) is the NATO's designation for the most powerful weapon a navy can own—a nuclear-powered attack submarine.

I was in command of HMS *Turbulent* (SSN 14), and she dominated my life for three years and four months of my time in the submarine service at the expense of everything and everyone else. During that time, we undertook two periods of the most demanding training the Royal Navy provides (and they are good at training!), eight covert patrols and one 10-month deployment. Exactly 484 people served with me (although not all at the same time), and we influenced one another in achieving outstanding results. It wasn't always smooth, but achieving success is like a marathon, not a sprint.

Command, the all-encompassing term for those who lead a submarine to conduct all these operations, is extremely challenging. The training and hours required to get you to that position are complex, thorough, and brutal. It has to be like this; in peace and war, people's lives are your responsibility. However, what a privilege!

The first time you dive in a submarine is unique. The first time you do it as a captain, even more so. You are in a platform more complex than the space shuttle, about to go into a void less explored than space, and on top of that, you have the responsibility of leading 130 other people into that abyss. The moment that the captain says, 'XO, dive the submarine,' a choreographed sequence starts that involves a 500-million-pound submarine, comprised of a nuclear reactor, thirty-seven major systems, one million separate pieces, and an arsenal of weapons. You and all that technology are making a complicated transition from the world we know to one that very few do. With half of my life spent in the submarine service, I learned to be comfortable never taking anything for granted and only trusting people who are as committed as you are. *Turbulent* was zenith of that career.

The focal point of my life aboard *Turbulent* was a 286-day deployment, where 237 days were spent underwater. During this intense time, all my leaderships skills were tested to the full, and we all, very nearly, didn't come back to tell the story. A series of challenges, many of which were presented to us by our ageing vessel operating in conditions it wasn't built for, challenged assumptions and refined what I thought I knew about leadership.

I am who I am. I can't change that, but I knew that if I were going to make the most of our people on that deployment, I had to be wary of mine and my team's strengths and weaknesses. I did that and got it down to a fine art, using that skill to create a strong team. Leaders must trust their crew to use their talents and then free them to do so. They will rise to the challenge and reward that trust. My crew certainly did that. Indeed, so successful was the team product and what we achieved on this deployment that I was selected to teach the world-renowned Perisher (submarine command course), where I mentored the student captains in the art. I used to tell my student captains, 'This is not about you and what you're going to do when you've qualified. This is about how you enable the next generation. Their success is your gift and your legacy. You must take people's development seriously and be seen to take their development seriously.'

While that long deployment only presents a snapshot of my time leading aboard subs, it is a perfect summary of the intense highs and lows of leading in a high-risk, high-consequence environment. It is for this reason that this book focuses on that particular period.

Many of the huge number of crucial lessons in both leadership and followership experienced on *Turbulent* translate perfectly into the outside world. It doesn't matter if you are running a submarine, a small business, or a multimillion-pound corporation; we all need to figure out how to work alongside people in a close, often-intense environment and help them grow. I don't claim to provide a silver bullet, a catch-all solution to every leadership challenge, but it is an honest account into how we achieved success and my personal input into that accomplishment. It's written from the unclassified diaries I kept during that period and shows the emotion I felt right then.

People let me take risk with their lives continually, and I was always aware of it, never taking that privilege for granted. A culture that discourages risk in their people will always be ineffective. In fact, you see it everywhere, even in the military, where the lack of appetite to take risk induces paralysis. It is impossible to learn what people can really do unless you allow them to properly explore their limits.

In the chapters that follow, I have described a progressive leadership and followership culture and the challenges that come with autonomous command. It tells our journey towards making *Turbulent* the best sub in the fleet. And it was! I have narrated episodes which have never before been described, and organised them around leadership ideas. It's both self-critical and critical of others. It has to be; otherwise, how do you learn? It is the truth, not fiction.

This book can help anyone who either is in a leadership position or aspires to be in one, not by telling you how to do it but learning from my experience. As a leader, we all have an opportunity to make a difference and change our piece of the world, but we must always remember that we can't do it without followers. If you are able to pull any idea from it that helps, make it your own and use it. This book will have achieved the aim.

This whole leadership journey was HMS *Turbulent*, and while my crew were everything to me, being part of her was at the expense of being with my family, who put up with me making the most of what I felt was my one *real* opportunity to make a difference. It is for this reason this book is dedicated to *all* the families of HMS *Turbulent* across the generations who let us do what we did and, in particular, my wife, Corrinne, and children Olivia and Theo.

Team Turbulent 2011

CHAPTER 1

Be Relentless in the Pursuit of Success

I knew I had been selected to command the attack submarine HMS *Turbulent* eighteen months before I joined, so I spent much of the time in the lead-up, thinking about how I was going to make a positive effect. At the age of 38, it was my first command after twenty years in the Royal Navy and the culmination of all my training and ambitions. I planned for it, I visualised myself in the new role, and I seized upon any information I could about how others had done it before me. Preparing myself both physically and intellectually was exceptionally important for me. Once I took command, people's lives would really be my responsibility. Until this moment, there was always another person I could turn to. Indeed, even when I was an executive officer or second in command, I could defer to my captain. Now it was me. I relished the challenge ahead and took great pride in knowing I would be taking command of this legendary submarine in January 2009.

She (and the navy always calls ships and submarines *she*) had an enviable reputation. Her motto was 'Turbulenta Hostibus Fiat', which translates as 'troublesome to our enemies', and she had always been exactly that since she was first launched in December 1982. I was acutely aware I would probably be the last captain as she was due to decommission a few years later.

At the beginning of November 2008, while at HMS *Sultan* in Gosport, Hampshire, on the nuclear commanding officers' designate course, which was essentially a nuclear-engineering refresher because Royal Navy submarine captains are not engineers, I received an unexpected call.

'Ryan, it's Captain SM,' the voice said. It was my future boss.

'We've had a discussion, and the decision has been made for you to take command on Monday,' he continued. 'We know that they are mid-training, and that's unusual, but now's the time. Are you happy with that?'

The abrupt change in schedule took me by surprise, but I replied without hesitation.

'Yes, sir, absolutely,' I said. 'I'll liaise with the travel people and get it sorted.'

The light at the end of tunnel was finally in sight after a long wait, albeit sooner than I expected and the context had now changed. I would now join one-third of the way through operational sea training; the team would be formed, although probably tired, and they still would not be fully trained or have demonstrated capability. That was good; we would do that together. However, it appeared they were behind the planned schedule. I hoped that light at the end of the tunnel wasn't a freight train.

Anyone taking over another person's team has to expect they'll be established in their ways, good or bad. If they're good, all that needs to be done is to adapt to be part of it. If they're bad, visible changes need to be made because they can't keep going in the same direction, thinking they are right. I would also need to communicate this with clarity. In different mediums, lead by example, both verbal and written, making sure that everyone understood in the manner that was best for them. If my team could understand the end state, then they can see success.

My task was not straightforward. *Turbulent* had been undergoing major maintenance, and the reality of bringing any submarine out of a situation like this is that it is always a struggle. Supporting organisations start focusing on the next project at your expense, and the team generally takes a dip in performance as they try to manage the physical aspect of getting the submarine back to sea. The whole process usually ends up being achieved at the expense of training. Then when the crew start the training process, they believe *they will train us*, whereas the reality is that it is more like—they will assist us with our own training. I knew this better than most because I had worked for the renowned training organisation Flag Officer Sea

Training (submarines) (FOST) as a command rider. I learned there it was all about ownership. Each individual needed to *own* their training as did the team.

When the captain is changed, particularly during training, it's usually because it is not going well and he is the cause. Anyone who takes over in a situation like that, stepping into something that isn't working, faces a challenge. However, rather like changing a football manager when a team is failing, it may not always be the case that the manager is indeed the problem. My predecessor's departure was purely an issue of timing and enabling future success; however, it would be easy for people to read it differently. I was aware that there might be misconceptions here. I was also conscious of my own approach. Some potential submarine captains fall into the trap of believing that because they've passed the Perisher submarine command course they should automatically be given respect and can step in anywhere and command. You can step into the role, but those who think there is no need to earn respect and it's about 'your moment' get it very wrong.

My eyes were already open—this wasn't about the position of 'captain'. I would earn the respect of my team. Even though at present my outlook already differed from theirs, we would be successful together. Their focus would be on becoming fully trained. For me, it was on success on the forthcoming patrol, which was months away. The training was just one step in that journey. We had time, although it would appear as though we didn't have as much as we needed.

Within hours of receiving the call, I was on a flight to Glasgow. I was met at the airport by HMS *Turbulent*'s coxswain, Chief Petty Officer Martyn 'Paddy' Parsons. The coxswain is without a doubt a key person in the submarine team. The United States Navy calls them the chief of the boat, and they genuinely are. If it didn't feel quite real before, it certainly started to do so now as I stepped into the front seat of the official car.

Unusual for the Royal Navy, I thought.

It must have been a hire car. They were obviously attempting to make what they believed were the right first impression. The superficial trappings of command don't interest me. They'd learn that in time.

As we headed north, away from the Glasgow suburbs, towards the Faslane naval base on the Clyde, I had almost too much time to think about what lay ahead of me that day. I knew that I had to get to know my team and my team had to get to know me. This was about *us*—but that would take time, and that was the one thing we didn't have. First though, I needed us all to get through the first day.

When a nuclear-powered submarine changes hands, there is a well-worn routine, which takes about twenty minutes. I knew roughly what to expect because I'd spoken earlier with a frigate captain who was about to 'drive' an aircraft carrier, and he had told me about what happened.

'It can be a bit of an emotional roller coaster,' he told me. 'It doesn't take long, but it is best to prepare yourself. Once you've taken command, your predecessor leaves, and the crew cheer him over the gangway. The size of the cheer indicates the popularity of the previous captain, and that can be a bit daunting. Equally, don't talk too long. Some talk way too much about what they are going to do/change—it's not necessary.'

I'd be taking over a well-established tough crew. They might well not be the same as me, and some might dislike the fact I was the new boss and relatively young at 38 years old. The position of commander itself represented an old-fashioned, increasingly obsolete authority figure. Being popular was not high up on my priority list though. What was essential for me was to be respected and to have the trust and loyalty of my crew.

I arrived at Faslane in the late afternoon. The ground was wet after a recent shower, and the clouds were dark and low in the sky. My first sight of HMS *Turbulent*, or Turbs as she is affectionately known, was incredible.

There she is, I thought. *Time to walk the walk.*

Except it wasn't. Even though I was itching to go on board and do something, anything, just to get my hands dirty, protocols had to be observed. All ships and submarines follow the same process. The new captain doesn't go aboard until he takes command, and as I discovered and sympathised with, the man I was taking over from seemed in no hurry to hand over.

I had to be patient and contain my enthusiasm. I went to the wardroom in HMS *Neptune* (the submarine base officers' mess). Dan Clarke, the second in command, came up to meet me.

'Good to see you, sir,' he said. 'We're having drinks with the current captain in the bar downstairs. There'll be a car to pick you up here at 08.45 and bring you down to the boat.'

'Cheers, Dan. Enjoy yourself and see you tomorrow,' I replied.

I stayed in my cabin (and yes, rooms are called cabins even ashore), preparing my kit and reflecting on all the advice I had sought and been provided with by others. I reflected on the words of my friend Mike Bernacchi, the captain of the USS *Alexandria*.

He said, 'Ryan, remember two things: Firstly, don't change who you are, but be aware of yourself. Secondly, you are not their friend, their brother, or their father—you're their captain, which is all of those and none.'

The next morning, when I arrived at Turbs, Dan met me with a salute as I went over the gangway. Then there was some polite briefing from Dan about what was going to happen next, which was simply part of a historical formal process of taking command.

Finally, I was shown into the captain's cabin. The captain's cabin is traditionally the only single cabin on board, but it is tiny. It is sited opposite the radio room, next to the control room and the reactor compartment. It's the same on most attack submarines the world over. It allows the captain to get to the control room instantly because when things go wrong, they generally go wrong quickly.

'Welcome, Ryan,' the captain said, stepping forward to shake my hand.

Even though the captain was friendly enough, I could sense immediately that this was not a great day for him. His demeanour was that of a man who was not ready to give up his command, and seeing me chomping at the bit to take over couldn't have helped his mood.

'Hello, mate,' I said with a smile, trying to sound friendly and relaxed. 'How do we take this from here?'

The captain stared at me hard for a few moments as though weighing me up, then nodded and replied in a flat tone, 'The submarine is in good material state, and the heads of department (HODs) will brief you.'

Then silence. The atmosphere in the room felt awkward. The captain turned and picked up a sheaf of papers from the desk behind him.

'Here are the combinations to the safes,' he said, speaking more briskly now, as though he had suddenly resolved to get this part over with as quickly as possible.

'Which one is which?' I asked, still doing my best to sound light and friendly.

More silence. Looking at him, I could see he was struggling. I retained my stance, pretending I hadn't noticed. I decided then that when I leave, I'm not going through this process. There must be a better way. I'll do it differently.

Our conversation continued on this stilted level for a mercifully short time before his XO, Dan Clarke, now my XO, came to say it was time to leave. The captain shook my hand along with a muted 'good luck' and followed Dan out of the cabin. I stood alone for a few moments, holding my breath and listening. Then I heard it—a huge cheer from the men.

I've got a big task ahead, I thought. That was quite a send-off. The captain might not have been particularly welcoming to me, but he was clearly a huge hit with *his* crew. I might have a long way to go before I really became their leader.

In a matter of minutes, Dan returned to my cabin. Sir, are you ready to meet your men?' he asked.

'Yes, Dan, I'm ready to meet our team,' I replied, relieved that part was now over.

As I followed him out, my mind was buzzing. I had no misconceptions about the scale of the task ahead. Out there, in the civilian world, the workplace has changed markedly over the past decade. Employees feel confident about telling their bosses what they think of them. Even though the runaway economic-boom years were over and we were now firmly in the post–credit crunch world, people were far less afraid of losing their jobs. Even half-decent employees knew they could move freely from job to job. Those with the most modest qualifications could rest assured that, all being well, there were always other opportunities elsewhere. This new way of thinking has seeped into the military too—although not fast enough in my view. The old order where the crew accepts the hierarchy of command without question had changed. People could and frequently did question things—a lot. For some leaders, that would be uncomfortable; for me, that culture was good.

This all presents a huge amount of leadership challenges. Those challenges are over and above the ones presented by leading more than a hundred men living together in a confined space for weeks at a time. Trafalgar class submarines present an environment like no other. It is 85 metres long, 10 metres wide, and about the same again in height (which is about the same length as a football pitch and about a fifth of the width). This is the cocoon in which more than one hundred people willingly spend weeks at a time without glimpsing daylight or speaking to loved ones. Stifling claustrophobia is a clear occupational hazard. Although potential sufferers are weeded out in the selection process, it is a challenging environment for even the most well-adjusted ones. Some people have compared life on board as similar to being locked in prison. It certainly has some similarities, being trapped in a confined space for months at a time. Then there is the daily threat of attack, drowning, or fire. Space is at a premium, personal space even more so. There is only room for a handful of personal possessions, such as family photos or a few books and CDs. The leaders and their men live in the same conditions, eat the same food, face the same challenges, and are constantly visible to one another for prolonged periods. The pressure can really take its toll.

I saw the task ahead as motivating the crew to work with passion, energy, and enthusiasm, ensuring they were armed with the right skills and right tools. First though, I had to find out what—or more importantly, who—I was dealing with. It was time to meet the team, together first and then as individuals.

I wanted to approach this differently from the start. Normally, most captains expect their entire ship's company to line up on the jetty and then provide a suitably rousing speech to the assembled group. I'd experienced a few of those from the other side of things, and while some of the speeches I heard were good, many of them were not. The trap that many captains fall into is to launch into a long-winded monologue all about him. They don't give out any real leadership message even though they are clearly trying to articulate one. It was these experiences that prompted me to decide to speak to smaller groups instead of the traditional inaugural address to the entire crew. I would get in front of a handful of people at a time and keep my comments to a minimum at the initial greeting stage. I didn't want to speak for anything more than a minute and a half. My kids were fortunate enough to have helped me practise this and could repeat it word for word!

I had told Dan this long before I stepped on to Turbs, and the crew had been duly arranged into small groups dotted around the submarine in their respective messes. The officers were in the wardroom, senior rates in the senior rates' mess, and the junior rates in the junior rates' mess. The routine was pretty much the same for each one.

I would walk into the room and introduce myself, after which I'd say, 'We've got a hard journey ahead. We will have some challenges, and we will be successful. In the coming weeks, I will take time to get to know you, and you will get to know me. In the meantime, I need your honesty and your commitment.'

The only variation in my patter was among the senior crew. I wanted to make specific mention about leadership with them because they were in leadership positions too.

To the officers gathered in the wardroom, I added, 'We are the leadership of HMS *Turbulent*. We need to lead by example, step up to the mark, and make our teams do great things. We are leaders because we are skilled and motivated. I look forward to working with you.'

That was it. It was as far as I needed, or wanted, to go for now. I also provided a written letter to each of the leadership team, incorporating a one-page outline of our ethos, with the instruction that this was a baseline and ready for adaptation. They could read it in slow time.

Although the introductions were brief, it was interesting meeting my crew for the first time. No submarine captain chooses his crew, and no crew chooses their captain. The team I met on that first day came from all rungs of the socio-economic ladder and was a fair reflection of society as it is today. There were those considered normal or average in approach, but equally, I was prepared for a fair smattering of men who would break rules or might be violent and have problems. There is a handful in every crew, and in my head, I already began to work out how I was going to deal with that challenge. In the briefing notes I had been given ahead of my first day, I could already see that the variation in standards of educational achievement was incredible, from master's level degrees in subjects such as nuclear physics to men who had a single GCSE to their name.

As I had brief chats on my journey around the submarine, it was good to see some old shipmates, whom I knew from my previous times on other submarines. I was careful though not to stop and chat too long. It was important not to impact on their daily programme too much on this day of change. One thought that I kept coming back to was that I had to find a way to lead and inspire each one of them, both individually and collectively. I needed to know about my crew, and that would involve making conscious time to learn about them and hopefully assist them on their journey.

The military is very good at training leadership and teamwork. It trains poor leaders to be average, average to be good, and the good to be the best. However, training is only one part of the mix; experience is the other. What experiences did I have to draw upon to assist me? Well, I am a great believer that your first captain has an enormous effect on you and sets up your future leadership style. He creates the norm, the placebo if you will. How they deal with issues—rationally or irrationally, with confidence or without, whether he controls events or allows events to control him, and whether or not he provides the example to his men—is the one that stays with you. Until you have developed sufficient knowledge from which to determine the effective or ineffective leader, you compare all future leaders against your first, and I was lucky enough to have had an excellent baseline.

My first captain was in command of HMS *Opportune*, and I spent eighteen months on his submarine. He was self-assured and very calm and measured even in the most trying of circumstances, which was, in part, helped by his tremendous sense of humour. He inspired everyone around him, although perhaps not in the heroic sense of the word. I didn't want to be him, but I did like his style. I really valued being part of his team and thoroughly enjoyed working for him.

While he was a brilliant starting point, one man truly stood out as *the* role model for me and made a real difference to my leadership style—an American called John Richardson. I met John while I was seconded to the US Navy in 2005. I had been selected to be the UK exchange submarine exchange officer with COMSUBDEVRON 12 (Submarine Development Squadron 12). This squadron of operational submarines develop and trial all submarine tactics for the US Navy, and there has always been a UK-command-qualified exchange officer there. It's a very privileged and sensitive position to be a Brit 'Perisher' in the US Navy. It was also a fantastic opportunity to be able to learn from a different group of submariners and provide an alternative view in return. By far, the greatest benefit from this experience, though, came from working with John.

John Richardson is an astounding man. He is a real people person, who was all about everyone else except himself. He is a truly selfless leader and a great mentor. His energy was incredible, and everyone wanted to follow him. He paid as much attention to the most junior submariner as he did to the admiral. He was an absolute master of the art of fighting the fights he needed to fight but then backing off and personally empowering others whenever was appropriate. He never became flustered. Indeed, I only once noticed the slightest sign of stress during a live torpedo firing against a hulk, but no one else did. Sometimes finding inspiration later on in life as a mature adult is not easy, but here it was, the example that I looked for. Nothing John did was to further his own ambition, yet his acts of leadership and followership did exactly that for many others, including me.

John encouraged me to be on board whenever a submarine command course was running. I was there ostensibly to assist with weapon firings and tactical development, but the real reason I wanted to be there was to watch those attempting to pass the course. By looking in and not participating, I got a real insight into leadership and decision-making, as well as what motivated a crew. I also spent a lot of time with the student captains and was able to learn from them too. Some were excellent, and some were not, but I did realise from my privileged position that the more engrossed you are in something, the less you are able to reasonably assess and decide. Sometimes you need to step back. I also improved my reading of people while they were acting under stress. It was an amazing learning experience, and John mentored me well, certainly more than anyone before or since.

What I most admired about John was the way he made a point of looking after the crewmen's families and encouraging the families' desire to be part of the team. He realised that it was a complete package. Often, very little is said about the families of submariners, but they play a vital role. Their partner/father/son might be away at sea for months at a time and often out of contact for weeks. That can put a huge strain on relationships and be stressful for all concerned. John had quite rightly surmised that easing this strain as far as possible was a vital part of the leadership role. It was an issue of respect. It didn't matter that the crew were being paid to do a job and put their lives in harm's way. They and their families had to endure a lot. I decided then and there that, when it was my turn, I would make definite steps in the right direction when it came to families rather than accept the status quo.

Aside from John, I also learned a great deal from the ten captains I served with before finally becoming a captain myself. The good ones definitely created climates of trust, but I experienced or observed many climates of fear as well. The worst example I experienced actually gave me one of the best lessons to take forward. I served for one captain who himself was the product of a climate of fear, and I often wondered why he had adopted this style, which seemed to me to be self-defeating. It suddenly became clear to me during a barbecue on a port visit in Gibraltar. This captain was reminiscing with a contemporary about a 'shouter' they had both served for way back when. They were both describing how awful it was working for him, yet here he was consistently replicating the same behaviour. He didn't realize, and nobody was going to tell him, but the coincidence was too much.

The ruthless reputation of this particular captain preceded him. Until I served for him, I had never really experienced this style of leadership. I had, however, seen the end product—fellow officers were 'maimed' by the same behaviour, or they turned into the same character. Of course, there are always positives if you look hard enough. He was good with the politics of readying a submarine for operations and managed the shore organisation very effectively. He was also an absolute gentleman when dealing with people outside his crew and when we had training staff on board. As soon as we were on our own though, he always returned to his ways. Serving under him marked the worst two years of my career. So bad that I very nearly gave up and left, but I decided against it in the end.

The first challenge was how he dealt with direction and guidance.

'You are to produce the plan to conduct surveillance of the enemy coastline,' he'd instruct. Broad guidance is great only if you are all aligned with the *how*. We all knew from the outset, we would be fighting not to find a course of action, or the right course of action, but *his* one.

This would almost certainly entail days of intellectual effort with no effect. We would culminate in the presentation of a reasonable plan, which would then be brusquely and negatively critiqued. There would be no advice on how to align with his thinking but just the assertion that it was wrong, not good enough, and needed to be done again.

'Is that the best you can do? If you think this is acceptable, you are absolutely mistaken,' he declared time and again.

Of course, he knew perfectly well what he really wanted. He just wouldn't share it. As a group, we would try again and again, and it would never be right. He also knew he had power in the management of his men's careers. Your future depended on his input. This cycle was destructive at best, and the lack of clarity in the purpose was soul sapping.

At sea, irrational anger became commonplace. If it were consistent, the team might have adapted to it over time, but it wasn't. He would rant about the smallest things; the team would then focus on fixing them at the expense of everything else. His style was very much to manage through his people, so the majority of his ire was directed at the officer cadre even though they were as powerless as everyone else to address the problem. When he woke, his mood would set the tone for the whole submarine. Unfortunately, it was impossible to predict. We could never tell what way he would go, but people were constantly on edge, waiting to find out. On many an occasion, while at periscope depth, nobody would change the lighting in the control room until he was awake, despite the fact it was broad daylight outside. It looked really weird—a dark control room, with two beams of light filtering through the optics of the periscope. But with the captain's cabin so nearby, no one dared risk it. The captain's cabin was linked to the control room lighting, and if he had not altered the settings, his lights would come on too. If they came on and he had been asleep at the time, we could all stand by. Perspective is lost when your world is a steel tube isolated from the rest of the world. If there is no external support to moderate the impact others can have, the pressure is acutely felt.

Inconsistency led to changes in behaviour. Some capitalised on the situation, while others did everything to avoid getting caught up in it. People suffered, and this cycle of toxic leadership had a massive effect. People became afraid to make decisions for fear of the consequences. We weren't paralysed; we were just not effective. The perception was the enemy was outside and within.

The gulf between the ever-increasing requirement for success and perceived achievement widened constantly, and it was obvious it was all going to come to a head during an operational patrol. Sure enough, as the patrol started, fear and anger stepped up a gear as the pressure piled on.

During this patrol against a very capable enemy, thousands of miles from any support, the true effect of fear, example, and imperative of action culminated in the most dramatic of results. Things went wrong. These moments are defining, and where leadership is needed most, the person on top needs to step in and take charge because the other team members can't. Rather than taking direct control and getting the submarine back under control, the captain let the team flounder while, at the same time, providing a barrage of criticism, which only compounded the problem. All intellectual ability to outthink the enemy was removed as he focused his own fear on his immediate subordinates. In turn, we spent most of the time attempting to respond to his reaction. No one was able to focus on gaining control of the tactical situation.

That event didn't end very well. Sadly, it was not a one-off either; it was one of many. This man thrived on providing fear; he saw it was his tool to achieve success. Sometimes people believe that style can work, but in reality, it didn't take us long to realise that the climate of fear was actually this person's own personal problem. He was transposing his own fears of failure into blame on others. The personal fear was that he had the ability to make/ruin your career—we were all career-driven, and therefore, we just accepted this as normal process. He didn't know any different and did not see it as either destructive or malicious, but that submarine was about him and not his crew.

This experience did at least provide me with the greatest preparation for command that anyone could have. I had visited the darkest place I could and survived. More importantly, I didn't change. One of the lessons I took away from it was how to delegate well within the capabilities of the individual and to make sure they understand. He demonstrated to me what happens if a leader doesn't provide clarity of purpose; a team can't give you what you need unless you tell them what you want. Most importantly, he showed what happens if you lose control of your own emotions and fail to set consistent examples.

My observations of over 100 captains from many nations revealed that there were two distinct leadership extremes and everything in between. Although many elements of their approach were the same, the most noticeable difference was focus—objective or subjective in emphasis. The objective leader focuses on his people and measures their success on what they achieve. The subjective leader, on the other hand, is only really concerned with his own progression and gains success from his team's success. There are, of course, some leaders who show a combination of both traits, but on the whole, people tend to gravitate towards fully embracing one style or the other. I had long since made up my mind that I would get personal reward from enabling others' success—that would be my legacy.

I had begun to mentally prepare a list of rules that would shape my leadership. I'd started to formulate them during my time with the US Navy, watching prospective submarine captains do their course. Then, as I returned to serve in the UK, I continued to hone them as I observed what worked and what did not.

My rules were:

- Be relentless in the pursuit of success.
- Serve your team—both leaders and followers.
- The need to succeed must overpower the need to avoid failure.
- Know the enemy—it's not always obvious.
- Plan, understand risk, decide.

- See simplicity in the complicated.
- Lead in defeat—it's the true test.
- Always have an exit—never go anywhere you can't get out of.
- Know the context—it drives how you operate.
- Celebrate success—theirs.

My view on being a successful submarine captain is to see the submarine through the eyes of the crew. It is often the only way to really find out what is wrong and to begin to empower the men to fix it. This is, of course, the sort of thinking you often see recommended in leadership books. The person at the top is encouraged to delegate responsibility and authority to subordinates so they can think for themselves and work together towards the common aim. In particular, it is the attitude everyone expects from the military. Officers are *supposed* to empower those further down the ranks. In reality, this does not always happen. Those at the top are on constant alert, scrutinising every detail and micromanaging each step. The long and the short of it is that the services don't like those in power to betray any sign that they don't know something or need to defer elsewhere. This can sometimes be at the cost of frustrating and disempowering the team. It probably goes back to the ancient perception of the leader wading into battle first, but that's not always necessary—it is necessary at the right time. If you don't delegate, people will never get used to taking decisions and enjoying responsibility themselves. You must train and support them effectively; otherwise, they will flounder, and that is destructive.

I wanted to ensure that the crew of *Turbulent* was the best team. By that, I don't mean the best we could be. No, I wanted us to be *the* best.

I wanted to create an environment where success was theirs and failure was mine alone, and I fully intended to make that clear at the start. The crew needed to know that I was not going to create a climate where mistakes weren't acceptable; mistakes happen because we are human. Negligence, however, was another matter completely, and I would not accept that. People need to know where they stand. After all, at best, it was maintenance of our reputation, and at worst, it was our lives at stake.

On the plus side, I already knew that the raw ingredients were there. Within the submarine service, there is a great leveller, and that is the earning of your 'dolphins'. You cannot be given them, and you cannot buy them—you have to *earn* them by demonstrating the requisite knowledge about the submarine. That means learning every system on board, understanding how they all interact in order to keep the submarine going, mastering all the processes and procedures that enable the submarine to operate, and recognising where you fit in to that team. To earn your dolphins, you have to demonstrate that you know this over a series of walk-rounds, showing a series of system experts and heads of department that you are knowledgeable. Once thirty-one of those walk-rounds are complete, there is then a board where superiors spend up to four hours, conducting a detailed examination of that understanding. When and only when the crewman is at the right standard will they receive their dolphins. By tradition, the captain presents the dolphins in a generous glass of navy rum, and the trainee has the option of downing the rum to get to the coveted prize. Most do. I still remember the defining moment I received mine. It was in 1991, and I was on board HMS *Opportune* in Copenhagen after a patrol. I also remember the sorrowful hangover the following morning.

Earning my dolphins was a significant moment because my pride in getting them confirmed to me that this was exactly what I wanted to do. I hadn't always wanted to be a submariner. Indeed, I had always believed I would follow in my father's footsteps and join the Royal Air Force. I had spent much of my early childhood on air bases and loved aircrafts. As soon as I was 17 years old, I applied to the RAF and was invited to Biggin Hill in Kent to sit an aptitude test. I thought I had done OK, but a week later, I was told I wasn't ready and should come back the following year. It was a huge blow, and I was bitterly disappointed. After drifting around for a few weeks, a school friend suggested I might like to try for the navy. To begin with, I dismissed it as I wasn't that interested in the sea and my naval knowledge amounted to next to nothing. There was a part of me that found it a little daunting too. I felt a bit out of my depth when it came to the sea, if you'll excuse the pun. Thinking I had nothing to lose since I had to wait around for a year, I applied. To my amazement (and shock), the

Admiralty Interview Board selected me, and in no time at all, I was off to the Britannia Royal Naval College.

After I left the naval college, I initially served on a hydrographic ship which I joined in Brazil. I found the tedium of going across the Atlantic as a midshipman with no apparent purpose disheartening despite the fact I loved the navy. On our return journey, we stopped in Tenerife, and the diesel submarine HMS *Otus* was alongside on the return from a South Atlantic patrol. The captain of the *Otus* came to pay his respects to the more senior captain on board the hydrographic ship, as was customary. The submarine captain was a lieutenant, yet it was immediately obvious to us junior officers that he had done way more than his very senior contemporary aboard our ship. His unsung confidence was very evident. The *Otus* submariners took us on an incredible night out in Tenerife. Even though it was their R & R time, their teamwork, loyalty to one another, and absolute singularity of purpose shone out. It was quite amazing, and I decided there and then I wanted to be a part of something like this. The surface navy was not for me—I already knew that. The submarine service, with its no-nonsense attitude and clear professionalism based on ability, not rank, was what I wanted. I consciously made a decision that night that I wanted to be part of a team like the *Otus* one. Not only that. I also decided that I wanted to be the captain of a submarine—nothing more and nothing less.

I learned a lot about myself while I subsequently worked towards earning my dolphins. I discovered, for example, I'm not good with detail, particularly technical detail. Most captains said that this needn't be a negative because, as I progressed to leadership positions, I could play to my team's strengths and compensate for their weaknesses. In order to do that properly, I had to get to know every individual within the team. On the plus side, I proved to be good at asking the right questions and developed the useful skill of reading body language and micro-expressions.

I didn't just accept my strengths and weaknesses as they were, though. I immersed myself in tactics to compensate for my lack of technical appetite and spent many thousands of hours of reading military histories, biographies, analyses of warfare, patrol reports, and tactical doctrines. Despite the fact that I had been a communications officer, a navigator, an operations officer, and a second in command, it was all preparation for one thing—submarine command. Now I had achieved that goal and hoped I was ready. Of course, now I was about to find out.

Submarines don't just sail off and 'do operations'. Teams plan, prepare, and rehearse. Whether they get it right or not is another matter. Tools used to plan change over time, but it became evident very early on that the planning process on board Turbs was complicated, serving itself as opposed to serving a purpose. This represented my first opportunity to make a difference, although I was wary about immediate change. Transition is a difficult thing to undertake or to experience; therefore, it was important to make some small but significant steps. If I could achieve some demonstrable positive change, the crew would see the benefit of looking for evolution too.

I decided to start with the planning process. I banked on the fact that the team would naturally assume that, because I had done advanced command and staff course and was therefore trained in that style of planning, I would expect them to do the same. In fact, they were already attempting to use that process without effect.

Simplifying everything and supporting the team were the first steps in rectifying this. I explained this to the team at the planning meeting.

'Men, the operational planning process you've been told to use is cumbersome,' I began. 'It's for a different level of planning. We'll simplify it by using an adaption of seven questions and warning order, which I have seen work well in other forces. The XO and I will start the process until you are all comfortable with it.'

Seven questions is a planning tool used by junior army officers; it is simple, keeps focus, and is very useful. I first learned about it in a bar in Helensburgh when I was chatting with an army colleague back in 2002.

'You lot are really awkward with your planning,' he told me.

He was in Faslane on Joint Warrior, a massive exercise involving many UK and NATO forces, and therefore, he'd seen it all happen in front of him.

'We use this tool called the seven questions,' he went on. 'At the end of it, there is warning order, and that tells the team what's going to happen and when.'

I was intrigued and asked him to demonstrate. 'We need something, and I'm certain that others would take this on.'

He proceeded to show me. Eventually, a long while later, indeed, just before I was in command, the Royal Navy took it on, although they added to it and changed it a little, renaming it the 'maritime estimate'. In my view, to get the most out of it, it was best to use it in its pure form as seven questions, which is what I now intended to teach my team. I judged it would give us more time, and in a time-deficient world where decisions are everything, this would help us.

After I presented the idea to the planning meeting, Dan and I then outlined responsibilities and how it would work. Looking around the room, I could detect visible relief that we were doing something positive about planning. I added two further points.

'I ask a lot of questions. I ask, not because I am testing you, unless it is a test of course, but because I need information and opinion to make a decision. We are a team. If the answer is "We've always done it that way", we need to question its relevance and value. We are a democracy right up until the decision is made – then we all go in the same direction. Let's enjoy the journey.'

HMS *Turbulent* was scheduled to sail at 9 a.m. the following morning. After a night in the officers' mess on Faslane naval base, I arrived at the submarine two hours before the planned departure.

'Dan, how are we doing?' I asked the XO.

'Sir, we're good,' he replied. 'The HODs will give you their department status briefs separately, but we're ready for sea.'

'Could you do me a favour once we depart? Can you arrange for five-minute joining interviews with each of the men, please?'

We were sitting in my cabin, and I was acutely aware we were probably both wondering how this was going to go. None of this would ever feel truly real until we went to sea for the first time together, with me leading. It would be another exhilarating yet nerve-racking first for me.

My first task was a briefing in the wardroom. This was the first briefing with my team, so I wanted to make the right impact. I had spent the previous evening looking at the charts, remembering all the times I had done this before and going through the what-if scenarios. What if we have a steering gear failure? What if there is a fire? What if the planesman puts the wheel the wrong way? How do I recover? I developed a mental model of how I would deal with each scenario based on what I had seen or done on previous occasions. Of course, during those times, I wasn't ultimately in charge.

After I had greeted the men, the navigator began the proceedings by giving his brief. He was meticulous in his presentation, going through all the necessary data in detail. We were about to proceed on operational sea training. This entailed a period of about four weeks at sea with a navy sea-training team on board to prepare and test us for war. These exercises are always absolutely exhausting for everyone on the crew. Aside from dealing with the constant threat of numerous opponents who are constantly trying to find our submarine, the sea-training staff simulates multiple damage control incidents and losses of equipment. It is all in the name of developing us as a team and normalising the worst-case scenario.

'Thanks for the brief,' I said once he had finished. Then, turning to the rest of the senior crew, I said, 'Men, we've got some challenges ahead. In order to maintain the programme, we need to make sure we do this safely. Take your time and make sure you talk to one another. Happy?'

My speech was short, sharp, and to the point. Everyone knew what they had to do. As soon as I had finished, I got up, walked out, and went to my cabin to get changed into my foul-weather kit.

Once I was dressed, had my binoculars around my neck and my hat on, I walked to the control room.

'Ship Control, I'm going to the bridge,' I said.

'Captain in the tower' came the reply over the microphone.

I have to say, hearing those words did feel very good, and I smiled to myself as I went to the bridge. When I reached my destination, I sat on the bridge roof.

'OK, Navigator, ready to go?' I said.

'Yes, sir' came the reply.

'XO, are you ready with the tugs?'

I heard the confirmation, and then we were ready to go.

Submarines are very difficult to move on the surface of the water, so we need tugs to pull us off the berth. As soon as they had done so, I gave the order to begin our journey.

'Half ahead, revolutions twenty-four,' I said.

I felt Turbs move beneath me. It's a great thing about nuclear-powered submarines underway on the surface. There is no noise, just an exhilarating surge of power as the propulsor bit into the Gaerloch and forced us forward. It felt sublime.

This is outstanding, I thought. *Now build the team's confidence–they'll be watching everything.*

I had a lot ahead. I thought back to some wise words from a former Perisher teacher: 'Prove yourself capable of driving or fighting the submarine once, then let them do it.'

He was right; basically, they needed to know that at that moment when it all goes wrong, I was going to get them out of it. For now though, this first part was about making sure that we had the team in the correct state in preparation for war. No one, including me, was capable of making every decision, though. I would have to train my crew to think and make judgements on their own. I would empower them. My job was to create the climate that would allow my people to unleash their potential. As far as I was concerned, there were few limits to what we as a team could achieve. We just needed to be relentless in the pursuit of that success.

CHAPTER 2

Serve Your Team—
Both Leaders and Followers

The journey to becoming fully operational and qualified to conduct standard operations worldwide was almost harder than preparing for our first patrol.

During the first phase of training, I didn't need to worry about searching for that opportunity to prove myself—they came thick and fast as we worked out how to adapt to one another in the demanding training programme. Sometimes it happens that the training is so complex that the situation can get away from the specialised team of trainers even though it has been planned with precision. This certainly happened in our case. Our greatest challenge occurred off the south coast of Devon, where we were honing our surveillance skills against our own forces.

It began when the periscope watchkeeper shouted, 'Go deep, go deep, go deep. Keep 60 metres.'

The ship control team went into their emergency procedures. As the submarine went through 22 metres, an alarm went off.

'Emergency stations, emergency stations, loud bang heard' came over the radio. 'All compartments carry out phase 1 damage control checks and report to DCHQ.'

The general alarm went again.

'Reactor scram, reactor scram, reduce electrical loads forward.'

Now there was no power. Then the alarm sounded again.

'Emergency stations, emergency stations, fire, fire, fire, fire in the WSC [weapon storage compartment].'

The officer of the watch (OOW) reported, 'Sir, the situation is we've hit a semi-submerged container, suffered a reactor scram, and are dealing with a fire in the WSC. Propulsion is still stopped, and they are attempting to go into EPM [emergency propulsion motor] drive.'

'Depth 42 metres, 44 metres, 46 metres,' the planesman broke in.

We're not in control, I thought. *The trainers can give us all our systems back, but propulsion will take a while. We don't have a while though. The depth of water is only 78 metres, which means we've got less than three minutes at this rate of descent before we run aground.*

'I have the submarine,' I said, announcing that I was taking formal control. 'Team, we're not in control of buoyancy. I'm going to use main blows and vents to control it. Ship Control, make a pipe to stand clear of main vents and blows.'

1.40 seconds remaining. Depth is now 58 metres.

'Put a two second blow into nos. 2 and 3 main ballast tanks,' I ordered.

We were still descending—*62 metres, 64 metres.*

'Put a 4 second blow into 2 and 3s.'

The boat shuddered as the air entered the tanks—*65 metres, 66 metres.* The rate of descent was slowing. I began thinking about the other parts of this problem. Firstly, we needed propulsion. Secondly, if we continued to pump out water from the internal compensating tanks, we were going to start rising. If we rose too fast, we would be heading into another danger because we'll be unable to manoeuvre out of ship's way. It was now a balancing act until the submarine was at safe depth and in control.

'Open 2 and 3 main vents. Shut 2 and 3 main vents,' I said.

'65 metres, 64 metres, 63 metres,' read out the planesman.

OK, we were going up. And so the balancing act continued. All the while, the other teams worked systematically at putting the fire out, dealing with damage control checks and getting propulsion back on line.

Once the submarine was in control, I said, 'Officer of the Watch, ready to take her back?'

'Yes, sir,' he responded.

I gave him the submarine back and went off to see how the teams were doing.

Hopefully, there won't be too many of those, I thought. However, we were back in control. Over time, the team would learn to deal with this and understand they had the freedom to do so without me having to jump in. Progression rather than perfection was key.

The other thing I was keen to do during the training period was to ensure normality and routine even in times of stress. I made a point of doing some form of physical activity every afternoon (as difficult as that is on a submarine) and frequently getting around the boat and chatting to the team. I introduced routines, such as the ritualistic cooking of steaks in the galley every Saturday night (there was no training on steak night!). It was sweaty work, but it meant I was experiencing what the chefs were and opened up a dialogue between us. I also played Uckers . . . a lot.

Uckers is a board game, which is a little like ludo, and had two roles—a break from planning and high-intensity operations and a way to overcome the boredom which inevitably happened during long transits. It promises strategy, tactics, and planning (and a little bit of sleight of hand) all in one neat package. It is just as enjoyable for both players and spectators, and we all played it a lot. It's a great leveller and a real stress buster, although when the finish is close, it can be stressful. I had a special travel board made so that I could play in my cabin against anyone who wanted a game. That, for me, was important because so many people walked past my cabin every day. It was reassuring for others to see I was 'relaxing', whether playing the guitar, reading, or playing Uckers.

It was at this time, during the training period, that the first of many challenges presented itself. Managing the team's individual focus versus the widespread fatigue felt by everyone became an increasing issue. They had been working with a high degree of intensity for nearly four months, and they needed rest. I had to take action. After some difficult conversations with my superiors, we stopped training without taking the final examination and returned to Devonport naval base. It was uncomfortable sending messages (or signals as they are known), attempting to explain my reasoning for delaying, but it was clear to me that the team was waning. Flag Officer Sea Training (FOST) Director

North, in charge of the training organisation, concurred, and we made our way back to Devonport. The mood on board was subdued. They all believed they could do it, and that was great as far as it went. Unfortunately, the trainers (and indeed I) were not as confident even though they did concede there was a chance they'd pull through.

I spoke to my team. 'Men, I've made the decision we're not going to do OPEX [the final assessment]. I want us to prove that we can be really successful as opposed to just scraping through. It may be difficult for some of you to understand, but it is the right thing to do at this stage. This is only one step in the journey towards operations, and we'll pick up the pace after rest and time with our families.'

Once we had passed and were fully operational, this would be forgotten about. People's memories are very short as long as success follows. Of course, if it doesn't, they remember forever! I was convinced I had done the right thing. I had shown compassion for my team and done what was right for them. I made sure that it was understood to be my decision and no one else's. The accepted view was that my team wanted to go on, but I wanted to wait and had been pragmatic in communicating that view. History shows my strategy worked. Fully rejuvenated, we passed well a short time later and went on patrol. I now had some great lessons for the next time I found myself in a similar situation.

After our first very successful patrol in 2009, we returned alongside to the Devonport naval base in Plymouth, buoyant in the fact that we had made a real difference and been an outstanding team. We had made some good changes to our team dynamics while away, aside from conducting demanding operations. Small examples of changes that had great effect were with the ship control OOWs and planesman. In the past, these two supplementary responsibilities were given to a specific job—for example, the leading stores accountants or chefs or medics were always planesmen, yet some just couldn't do it. It was unsurprising really, considering you need similar aptitudes as those of a pilot because you 'fly' the submarine. Unlike pilots though, there is no aptitude test, so predictably there were some really poor planesmen. Then, because they felt they weren't doing well, they became stressed about the fact they were letting the team down or that it might have an adverse effect on their career. Inevitably, the stress induced more errors, and the cycle continued.

I encouraged a change to the system so the right people, who were motivated by the challenge of the position and not by the fact they had to do it, were given an opportunity. In turn, this released others to go off and put their energy into the roles that they were mandated to do and wanted to do also. The net result was we enhanced our capability and had greater operational success against the most capable adversaries.

So powerful was our success that after the patrol, I was invited by the US Navy to brief the Pentagon on how we achieved the results we did. As I did so, I was careful to focus on the *we* as opposed to the *I*. I've heard a lot of mission debriefs, and in far too many of them, the captains talk as though it was only they that did it.

They'll say things like: 'I detected the warship and decided to close.'

What they actually should say is 'We detected the warship, and I decided to close.'

The captain didn't sit on the sonar set, report it through to the operations team, get on the periscope to identify it (although some of them do), put the navigational fix on to check he was safe, ensure that power was continuously available. *His team did.* He led his team.

I always use *we* unless it's describing failure, in which case I use *I* to talk about a specific decision that I took. Therefore, when I discussed our success on operational sea training, I was telling *our* story, and it was well-received. On a personal level, I was buzzing. Seeing people singing the praises of HMS *Turbulent* was great. We were rightly proud.

I returned to my home in Plymouth later on that week, and we all slipped into the rhythm of maintenance alongside. As a group, we all attended the Royal Navy Wardroom Summer Ball, which was being held in Devonport. It was always a great event, and this time was no exception. The officers and I, together with our wives and partners, soaked up the atmosphere, knowing that we would shortly be departing on a planned nine-month deployment after our successful training period.

I was standing at the bar, feeling relaxed and happy, when one of the shore support engineering commanders came up to me.

'Hey, Ryan, how's it going?' he greeted me. Then he said something that made my relaxed mood change in an instant.

'Have you heard? They've decided to put you in for a major repair. It could take up to nine months to complete.'

My first reaction was one of complete disbelief. I could barely process it, particularly after the high of the patrol. It didn't seem possible, and I'd certainly had no indication of this bombshell before now.

He could be wrong, I thought. Either way, I had to put on a brave face.

'Let's see how that works out,' I said, keeping my voice even. 'Right now I am just going to enjoy the evening.'

Of course, after that, the evening was spoilt. I was consumed with trying to work out the what-ifs. I could concentrate on nothing except contingency. Military officers are really effective at contingency planning. Years of training and anticipation make us really good at it. I plan contingency for everything in life, which allows me spare capacity for an unanticipated event so I can deal with it quickly and efficiently when it happens, hopefully without too much drama.

The next morning, there was nothing I could do. It was a Sunday, and there was no one around to answer the questions that occupied my every waking thought. It felt like a long day.

Early on Monday, I went to the *Turbulent* and moved around the submarine, chatting with my engineering team, attempting to keep the mood light. They had no inkling about the rumour, and it was best to keep it that way until I knew for certain. There was no gain in getting them to second-guess the options and decisions just because I was doing exactly that.

Pretty soon the message came through that Captain SM wanted to see me, and I walked up to the shore support offices. As I knocked on his door, I already knew what he was going to say.

'Ryan, sit down,' he began. 'They've made the decision, and you are going to go into long-term maintenance. Kevin [the captain of HMS *Trenchant*] will stay in position East of Suez until Simon [the captain of HMS *Talent*] is ready, and then he'll take over your programme. You're probably disappointed, but it is what it is.'

Disappointed didn't come close.

Unsurprisingly, submarine maintenance is complex. These ships of war have to operate autonomously, and the crew deals with much of the ongoing repairs effectively alone. Alongside, there are different challenges as submarines undergo standard maintenance, upgrades, and repairs. In the most part, the work is subcontracted out to civilian companies, who have different work ethics and entirely different priorities driven by economic and personnel factors. While my natural focus would be to drive everyone hard to get the submarine out as quickly as possible, the agenda of the outside contractors are different. These private workforces are never as motivated as a tight-knit submarine crew, although there were, of course, exceptions. Pushing the maintenance through to a speedy completion was going to be an issue, and it didn't help that we also needed decisions and consensus from a variety of sources.

Although I was gutted and apprehensive about the time ahead, I had to heed the captain's words. It was what it was. I just had to change my plan and fight for what I could.

By far, the greatest problem I faced was what would happen with my team. By the time I arrived back at the submarine, personnel management teams from HQ were already at work, removing people to put on other platforms.

A constant change of personnel is part and parcel of life in the submarine service. My job was to make sure that my crewmen's careers progressed and then let them go. Initially, that can be quite difficult, or at least, I found it difficult. If you shape a team effectively and they achieve results, of course, it's a comfortable place. However, right now I faced the prospect of losing nearly everyone, and there was nothing I could do about it.

Within three weeks, the team that we had fought so hard to form was ripped apart. I was left with a very small core crew of people. My challenge was now to form a team out of the crew I had left and those who had been assigned to me, to instil vision and purpose within them, and to train *us* to get back into operations as rapidly as possible once the maintenance was done. The more I thought about it, the more I grew to like this challenge. Now that I had got over my initial disappointment, I realised I had an opportunity ahead of me. I could use this protracted period of maintenance to build a formidable team from scratch.

Leaders generally have to make their mark with the team they are given, and this case was no exception. Once in a while though, there is the odd occasion when you can make some tweaks, and this was one of those. Although I would pretty much have to take the hand I was dealt, in terms of the crew I was given, there were a couple of names I really wanted along for the journey.

I had lost most of my officer corps and had done so willingly because they needed to progress their own careers and being in this state of maintenance would not enhance their prospects. I did, however, want to keep a couple of key people. The first person was Gareth Jenkins. Gareth was my new XO, replacing Dan, who had moved on following our first patrol. He had served with us as a watch leader with *Turbulent* during our first patrol, prior to going to do the submarine command course (SMCC) Perisher. I knew he would be successful, so I asked for him back. The second man I requested was Paddy, the man who had met me on day one. He understood his people, was exceptionally loyal, and would also challenge correctly. These qualities made him a great leader and follower. He had also demonstrably bought into the vision I had. The characteristics and skills of these two would supplement the current HODs, who would change soon. He was by far the best coxswain I had served with and would be instrumental in our success.

Now that the key members of the senior team were in place, it was time to plan, communicate my vision, and start the process of recovery back to operations. This would entail extended maintenance, rebuilding and training the team, ensuring we are prepared to pass the operational readiness examinations and then go on operations. I am a great believer in planning. 'Plan, plan, and then plan again' has always been a fundamental part of my psyche. We had to look further ahead than the repair. Our mission, once the repairs were complete, was 'to successfully regenerate and be fully prepared for an Indian Ocean deployment'. This meant HMS *Turbulent* had to be at full operational capability and the crew trained and ready to conduct all submarine operations. We had to be materially ready, have confidence in our systems, and fully satisfied that the basic skills and routines were in place.

In short, this was no time to sit back on our laurels. Learning lessons from when I joined Turbs, we would use the next nine months effectively. This was a crucial period of training, team building, and preparation.

I had a number of considerations to take into account. Firstly, there was routine. We needed routine to make the best progress. This meant matching the other organisations we would work with.

I addressed the HODs, saying, 'Team, there's going to be a great deal of change. We know how we work, so we need to make sure that others rapidly adapt accordingly. We can't have people second-guessing how we, as a group, will operate. Make sure we communicate so that they know and we all adapt. Executing the repair is vital, but so is establishing ourselves as our *Turbulent*.'

On a personal level, I also needed to be busy and constantly challenged, which can present difficulties. Most people might see this is as a strength, but in some cases, it's a weakness, particularly if the team feels compelled to try to adjust to match your approach. I'm a 'lark' and always arrive at work early—I mean very early—but I made sure that the team knew they didn't have to. I also take on as much as I can. When I passed Perisher and established spare capacity while I was an XO, I immediately looked for the next challenge, which turned out to be boxing. At 30, I took up boxing until I won a navy championship and then stopped. When I was with the US Navy, I filled my spare time after I had fully integrated by taking up flying. This cycle continues for me still. Those that could operate like that would take my lead; those that didn't, needed to understand that I didn't expect them to emulate me.

Overall though, team building was my priority. If you can build the team, enable the right ethics, and focus, you can achieve anything. Attitude is everything and, in some cases, can overcome capability. My thoughts initially turned to fitness training. I like to stay fit; if you are fit, you can fight. More importantly, if you are fit, you can think. I identified a new junior officer, the casing officer, as the man to take that challenge on. He was motivated, responsive to the challenge, and wanted to learn. Until we had another focus, sport could be it.

These activities might seem insignificant, but identity and focus were so important, and they worked. Peter started by taking the team on squad runs all wearing their HMS *Turbulent* T-shirts. HMS *Turbulent* was everywhere. If you weren't involved in it, you felt like you should be. The casing officer had done an outstanding job.

We used the simulators as often as possible. In each submarine base, there are a variety of simulators for tactical war-fighting, ship control, damage control, firefighting, and marine engineering. They allow crewmen to practise every credible and sometimes incredible situation, with the knowledge that they can reset it if it all goes wrong. The fidelity is so good that often when you get to sea, there is no difference.

Meanwhile, Gareth and the other HODs began a programme of volunteering for anything and everything as long as it involved the *Turbulent*. We hosted as many visits as we could, which went down very well with all parties. There are so few submarines in the Royal Navy today that all those who interact with them want to visit at some point. From a crew's point of view, these events can traditionally be really laborious because VIP visits take a lot of preparation. However, at a time like this, it was an ideal activity for us. Plus, it minimised the impact potential visits might have made on the other submarines. Best of all, it gave me the opportunity to sell HMS *Turbulent*. We took great pride meeting everyone and treated each visit, whether it was the most junior school trip to the most senior admiral, with the same intensity and preparation.

We marched in the Armed Forces Day 2010, not with the rest of the military at the main event in Cardiff but in Plymouth. It felt good, and we were proud. At the heart of every activity we pursued was the need to show the crew we were a success and should be seen to be so. Whether it was participating in a charity event or damage-control training, success needed to be recognised. We sent people to sea on other submarines, particularly in areas where we might eventually operate, to ensure that everyone was building experience from which to draw. In a short space of time, the team was looking for opportunities of their own without my prompting.

I also made sure that the crew took leave. They needed to be rested, and this was a perfect opportunity.

All the while, the engineers and I fought the fight to get the mighty Turbs back to service. My engineering officers used me well. They would argue cases and bring me out when the fight needed more punch to achieve the aim. One of our biggest challenges was that there were a variety of external stakeholders involved in this repair process. There were nuclear regulators, Babcock (who conducted maintenance), the MOD, Defence Equipment and Support, and so on. The list seemed endless. Each organisation had a different focus and rightly so; however, our objective was to refocus everyone to the fact that this was not an engineering project—this was about provision of defence. The chief requirement here was to return a war-fighting machine back to service to protect the country. I was not certain that we ever managed to convince all of them, but those that dealt with us couldn't help but be aware of our passion. We concentrated on this being *their* success story and not *ours*, but it was frustrating. Al and Ben were excellent, and their resilience in staying motivated despite having to fight process was incredible.

In March 2010, Gareth organised for the officers to undertake the gruelling Royal Marines assault and endurance course in the Commando Training Centre Royal Marines, in Lympstone, Devon.

'Why are you doing this?' Corrinne asked the night before.

I have to say I was starting to have a bit of doubt about this particular effort to 'lead by example', but I'd committed, and the reality was that deep down, I knew this was going to be a great team-building event and I didn't want to miss out.

It was a bitterly cold day, but we were all mentally and physically prepared for it. While we all accepted it was going to be painful, we also looked forward to the sense of achievement at the end, which we expected to be amazing.

Unfortunately, in the first part of the course and unbeknown to me at the time, I managed to slip two discs when I jumped off a 12-foot wall. The pain was excruciating, but adrenaline kicked in, and I carried on finishing the course before going home.

The following day, I knew something was seriously wrong as I could barely move, and I ended up in hospital, where I spent the next five days in a morphine-and-pethidine blur. I vaguely remember seeing Corrinne and the kids occasionally, and Gareth came in to visit. The bleak assessment was that this would take months to recover from, but I persuaded them to give me a 'quick fix', and I discharged myself at the first opportunity, promising I would return if it proved necessary. I had to get back to Turbs. Despite the fact that she was not in the best of positions, I was acutely aware others would seize upon my incapacity and use it as an opportunity to try to take over my command. I am certain that if the admiral had called me in a similar situation and told me to take over, I wouldn't have hesitated.

There was no way I was losing being part of this team that we'd worked so hard to form. This was just another challenge, and I would deal with it myself. I found a chiropractor who was able to help with my recovery one week later, which was just twelve days after the incident on the assault course. I went back to the submarine for the first time, albeit very slowly and carefully. It wasn't easy, but I wanted the crew to know that there would be no change. We were one team.

After I had made my rounds, I then went to the Submarine Commanders' Conference at the Britannia Royal Naval College in Dartmouth, much to the visible surprise of many there. Although I was in constant pain, I made sure no one could see it. I could tell that some of my fellow officers were really happy for me, but equally, there were others who were not because their window of opportunity was no longer available. You couldn't blame them; Turbs was a great submarine with an enviable reputation.

Six weeks later, I ran Plymouth's half-marathon against the doctors' orders along with a team of fourteen from HMS *Turbulent* (proudly wearing our T-shirts, of course). We raised thousands of pounds for the Children's Hospice South West and made sure that everyone knew; newspapers and social media were used to reinforce pride in my crew. Despite the fact that we still weren't doing the tasks we were trained for, our real job, we were still doing something worthwhile.

As the weeks rolled on, it became a constant battle to maintain the motivation in our close-knit crew. Everyone had one eye on the mission ahead, but that day never seemed to come. Gareth and the other officers continued to weigh in with as many initiatives as they could, but to be honest, we were just as impatient.

In July, I volunteered *Turbulent* to take part in a *Heston's Mission Impossible* series for channel 4, which is a show where he tries to shake up the menu in British institutions. The TV chef, renowned for creating quirky dishes such as snail porridge and egg-and-bacon ice cream, wanted to tackle the challenge of producing fresh and tasty food within the confinement of a submarine. Gareth and I vigorously pursued the opportunity despite our other challenges. We were nearing the end of the maintenance and repairs and starting the regeneration process training and getting back to sea; however, we could both see the enormous morale-building value the show might have.

Our dogged determination was rewarded, and we were selected for the show. Heston proved good fun to work with, and I liked the fact that he had the same attitude as us—he wanted to make a difference. The basic premise for the programme was we were not being fed well, and Heston came along to turn things around so we all ate healthily. Of course, from the film production company's point of view, the fact we were so pro Heston's ideas and got on so well was not 'good TV'. Great meals aside, what makes these shows a success is a little bit of friction. The director needed to create some tension; otherwise, there wasn't an episode, and to his credit, he did it very well. The defining moment of tension came out of the blue. On camera, Heston came in and asked me how he was doing, and I gave him some feedback. Then, without warning, the chef said something to the effect that I didn't know my crew very well.

His comments took me aback. I was passionate about knowing my crew, and this criticism hit really hard. It felt rather like that moment in the film *Lock, Stock and Two Smoking Barrels* when card sharp Eddy loses £500,000 of his friends' money at the poker table. The room seemed to spin uncontrollably. That, for me, has always summed up the sensation of how I feel when things go wrong. It was certainly how I felt then, with the TV cameras on, greedily waiting for my reaction.

Unlike Eddy though, I retained my poker face. I didn't react at all. Nothing.

Years of challenging experiences have enabled me to outwardly deal with moments like this. I consciously avoid any sort of expression wherever possible, despite how I'm feeling inside. During my brief time with Turbs, I had already had to deploy my poker face on a number of occasions, whether it was when I injured my back or though the disappointment of the lengthy maintenance. These events had to remain personal to me. Again and again, I told myself, 'It's never about what the issue is—it's how you deal with it that counts.'

Despite my refusal to play ball, the filming ended well. Heston gave us a potentially revolutionary way of increasing the endurance and standard of food using an adaptation of sous vide. In basic terms, we cooked the food first, either alongside or in the early stages of a patrol, stored it in a vacuum pack machine, and then froze it, bringing it out whenever we needed it. He also managed to secure us a machine for the entire deployment which we could use to demonstrate how successful this system could be for the broader navy. We knew it would prove successful, and despite the fact that the navy logistical hierarchy wasn't enamoured with the idea, the admiral was, so we were able to use it anyway.

On the final day, Heston threw a barbecue for our team and their families. The chef was very relaxed; he signed books and posed for photos. It was a great afternoon, and the families enjoyed it, which was perfect because *Turbulent* was nothing without the families.

The maintenance was now almost over, and we were not far from getting ready to go to sea. The *Heston's Mission Impossible* TV series would air during the first phase of our deployment, which was enormously positive. Our families would see what their loved ones did at sea and would now also be able to relate to some of it because they had met Heston. This would play a part in mitigating the long-term separation that was about to happen too.

It was now time to plan and prepare in earnest for the year ahead. We were to go East of Suez and arrive in theatre, contribute to the counter-piracy effort (among others), and provide UK Tomahawk (first strike) coverage. This was clearly a huge responsibility. If politicians decide they want to strike somewhere, they can do it rapidly, and that was down to people like us. It's worth noting here that the first offensive weapon into Afghanistan was from a submarine. Not us, unfortunately—it was HMS *Trafalgar*.

Our operations are exceptionally complex. We don't just set off and hang around an enemy coast somewhere, hoping for the best. We need to test all the equipment, test our quietness on an instrumented underwater range, test our sonars, conduct special forces training, practice Tomahawk cruise missile launches, and meticulously plan the journey from A to B, which may involve transiting through choke points. All this takes time, and it needs to be done in advance before we can brief the commander-in-chief that we are ready to go.

Although I don't generally have those moments when I gather the crew on the jetty, the time had come when it felt appropriate. I felt confident in doing this because I knew all my crewmen now and they knew me. They recognised *Turbulent*'s energy and motivation. They knew it was *the* team to be part of, and they were proud of it.

Surveying the crew in front of me, I felt a glow of pride as I began to speak.

I said, 'Men, you know I don't do this normally. Well done on where we are today. We've come a long way, but the hardest part of the challenge starts shortly. The commander of operations needs us to deploy as soon as possible. Therefore, we need to complete operational sea training (OST) rapidly. I've told him we will be ready in twenty-six days. I've told him that because we *can* be ready in twenty-six days, because we are motivated. We thrive on success, and we will not fail. I need you to buy into that success, prepare your families for your departure, prepare yourself, and get ready for this difficult journey. That is all.'

Looking around my team, I found two who clearly didn't buy into the vision. Body language and micro-expressions give away a great deal, and I am always keenly attuned to them. It's also a small world inside a submarine. The crew have conversations which eventually find their way back to me. After observing their reactions, I made a mental note that I would find out what needed to be done to help them buy into the vision or isolate them if they still couldn't. If the naysayers are strong enough personalities, they can be cancerous to team dynamics in any environment, and that goes doubly so in the close-knit, isolated environment of a submarine.

In most teams, there is a bell curve. At the right-hand edge, there are those who don't need direction and motivation who will proceed well. In the middle, there is the majority, who want to get to the end goal yet need to be shown the way. Then there is the third group comprised of those who aren't going to go whatever the situation. The problem is that leaders invest so much time trying to convince and change the last group without realising that it's at the expense of the second and even the first. Before you know it, the complexity of the challenge increases. The skill is to realise when you can't change the last group and adeptly isolate or remove them. Most importantly is to do so fairly and compassionately.

We achieved success on OST with a 'very satisfactory'assessment, and my team's hard-earned effort was also rewarded. We won the Rolls-Royce Valiant Trophy, which is awarded to the submarine that achieves the best result of the year.

All going to plan, I thought. Nothing was going to spoil the anticipation of our much-awaited departure. We were due to sail in the first part of January, and everyone was desperate to get going at last. We'd done a great job sustaining team morale during the long months of maintenance, but the time had surely come to do the job we were paid to do.

Of course, the thing about planning is that something will always happen, the plan will change completely, and you have to start again, adapting the plan to match the new situation. In the final few months, for example, I had had to make adjustments in aligning the maintenance and the crew-training plans because it was proving very difficult to schedule in everything towards the end of the period. We faced a number of challenges. It is not possible to go to sea unless everyone has completed the FOST training package successfully. In order to get to that level, there is a requirement to conduct a great deal of self-training where trainees integrate their team, learn new team skills, and learn forgotten lessons. At the same time though, I didn't want to burn out my crew before we started the OST programme. OST is a world-recognised, intense package that, while exhausting for everyone, prepares you for war and tests whether you are battle-ready for the most extreme situations. Meanwhile, I was trying to get the balances right on training when we were faced with a situation where the predicted maintenance schedule for January 2011 was slipping. At the same time, we were being pushed by the HQ to get on operations because they needed to plan strategically.

There wasn't just a requirement to be in two places at once; it felt like we had to be in up to half a dozen different places at times. It was tough on the team that had to take up the slack, particularly the engineers. When the engineering systems backup got started, they were obliged to remain in sea watches alongside. They would have obviously (and quite rightly) preferred to go home to see their families rather than staying on board during their 'off watch', and unsurprisingly, people started to get tired. When people get tired, they make mistakes. While it is understandable wanting to spend time with family, mistakes aren't acceptable.

Learning from these observations, I started adding days to the deterministic plan, which had the knock-on effect of changing the dates we booked in the FOST team. I told the HQ they should plan for a revised date, and even though they would have preferred we brought it forward, I stood firm. It would be impossible to do it any other way. We were, however, moving in the right direction, although to be fair, we weren't moving at all!

When I start planning something, I always start with the exit. My major rule for operational planning is 'Always have an out'. The mission doesn't end until you are safely home, and you don't enter into anywhere where you have no contingency. In the beginning, working in this way is tiring, but being adaptable, flexible, and dogged in your approach is hugely effective once you have mastered it. I've normally got a pre-planned response for nearly everything because I've invested intellectual horsepower in the first place. I have even found that it helps in the 'normal' world too.

Despite all my preparedness, I was being sucked in to success-based thinking. We had achieved operational competence, maintenance was going well, the team had had Christmas leave, and we were ready to deploy. What I didn't expect at all was for it all to go wrong in the final few days. Inexplicably, just as we were in the final phase, we had another setback. It turned out the Old Girl didn't like being alongside for such a long period of time.

I was off base when the problem was discovered. I had gone to the Royal Navy Northwood headquarters in Eastbury, Hertfordshire, to discuss our pre-patrol brief. One of my seasoned sailors had accompanied me, and after the briefing, we had dropped in at his aunt's house near Tottenham, North London, for a very welcome and enjoyable lunch before embarking on the four-hour drive back to

Plymouth. He was a very positive and funny guy, the life and soul of the party—now I understood where it came from.

I had mixed feelings as we chatted while speeding along the M4 towards the West Country.

'You don't drink much with the lads, sir,' he said.

'You're right, I don't,' I agreed. 'I don't mind telling you, but I've got a theory about it. Some captains can do it well, but I'm not that good, so I only do it occasionally. I did do it in Norway!'

'Yes, you're right,' he laughed, remembering our night out.

'The other thing, of course, is that when it goes wrong, I'm responsible for discipline' I went on. 'Roger, sir.' He nodded, hopefully understanding the point.

I thought of the fact that we weren't far off departing. I was eager to set sail, and with all the preparation nearly complete, the moment to deploy was tantalisingly close. This was our chance to prove how successful a submarine could be at making a difference. At the same time, I was saddened because this was going to be the start of an epic period of separation from my family. I had thoroughly enjoyed my weeks in Plymouth because it was my home town and I was with my loved ones for the optimum amount of time.

Then, just as we reached the outskirts of Reading, my mobile phone rang.

'Sir, it's Ben,' said the caller. Ben was our immensely capable marine engineering officer (MEO).

He got straight to the point.

'We've got a real engineering problem. You'll know I can't discuss the detail over the phone, but I'm shutting the plant down to start the investigation.'

My heart sank, and I let out an audible sigh. This was all we needed. I couldn't help myself and pressed Ben for more details even though I already knew there was little we could do other than to leave him to get on with it. Ben was exceptionally energetic in attacking issues, and most importantly, he had the intellect and intelligence to present arguments and solutions. If anyone was going to tackle this problem, it would be Ben and his team.

'OK, can you keep me updated?' I said, concluding the brief call.

Over the next few hours, a number of further calls were exchanged, and it quickly emerged that the prognosis was not good. While the repair itself would only take a day, which was well within our planning margins, it would take over *five weeks* to get the paperwork and consensus in place to achieve it.

Five weeks might sound like an inordinate amount of time to source and sign off parts, and it is. Unfortunately, this is the way of things in the modern world. Like most contemporary organisations, the armed forces are under-resourced and overcommitted. To be fair, the services have always been that way, but the real challenge in the twenty-first century is the increasing levels of bureaucracy and process. Process has become the enemy, engulfing the entire service and those who support it, instead of being the bedrock of support it should be. An increase in litigation, a growing claims culture, and the ever-present threat of negative PR from multiple sources, including digital media, have meant that more and more safeguards have had to be put in place. Unfortunately, these safeguards slow everything down to a snail's pace, even when the event in question has no possible threat. While eliminating the inevitability of mistakes in a high-risk environment, we've become overly restrictive and overprotective.

We've been left with an impossible scenario. It is not possible to entirely eliminate risk, yet as power has shifted from achieving operational capability to an individual's interpretation of health-and-safety compliance and budgets, the only people who suffer are those on the ships and submarines, who generally sail exhausted following the unnecessary fight against process. It is an indictment of our current state of affairs that it is generally easier to get maintenance done East of Suez than in our own home ports.

Despite the best intentions of many, we now had a real fight on our hands.

HMS *Turbulent* couldn't sail as planned, and it was a huge blow. The delay had consequences for so many people. I was really disappointed on a personal level, but what discouraged me most was the feeling that I was letting the crew down. After months of enduring the protracted period of maintenance and repair, as well as achieving real success with OST, they had been preparing themselves mentally and physically for the deployment for days. It wasn't just us that would be affected either. We were also creating an issue for HMS *Tireless*, the submarine we were supposed to relieve in one week's time. Its crew would have to stay out longer, and that would put its captain in a poor position. He too would have to let down his crew. I knew what it was like to have to tell your team such disappointing news. They'd get on with it because submariners are a resilient bunch, but they would be downhearted and anxious about their families who were expecting to welcome them home at any moment.

As we covered the final few miles to the naval base, I resolved to fight against the process, which dictated another five weeks of delay. It was absurd that it would take that long and, in my view, entirely preventable. I would tap on relationships and friendships that I had established over twenty years in the Royal Navy. I would concentrate my energies on finding out what needed to be done or where I should focus my lobbying to achieve it. Right now, if we wanted to get HMS *Turbulent* moving, we had to fight against process, and this was becoming an engineering project.

By the time I walked back to Turbs, I had a renewed bounce in my step. All the disappointment and negativity I felt when I first heard the bad news was gone.

I'm always aware of how profoundly my attitude and moods affect those around me. Optimism and pessimism are equally infectious. A leader's demeanour sets the tone for how everyone reacts. If I had walked over the gangway, shoulders hunched in despair, I would have made a bad situation drastically worse.

All leaders need to think about the effect their attitude has on their people, whichever situation they find themselves in. A boss who fails to look up when a member of his team walks in the room or who will willingly interrupt a chat to pick up a call is setting themselves up for a fall. They are showing that they don't rate their team. At best, this is mediocre leadership; at worst, it is rude and short-sighted. We all need to recognise the influence we have on our teams and use that knowledge wisely. Once you understand the powerful effect you have, you can help everyone around you to be more positive and achieve more.

I was glad I adopted an optimistic stance because the disappointment aboard the Turbs was palpable by the time I arrived.

The crew was visibly struggling to deal with the repercussions of the setback. When a defect like this is discovered, it doesn't take long for it to get around a small community like a submarine. It didn't take long to spread throughout the base and headquarters either. The greatest yet, at the same time, the most destructive quality of the submarine service is that everyone always has an opinion or has 'heard something' and all want to share their view. The anecdotal solutions I heard on board ranged from a quick fix to decommissioning the submarine immediately as a cost-saving measure. Hearing the diverse range of views only served to stiffen my resolve to sort out our problem as soon as humanly possible.

The final straw came when I was walking through the naval base and passed a young chief petty officer from another submarine.

'Hi, sir, so it's over then, I hear,' he said cheerfully as though he was discussing the end of a football match not the future of my team and our submarine.

'We've got some challenges ahead, but let's see what happens, shall we?' I replied, trying desperately to sound calm and measured.

I was a bit peeved to say the least. Avoiding any sort of reaction was a conscious decision, just as it had been during the Heston Blumenthal confrontation. I'd been in the Royal Navy long enough to know exactly what happens when these rumours take hold. Pretty soon, they become self-fulfilling prophecies. People get hold of the gossip, and before you know it, they start making decisions based on what they think they know.

I was right too. Within a matter of hours, the Chinese whispers took on a life of their own. We started receiving calls from navy career managers asking if they could remove crew members and place them in other units. Now, I wasn't only dealing with the challenge of getting Turbs fixed; I also had to manage an internal PR campaign to ensure decisions were not made based on speculation and hearsay. After months of building a team and maintaining their morale, I wasn't about to let them go easily.

It was quite a balancing act. I wanted to send a positive signal which said I was on top of things and would move mountains to get the parts we needed to keep us on schedule. I believed in the team and wanted them to know that. However, all the while, I was fighting a negative backlash. I honestly felt that there were people around us, from other crews on the base and elsewhere, who truly wanted us to fail. It felt like the world was against us—but that in itself is an opportunity waiting to be taken. At times like this, the best option is to draw strength from the negativity and use it to add to your resolve. I didn't ignore what was going on elsewhere; I positively encouraged the crew to acknowledge it.

'We know what we are capable of,' I would tell each person I would discuss it with. 'At the end of this, we'll have to prove them wrong, and on our own, we've done it before, and we'll do it again.'

The negative sentiments turned out to be a great vehicle to get my team entirely focused on the matter in hand. A competitive bunch, they couldn't bear it that other crewmen were talking them out of the game. They re-harnessed their energies and worked around the clock to resolve the problem, and I hit my contacts book with vigour.

I have always found the approach of the worlds against us. 'We're better than them—let's prove them wrong' works well. It is not advisable for a leader to use it all the time, but if you know your team well enough, it can provide a competitive edge when you really need it. The fine line is making sure it is used constructively, and the rhetoric has to be well considered. There is little point going in and saying everyone else is all wrong and you are right without any justification or backup argument. People can see through that.

The approach that proves effective is to say, 'This is an opportunity to prove to others that we are as good as they know we are. They'll want us to fail because they already know we're better than them. We have earned that reputation. We have earned it by hard work, dogged determination, and being the best at what we do. We may feel a little deflated—I know I do. The true test of what we do now, though, is how we handle this. We must focus on our own challenge and our own success. The enemy has shifted, but the challenge is the same. Let's do what *Turbulent* does best: deliver.'

Although we were still battling with process, on the plus side, there were a number of key players who were helping our cause. Some were in supporting companies, and a good number of others were from within headquarters. Within a short period of time, there was a feasible plan to rapidly fix the problem and make us the priority.

It was a good thing too. While all this was going on, it was evident that the situation in Libya was not going well for anyone. In 2008, before my command of the *Turbulent*, relations had looked to be getting better with Libya. It had taken a one-month rotating presidency of the UN Security Council, which was widely seen as a step back to respectability after decades of being shunned by the West. The US had even signed an agreement, committing to compensate victims of bomb attacks in the country, and US Secretary of State Condoleezza Rice had made a historic visit to Libya, where she said relations had entered a new phase. Less than a year later, in August 2009, things had begun to unravel when Lockerbie bomber Abdelbaset Ali al-Megrahi was freed from a Scottish jail on compassionate grounds and returned to Libya. The hero's welcome he received caused a storm of controversy. Weeks later, the West was on high alert when it was revealed that Russia had sold Libya weapons in a $1.8-billion deal. The haul included fighter jets, tanks, and air defence systems. Meanwhile, the Libyan domestic situation was unravelling with violent protests which began in the eastern city of Benghazi and then rapidly spread to other cities. Despite escalating clashes between security forces and rebels, Colonel Gaddafi remained insistent he would not step down and said he was in full control of the capital Tripoli.

It was now 2011, and it was not difficult to work out where this was going. As we watched events unfold from the UK, we were all too aware we might well end up a part of the military solution. My personal view was that the real tension began the day the UK naively released the Lockerbie bomber and, in so doing, upset our American allies. However, no one really paid this any proper attention until the 25 January uprising in Egypt in 2011. The scale of the revolution there and the dissolution of government made the West sit up and take notice of the potential for significant change elsewhere. It was inevitable that at some point soon Libya was going to become a target of those interested in regime change. Colonel Gaddafi's narcissistic approach would inevitably make it happen, and it appeared that that time had come.

At our current rate of progress with the repair, it seemed that HMS *Turbulent* and our sister submarine, HMS *Triumph*, would be ready to sail at the same time. We would both, therefore, be available for strike operations, and the question now was going to be 'Which one of us would go?'

The repair was completed by early February, just days after the defect was discovered and was in no small part down to the dogged persistence of everyone on board. We were scheduled to sail on 26 February in the full knowledge that the political situation in Libya was escalating and we were to go straight into pre-deployment training.

The reactor was finally started up, and to our relief, everything was in working order. The engineers had done an incredible job with the help from both Rolls-Royce and some of the Babcock team. We were now in a position of awaiting orders. HQ was mooting very broad intentions—mainly because they didn't know anything more than there was a desire from the government to be part of the effort to enable regime change. If Libya was to be our hunting ground, Tomahawk would be our weapon.

CHAPTER 3

The Need to Succeed Must Overpower the Need to Avoid Failure

The Old Girl appeared to be all right. My team and I had performed well during the really demanding training package that the navy had put on. Actually, that last sentence is an understatement to say the least. OST is probably the most difficult event that submarines undertake. The submarine service wants to know that their submarines can be deployed on any mission type anywhere; therefore, it is a continual war being fought, both internal and external. The sea training package does prepare you well though.

On the last day of the training, we were approaching the Cumbrae Gap, just off the rugged coast of Scotland. It is very narrow, with a lot of traffic from yachts to vessels going to and fro the oil platforms. We needed to conduct reconnaissance on a building on the Scottish coast for special forces insertion. As we closed, the first incident happened.

'Emergency stations, emergency stations,' rang out in the control room.

There was a loud bang.

'All compartments carry out phase 1 damage control checks and report to DCHQ,' I said.

We had struck a simulated mine.

'Hydraulic burst on the forward escape on the main hydraulic systems,' the voice of one of our engineering technicians came over the main broadcast. Then almost simultaneously, a succession of others came in over the main broadcast system.

'Casualty, casualty, casualty, casualty on the forward escape.'

'Fire, fire, fire on the forward escape.'

As I was putting on my emergency breathing mask, a sonar report came through.

'Ops [manages the tactical picture], controller [sonar controller leading the sonar team], new contact, bearing 010, two shafts, five blades, whine, possible warship.'

'Roger, that's contact 210, standard cuts, 210.'

The warship we'd been desperately trying to sneak around to get in and do our reconnaissance was now in the game.

'Team, listen up,' I shouted through the breathing apparatus. 'Command priority is extinguishing the fire and returning main hydraulics. We need main to get the mast up. We're going to 30 metres, which enables depth separation from the warship until we're sorted.'

If we can deal with this–and we will deal with this–we can deal with anything, I thought. *But first, we need to get to periscope depth safely!*

We did, of course, deal with it and with aplomb. We were way past that now though. Now we were doing it for real. We had our long-term tasking. We were to sail, spend ten months East of Suez, providing the UK's first strike capability in an area that was transitioning violently politically, lurching between Middle Eastern ideology and Western principles. Anyone going into this area needed to understand what they were entering. The situation was too complex just to arrive and imagine that you would be able to achieve what needed to be done, learning on the hoof. Within this 'theatre', there would be one major complicating factor—our submarine. At 28 years old and in warm waters, it would be operating outside its original design envelope. These submarines were never designed to last this long.

It was hard not to feel uncomfortable about operating in an era of constraint, where reduction of military forces did not match the increase in commitments. My personal view was that the unconvincingly named Strategic Defence and Security Review did not reflect the fact that there was little review about what was required and that nothing had been learnt from history. None of this mattered though. It was not possible to influence that political process; therefore, we had to work within it. We had to compensate for the lack of forces by the timely provision of intelligence to enable strategic thought, and we were well prepared to do this. Submarines have always been a 'force multiplier' in that role.

We were a team that had conducted many operations and had extensive, high-end training behind us. We also had the unrivalled advantage of our own particular ethos: 'We are HMS *Turbulent*, a brotherhood that neither retreats nor fears. We fight together, and we win together.

We needed that approach because there is nowhere to go when things go wrong on board a submarine, and they do. If there's a fire, you can't call the fire brigade thousands of miles from home.

In the frantic final days before our deployment, we returned to the south coast to conduct a period of what's known as independent exercise, which is a process of really getting to know the submarine and ourselves in preparation for operations. We also had to squeeze in pre-deployment training, which is when external teams come on to train, and assessment where Devonport flotilla staff and FOST join us before reporting back to the HQ that they are content that we are ready to deploy.

The day of deployment itself was an extraordinary one. We were surrounded by press and TV crew, recording every second of the bittersweet moment we said goodbye to our families and went off to go and do what we were trained to do. It did, however, feel great to sit on the open-air bridge of the submarine and deliver the final instructions for our departure.

'Navigator, are you ready?' I said.

'Sir, obeying telegraphs, they are at stop, thirty revolutions rung on, the tugs are attached, ready in all respects.'

'XO, happy?' I said to Gareth.

'Yes, sir,' he replied.

'OK, let's go. Let go all lines, have the tugs pull dead slow, please, Pilot. When we're in the middle of the river, we'll propel.'

The tugs pulled very slowly, and Turbs lurched gently sideways. As soon as we were in the centre of the river Tamar, the tugs were released, and the navigator started driving her out. I saluted at the team on the jetty, waved my hat, and we were off.

Plymouth is one of the most difficult harbours to get in and out of, and it takes some real concentration to do so. It does offer some quite rewarding navigation and ship-handling opportunities though as long as you get it right. My focus had to be elsewhere though. The longer-term programme was pivotal to how this tour was going to go, and one of the most crucial elements would be transiting through the Suez Canal. The date for this part of the journey had already been decided and paid for. It costs a great deal of money to transit a nuclear-powered submarine through the historic canal, so it needs to be meticulously planned out in advance. Everything else has to be matched to arriving at the right position, at the right time. It constantly played on my mind.

Once we'd reached open water, the team quickly settled down. We were ready to be assessed within a few days, and I let the commander of task force know so that they could deploy us if they needed to. In the meantime, we continued exercising.

We were just about to start a submarine-versus-submarine exercise with HMS *Triumph*. I had long used our relationship with HMS *Triumph* to focus the crew. We had exercised together a great deal during training and *Triumph*'s captain, Rob Dunn, was a good friend of mine. He had been the command rider during one of our patrols, so he knew me very well, and I him.

'Team, we need to not just beat *Triumph*, we need them to know that we beat them,' I often told my crew during training. 'Do not stop until they realise that we are in absolute control.'

Using this desire for the competitive edge always worked well. But now, off the south coast, things were going to change.

'Gareth, you're not going to believe this, they're sending *Triumph* down to Libya ahead of us,' I told the XO. 'We've qualified, whereas they're not fully. I don't understand the decision, but it is what it is.'

'Sir, I'll tell the crew this evening,' he replied.

'I expect there'll be disappointment,' I began. I certainly already felt that way.

'You're not kidding.'

'We'll need to focus on the longer-term stuff,' I said, doing my best to sound upbeat. 'What we don't want is the team to come off the boil. We still need to integrate the additional personnel. How we set the tone will be vital.'

Then to add insult to injury, as we continued the assessment phase, we suffered another defect. This time, it was on the attack periscope.

It was a ridiculous defect too—a small piece of rubber came off one of the external seals. Sadly though, it was enough for HQ to instruct us to come back alongside to Plymouth in order to change the periscope.

'You are kidding,' I said to my warfare counterpart in HQ as we discussed it over the SATCOM (satellite communications). 'You and I both know this is nothing.'

'Unfortunately, the engineers disagree, and the view is it has to be changed,' he replied. 'I know you want to get on with this, but the decision has been made.'

I could hardly believe it. Everyone had said goodbye for the deployment, and there had been plenty of tears. Now, although there would be joy and surprise as we came home, we would have to go through that pain again.

When I discussed the news with the crew, I concentrated on the long term.

'Libya is not our fight,' I said. 'We were only ever contingency. Our challenge is East of Suez. The world's a pretty unstable place, and we need to take our weapons and our skills there.

'Think long term, people. We'll work this problem through and get to where we're supposed to be.'

Even so, reaction was mixed. I could see some of the men's heads were down. Some felt like it was their fault, which it wasn't, but I was confident that they would fight this through. We went back alongside Devonport, and I paid a surprise visit home, which was excellent. The joy of seeing your family again cannot be understated even though it is tinged with the sorrow of knowing that you're leaving the next day, and trying to explain it all again to the kids is awful.

Within twelve hours of arriving back at Devonport, Ben, the MEO, called me at home.

'Sir, we have a defect with one of the secondary systems, but we need to shut the reactor down to fix it,' he said.

As we spoke, it occurred to me that my conversations with Ben about the state of the submarine were either really bad or really good. In essence, they boiled down to two things. It was either 'Sir, it's broken' or 'Sir, it's fixed'.

In recent times though, it seemed like it was increasingly more of the former. I was really disappointed as I knew that once again we were going to have to negotiate a number of hurdles to fix the problem. Even though the trials and tribulations of earlier in the year had demonstrated a widespread will to fight to help the Old Girl, she was really beginning to struggle.

Meanwhile, we were on the brink of a major conflict yet nowhere near the action.

Early estimates were that it would take three days to fix Turbs, and although that felt a very long time, at least it was a lot better than the five-week estimates during the last breakdown. Nevertheless, it was still very frustrating, and I had to fight hard to retain my composure and not give way to the angry disappointment I felt deep inside.

Fate is against us, I thought. I had worked hard to win the trust of the crew, and I knew they would be watching my reaction closely, so continuity is key. They were always watching.

I've spent my life hiding negative emotions. It probably began when my parents sent me abroad to boarding school at age 5. It was not an enjoyable experience, and slowly and resolutely, I learned how to conceal sadness and disappointment. This occasion was no different. I've always believed that one of my greatest weaknesses is taking everything personally. The failure of our submarine was completely out of my control, yet it felt like I had failed. The feeling was exacerbated by the thought that we were no longer able to contribute militarily.

Whatever I felt like saying about the ongoing problems of HMS *Turbulent,* I contained my own emotions about the emotional roller coaster we were all on. I focused on retaining a positive outlook and working relentlessly towards a speedy resolution.

The team again pulled out all the stops to find their way through all the red tape and bureaucracy. We were also helped by the effort of some amazing individuals who pushed their teams to support mine. In less than the expected three days, we were able to accomplish what we needed, and once again, we were ready to set off.

I now had to say goodbye to my family for potentially the last time. That statement sounds dramatic, but although I knew my agenda for the whole trip, I could never be sure of exactly what was going to happen—it is a troubled world. I hated saying goodbye. My daughter

Olivia played it pretty 'cool' (probably for my sake), but my son Theo was visibly unhappy, and that was exceptionally painful.

Once I kissed my family and got on board the submarine, I focused quickly.

'Gareth, are we ready,' I said.

'Morning, sir. Yes, we are, and the film crew is back on board,' Turbs' XO replied.

Channel 5 was filming a documentary called *Royal Navy Submarine Mission* following a Royal Navy submarine on active service for a period of time. HMS *Turbulent* had been chosen as the subject for this three-part show, and remarkably, once the Admiralty had agreed to it, they had largely left me to get on with the detail. Gareth and I had actively encouraged Turbs' involvement. We were focused on the PR potential for the submarine service—and of course, Turbs— and therefore encouraged every opportunity to overcome the 'silent service' persona. We felt people should know what submariners do and the challenges they face. We were also motivated by the opportunity of letting families see what we did. Following our protracted period of maintenance, we were quite used to trying any method possible to get exposure, including radio, papers, magazines, and TV.

When the discussions with channel 5 first started, we weren't earmarked to go to Libya, but now, clearly, the situation had changed. Over the past few weeks, I had held serious talks with the programme producer, Rosie Kingham, and director, Geoff Small. We agreed a strategy where her cameramen could film everything on board, but if I asked him to leave an area, he would do so immediately without question. Now, the film crew, like everything else, was set to go.

'OK, let's get on with this,' I said, signalling that we were finally on our way.

We needed to sprint to get to the action. HMS *Triumph* had already fired missiles into Libya, along with the US Navy. In fact, an excess of 100 Tomahawk land-attack missiles had been fired in total. If anything was going to make Gaddafi go, this would be it. We had a long transit down to the Mediterranean to mull all this over, but more importantly, to make sure we were fully ready and capable of doing anything we were tasked to do.

Once we finally got going, we quickly slotted into the daily routine that would be repeated ad infinitum; things needed to be done even when on occasion there may have appeared to be no reason for it.

The submarine is divided into two major sections—*forward* (where people live, sleep, eat, and tactically operate the submarine) and *aft* (where the reactor, main engines, turbo generators, propulsion shaft, and a variety of supporting systems are run to allow us to live effectively). Neither section can function without the other. It is a symbiotic relationship. Just over half of the crew work 'back aft' in the standard maritime watch-keeping cycle that has been handed down from generations of sailors.

In forward, there are ninety-three bunks for 130 people. We sail with far more people than the submarine was designed to take, which means that at least forty people have to hot-bunk and share the bed of their opposite number. While one is on watch, the other is asleep. At watch handovers, one will wake the other. It is an extreme way to live, and it is different to any other form of living.

The submarine day is continuous. We all work a six-hour on-shift and six-hour off-shift cycle that lasts forever. It's incredible to think that people can last for over ninety days in that routine.

The submarine forward is divided into first watch and second watch. I've always felt second watch to be hardest, working 01.00 to 07.00 and then 13.00 to 19.00, one of the times when your body naturally wants to sleep. The daily sequence for anyone in this cycle is to get up at 00.15, go and wash in one of nine washbasins on board (one for up to twenty-two officers, four for the senior ratings, and four for the junior ratings). People have to queue up in order to wash, and even when they reach their goal, they are allowed very little water to clean themselves. There are three showers on board, and a submariner's shower is a very rapid affair. Thirty seconds with water on, switch it off, lather up, switch back on, aiming for about one minute to one minute and thirty seconds to wash the soap off. Longer showers are referred to as Hollywoods and are greatly frowned upon. The issue here is not how much water a submarine makes, because it can make a lot using its two on-board distillers—it's about the noise put out into the sea while emptying tanks of used water. Noise is absolutely our greatest threat in counter-detection when operating against other submarines.

Once the submariner is washed, he'll go for food, or scran. At 00.30, that meal usually consists of soup and rolls. He'll then take his handover and go on watch to whichever position he is in. When you are on 2 deck, where the messes are (where people live and eat), it's light, but as you head to towards the ladder to 1 deck (control room), it goes into red and then black lighting. Red lighting is there to keep eyes adjusted to darkness, and that is what you usually see in war movies involving submarines. Black lighting is no lighting at all, except what comes from the indication lights and dials (which are all dimmed down to just about visible).

The noise is constant. If it is not the air-conditioning, it is the continuous reports:

'Ops Controller.'

'Ops.'

'New contact bearing 210, showing two shafts, four blades, 110 RPM, classified possible merchant vessel.'

'Ops, roger, cut through.'

Meanwhile, the planesman and ship controller are constantly reporting too: '17. 5 metres, 1 up, 4 knots, 18 metres 2 up, 4 knots, heavy, increasing to 2–4 revs and pumping out.'

In the centre of all this is the man at the periscope, shrouded by a dark curtain, constantly looking around into the dark abyss, searching desperately for any lights, and reporting if he sees anything. The navigation team continues plotting course, collating intelligence, and reporting back.

'Officer of the Watch, Navigator, LOP has been run on track 56, the merchant vessel. Solution is bearing 205 range 10,000 yards, course 110, speed 16. He's following the standard shipping routes.'

'Officer of the Watch copied.'

We acknowledge every report and every order. In fact, there's a submarine saying that 'an order is not an order unless it's been acknowledged'.

There is a continuous cycle of positions so people can stand down for short periods to revitalise with a cup of tea or just focus elsewhere. When it's quiet, such as when we are transiting deep, there are more opportunities to stand down, to catch up on administration, training, and other activities. Off-watch activity is, however, frowned upon during stand-down time.

The last hour of any watch always drags unless you are in contact with the enemy, which always focuses the mind because you need to make sure that you hand over to your relief in a position of control. You don't want to hand your opposite number a hospital pass. The next relief turns up having got up at 06.15 and repeats the process described here. Once they're in position, the first person can go off watch. Some will need to collate records of what has just happened (always done after breakfast), and some key players will need to prepare for Operations Group (O Group).

O Group is attended by those involved in planning and execution. The captain, heads of departments, ops officer, navigator, logistics officer, radio supervisor, intelligence officer (an additional duty normally held by a junior officer), strike officer (if we are doing strike operations), and others who contribute specifically depending on the operation. During that meeting, we lay out the facts about what has happened in the last twenty-four hours and discuss the state of our submarine, and then we project what we expect to happen. There is always more than one option, so they present plans to match each option with risk, advantages, and disadvantages for each. We then have some discussion before I decide which plan we will execute. Some captains did that differently, but for me, *Turbulent* was a democracy right up until the decision had been made, and we all moved in the same direction.

Those that have gone off watch may go and do some physical activity (phys.), but only when there is no submarine threat. They may use one of the two rowing machines squeezed in between switchboards or the one cycling machine up in the forward escape compartment, right by the weapons embarkation hatch and perilously close to the ladder down to 2 deck. Alternatively, they may use the weights located in a variety of places on board. Some choose to watch a movie, play Uckers, or read a book, but it is more likely they will choose to sleep because you never know what's going to happen.

Then they'll wake up at about 12.15 and repeat the whole process before going to lunch. Lunch is generally filled rolls made on board (sometimes great, sometimes not) and soup. Then it's off watch at

19.00, a choice of two dishes for dinner before using off-watch time as they wish.

This routine continues endlessly until there is an emergency. If there's an emergency, you'll know right away, almost before the alarm goes off, because the constant hum of the ventilation stops. The men get up quickly, get dressed, and move to their emergency station. If they're in one of the twenty-seven-man messes (twenty-seven people sleeping in a room about the size of an average living room with only six-foot-three headroom), it's always a time of confusion because everyone's trying to do the same thing. However, once fully trained, people are generally in position within about two to three minutes. The wardroom transforms into a complex damage control HQ, with a damage control officer (one of the watch leaders), two specialist cells of people (marine engineering and weapon engineering), an incident board operator, and a communications number. The team gathers information from around the submarine, pieces together issues, and finds solutions while all the instant response activity is going on.

Fires are really bad, and I've been in a few. Smoke fills the submarine rapidly, and emergency breathing system masks have to be put on almost immediately to ensure we can breathe, fight the internal battle, and fight the external one against the enemy. We are trained to multitask, and we do not stop other essential activity unless we think it's no longer sustainable—in which case, we look for the opportunity to disengage from 'contact' and find a safe place to sort ourselves out internally. It can be quite frightening, particularly if you've never experienced an emergency before, but the training is incredible. OST prepares you to take on more events than you should ever experience simultaneously.

On a normal day (and skipping meals), the men could get 9 hours of work in two 4.5-hour slots, but more likely is that they'll do one 4-hour and one 3-hour session. Some men get less time to sleep, particularly some of the key officers (navigator and operations) because they are planning and training. There are also those who have other responsibilities, whether it is that they need to write reports and manage their subordinates' careers or carry out internal audits, run accounts, provide academic training to others. There's always a lot going on.

The amazing thing is that, in general, people move around each other continually. There's a natural sense of order. People are polite and always offer to let others through first when they pass in the cramped corridors, except when there's an incident or urgent action is required. In that case, those who need to get there first go there. In the event of an incident, the first wave of firefighters (attack BA as they are known) takes preference over everyone. Those that are going to key positions—the damage control HQ team, me, and others—get to theirs. In an urgent tactical situation, people automatically move out of the way even before I get to 2 deck to let me move rapidly through the narrow corridor (one person wide) to get to the control room. People generally get on. Even if there's the odd conflict, it's always resolved quickly. I've always thought that if the world was like a submarine, there would be no reason for submarines.

The best way to keep a sub, or indeed any sort of organisation, running smoothly, is to give the team all the responsibility they can handle and then stand back. Trust is the bedrock of any human contract. It is what turns inexperienced sailors into seasoned shipmates and troubled companies into dynamic ones. Of course, it is always a bit of a leap of faith. Trust is something that has to be earned, yet you can only earn it if you are given it in the first place. To make matters even more complex, I don't think it is right to expect everyone to do things in the exact same way that I would. In fact, I actively encouraged them to think of alternative solutions.

The other side of this unwritten contract of trust with the crew is that a leader needs to allow everyone the courage of their convictions. The only way to achieve this is to accept that occasionally mistakes will be made. The reaction from the top to screw-ups sets the tone for everything.

It is critical to demonstrate there is adequate room for redemption. It creates an environment of independent thought, where the team is not afraid to take the odd (calculated) risk, and a generally positive attitude throughout. Likewise, it is vital the boss doesn't shoot the messenger who brings any bad news. A measured approach is what is required. The alternative? Well, any leader that systematically bawls out somebody delivering bad news will soon discover he or she doesn't hear about problems any more. That doesn't mean the problems are not happening though. It would not be an over-exaggeration to say it is a matter of life and death to know about everything that goes on aboard a submarine, good or bad.

I encouraged everyone to be open about mistakes, and whenever one was made, I felt responsibility. I'd ask myself, 'Did I articulate properly what needed to be done? Did I give them tools to do it? Did I ensure they were trained?'

One of the first mistakes occurred not long into the deployment, and I was very aware that the way I dealt with it would set the tone for the remainder of the 286 days we would spend together.

The submarine has two watch leaders, who are also known as ops, TASOs, TSOs, OOWs, depending on which submarine they are on. They lead their smaller teams executing the day-to-day operations of the submarine. They are a key element to success—you could have the best plan in the world, but unless these leaders own it and execute it, success becomes a struggle. They are supported by a variety of other departments on board—marine engineering, weapon engineering, logistics, etc. My approach was to tell someone what needs to be done rather than tell them *how* to do it, but I would make sure they were armed to be *able* to do it. Training was key to this; however, natural ability and capacity to learn is vital. We were off the south coast of the UK, but the terrain could not be underestimated. It's a great training ground, but it's also very real. While at sea, every military and merchant vessel becomes a hostile. It is easy to collide with other seagoing traffic, and if we got it wrong, we could run aground. Things can go wrong, particularly if other forces don't know exactly where you are. Plus, since we are trying to remain covert, the risk was even higher. It's partly why Royal Navy Submarine Service is so good at what they do. It doesn't matter whether its peace or war; they always operate as though it is war because they have to. Counter-detection could result in real issues.

After returning to periscope depth (PD) to receive our broadcast routine (messages or signals), the team concentrated on the military activity in the area while managing to stop focusing on the neutral traffic.

I had screens in my cabin that displayed sonar and tactical information, as well as speakers where I could normally hear the communications between all the different sensor operators. I could detect when something was up by the inflection in the voice I heard and judge the right time to intervene. On this occasion though, I was in the wardroom with none of that information to hand, so my first indication that things were not right were when I heard the words *close quarters* over the main broadcast public address system. *Close quarters* is the term used when something has got way too close to the submarine and there is a risk of collision. This was serious.

I went straight to the control room with Gareth close behind. My senses were rapidly arrested by the sound of a number of reports being made, and the voices of each speaker betrayed real tension. It was dark, with the control room bathed in red lighting. Looking around me, I saw the periscope was down. The sonar screen to the left of me showed that something was moving very fast down our left side. This indicated that, whatever it was, it was either travelling fast or it was close. In this case, it was very close.

The OOW was sitting in the captain's chair, watching events unfold. In a second, I took in his demeanour and realised he was responding mechanically. He knew the drills, and he was acutely aware that we had seriously dropped the ball. His greatest emotion was fear and shock. He was genuinely frightened by what had happened; there were 130 lives at risk.

He got up out of the chair, and moving purposefully, I sat in the vacated seat and studied the screen. It's a great anchor position.

Turning to the planesman, I spoke calmly but firmly, 'Starboard 10, steer 030. I have the submarine.'

I didn't have to say the last part because by the rules, I'd taken the submarine off him, giving the order. I'd deliberately said it to make sure that people knew I was in control.

'Officer of the Watch, work the fire control solution on the contact, keep the reports coming, but make sure we calm down,' I said to Tom, keeping my voice steady. 'Team, we are safe. Focus on avoiding counter-detection. Navigator, report distance to the nearest point of danger and depth of water.'

I didn't need the last two pieces of information. I already knew them because I had looked at the chart as I walked in. I just wanted to compose the team to give them breathing space to work the problem through. The crew looked visibly more relaxed as they understood we had regained control. We hadn't been detected, and we were unscathed.

My priority now was to build his confidence rapidly. He had to drive the submarine for the next few hours, and we could debrief later. I knew negative thoughts would be flooding his brain. He'd be thinking, *I have really screwed up. That's not going to help my selection for the submarine command course. That was really close. What if it had gone wrong?* I used to think like that when I was in the same position, and I too made mistakes. Back then, my captain, the shouter I described earlier, invariably took the hostile approach, publicly berating me and screaming in my face even while I was trying my best to recover my error. He did not hesitate after the event to tell me that I had personally cost the submarine the whole mission and it was my fault entirely. I could still recall the feeling of hopelessness and humiliation and the looks from the team, which were a mixture of pity at my predicament and abject relief that it wasn't them in the firing line.

I calmly got out of my seat.

'Officer of the Watch, are you happy?' I said, turning to him. 'You're in control. Let me know when you're ready to take the submarine back.'

His answer would tell me a lot about the man. If he was reluctant, he would have a personal challenge to regain self-confidence, and I'd have a challenge to help him. Fortunately, he bounced straight back.

'Ready, sir, steering 240 at slow ahead, revolutions 16,' he said without hesitation. 'Keeping a depth of 17.5 metres, safe depth 60 metres. I have the submarine.'

Relieved, I went back into my cabin, sat down, and pulled out my guitar. I played one of my favourite classical pieces (poorly). The fact was that the team knew that I was obsessed by learning it and that I played when I was relaxed, therefore crisis over.

Later on, at the end of his watch, the OOW came to my cabin.

'Sir, the ops officer has the submarine,' he said as he walked in. He looked ashamed. He knew he had let us down.

'Sit down,' I told him. 'So how do you think that went? What do you think you could do differently to avoid that?'

I took a deliberately calming approach, and he responded well. We talked for no longer than five minutes. He was tired and wouldn't take it all in. Things will go wrong, and the consequence on occasion can be fatal. He didn't go out there with the intention that, during that watch, he was going to find the vessel close to a point of near collision. He made a mistake, albeit a near-catastrophic one. I didn't need to tell him I was disappointed—he already knew. He was a good follower. The need for success always needs to overpower the need to avoid failure, and this experience would teach him to embrace failure, deal with it, and move on. I would show him how to do that without it ever being evident to others.

CHAPTER 4

Know the Enemy—It Is Not Always the Obvious

A submarine patrol is an exceptionally strange and exciting beast. A day can be full of action, or it can be devoid of activity, but rarely is a day neither one thing nor the other. The trick to getting through the tedium on quiet days is to remind yourself of the exhilarating ones.

One of the first times I had to really put this philosophy into action was in 1994, when I was watch leader for the Dutch Navy on board a diesel submarine in the Caribbean. When it is written like this, it doesn't sound so bad. Readers would be forgiven for conjuring up images of blue skies, azure waters, relaxing on the bridge in the warm weather, and looking forward to sundowners at the end of the day. Well, it wasn't like that at all. Certainly not for me and the rest of the crew on board the diesel submarine stationed at PD. Our brief was to pick up drug smugglers and report as they transported their illicit cargoes from producers to users. For four weeks, we 'patrolled' the Caribbean. In reality, we stayed in the same area for three of those weeks. In fact, we almost stayed in the same position. The intelligence we were collecting undoubtedly contributed to some greater effort, but few of us on board knew anything about that because of the stringent security requirements. We didn't even have that crumb of comfort to encourage us through the endless hours of tedium.

Most of the crew managed it through the first week OK. The work felt new, and we were operating in a different region from usual and doing something that we hadn't done before. There was also an element that we were going to make the most of it because it had taken us nearly a month to get to the Caribbean from the Netherlands. We'd invested a lot of time and energy into all the preparations beforehand, learning about the threat of other nations in the region and in understanding the drug runners and how they operated. Indeed, I would go as far as to say we approached the first week with huge energy as we eagerly looked for anything that might lead to a potential bust. However, after a week of absolutely nothing, it was evident that we were nowhere near the action. I quickly surmised that the real challenge would be keeping motivated during this time.

People naturally slip into routines; it is human nature. In fact, routine becomes the reason to exist, particularly in the less-than-hospitable and cramped surroundings of a submarine. Half the time, it is difficult to judge if it is morning or night, and the only way to tell is by the food that is served. I took the conscious decision to create a routine for myself to get me through the monotony of my time in the Caribbean. While ensuring that as a watch leader I was always prepared for the next watch, I filled the rest of my time with physical training. In fact, the training routine began to dominate everything, sometimes at the expense of sleep. Nonetheless, by sticking to my routine, I was motivated enough to perform my duties with energy and enthusiasm.

I thought of that Caribbean patrol as we made the fast transit towards Libya, knowing that was only one step on the long journey ahead. It was now April, and the quiet steady journey in the Atlantic was a marked contrast with the busy time in the run up to the departure from the UK.

Transiting deeper than 200 metres underwater is a surreal experience. It feels much the same as being alongside in a port. There is no change between day and night. All the lights are on, people go about their business, and there is little movement during the high speed transit phase. The only real difference is when the submarine needs to manoeuvre and then there is a sense you are getting somewhere. Otherwise, there is no real feeling of achieving any distance at all unless you look at the chart. We spent most days deep, returning to PD once in every eighteen hours to ensure we received all our messages from HQ. One of the best aspects to being on operations is that the HQ reduces information down to only what is absolutely necessary. All the superfluous stuff (although probably important to someone) arrives a lot later when we get into harbour.

We ran drills to make sure that we were ready for any eventuality, paying careful consideration to the potential for mines and asymmetric warfare when we entered theatre. Looking around, I was pleased to see the team was professionally effective and motivated. It gave me confidence that when the time came, we would be ready.

I was still dealing with the personal disappointment that we were not the first shooter to be activated. I didn't even know why. Perhaps pride? A desire for glory? Either of those were not good reasons. Ours was to be a different battle. Until we were East of Suez, we were to conduct surveillance operations off the Libyan coast. Although I had no control over it, I was genuinely concerned about coalition command and control and how that would work. NATO had become fully involved in the Libyan issue in February 2011, following news that Colonel Gaddafi's regime had begun targeting civilians. The United Nations (UN) had called upon the international community to help the Libyan people, and NATO had responded. In March 2011, a coalition of NATO Allies and partners began enforcing an arms embargo, maintaining a no-fly zone to protect civilians and civilian-populated areas from attack under Operation Unified Protector (OUP). The rumours were that not everyone in NATO agreed with the operation, which was not a strong starting point. Added to this was the fact that a great deal of OUP activity would be conducted on Arab soil. The religious implications of this intervention were bound to get in the way. It would inevitably be seen as the West trying to impose itself upon Islam, and if that view did not occur naturally, the Colonel would do his best to make everyone aware of the full implications of our response.

Our instructions were to integrate into the NATO OUP operation, in addition to Ellamy, the code name for the UK mission in support of military intervention in Libya. Ellamy was part of the international coalition enforcing a Libyan no-fly zone in accordance with the UNSCR 1973, which said that all necessary measures should be taken to protect civilians. Our sorties were under operational command of the United States, although they still came under the Ellamy banner. I was curious to see whether this structure allowed indecision and lack of resolve to enter the equation because most decisions needed to be made with consensus, and that is always difficult to achieve at the best of times. There were certainly signs HQ was struggling with this process. My personal view is that when action involving loss of life is involved, small coalitions work while large ones fail eventually, particularly when no results are visible, but I would never articulate that to my crew.

Just before we started the sprint to the Mediterranean, we experienced the first in what was to be many instances of a change to the crew. My crew numbered 160 people, although we usually sailed with around 130 personnel. There was a need to rotate people because we were away for so long. They might need to return for courses to enable their career progression or take leave with their families and friends. We took considered risk with whom we released to go home and whom we took in their place; therefore, only two people, I and the operations officer, did the whole trip in total. There might also occasionally be specialist riders necessary for particular types of operations. I might be required to carry trainees from other submarines too.

It is surprising how different a team looks after even only a few crew changes. We might be joined by people who have never been on *Turbulent*, although they might be qualified submariners if they'd come from another submarine crew. My challenge was to manage personalities of both the old and new hands and ensure that the whole team integrated and settled down quickly. The best way to do this was to rapidly get around the crew, see everyone, and find out how they are. Fortunately, most of the new people had completed OST, so it was relatively simple to integrate them into the existing crew.

At the heart of successful leadership is the ability to communicate effectively, and this is crucial when incorporating new crew members. How you communicate is much more powerful than what you communicate. Everything else is wasted unless you can articulate a common goal that inspires a diverse group of people to get the job done and ensures others leave you to get on with it.

To communicate properly, you need to understand your audience; one size does not fit all. Firstly, I had to consider how I was going to deliver my message. In submarine operations, there are four distinct groups that need to be communicated with: HQ, your command team, your crew, and their families. Now there were five if you counted in all the new people. Communication with each of these sub groups needs a different approach to ensure that they were receptive, received, understood, and acknowledged the goals. I was wary of over-briefing and worked hard to find a way of communicating that the team responded to well. My solution was to allow plenty of interaction and ideas from everyone in the team; some of the best ideas come from those you least expect them from. Esprit de corps and team spirit are a great force multiplier and aided our success in operations.

It was handy that integrating the new crew was relatively straightforward because we needed to surface in order to go through the Straits of Gibraltar, or STROG as it is affectionately known in the service. STROG was the first of three major choke points we would be negotiating on this patrol. Choke point is the term for areas where an enemy can engage you but there is little room to manoeuvre. In the eighteenth and nineteenth centuries, it was common for the enemy to have gun emplacements on either side of a choke point to engage slow-moving sailing ships. They can still do that today, but modern warfare has changed considerably. Terrorists in small fast-moving crafts are a far greater threat because submarines are not very responsive on the surface. Terrorists could rapidly launch an attack from the shore, and we would be limited in our ability to deal with them. The best strategy to avoid an event like this is exceptionally good intelligence-led planning—that and a couple of strategically placed general-purpose machine guns (GPMGs) to deter would-be attackers. It was not that there was too much chance of attack here, but we needed to be ready just in case. You never know with terrorists. The uncertainty of their resolve is the real genius of their form of warfare.

Our best defence by far was to get back underwater at the earliest opportunity and to do so as quickly as possible. However, this all had to be done with one eye on the depth of water because if it was too shallow, we couldn't dive.

'Captain, we are in the position ready to return to periscope depth and surface,' Jon Lewis, the OOW said. 'I have twenty sonar contacts. All of them have been ranged and are outside of 8,000 yards.'

I had been watching the sonar screen in my cabin while Jon had skilfully manoeuvred the submarine to detect and range all contacts. There is an art to doing this because we couldn't use active sonar to judge the range of what was around us. Doing so would pose a counter-detection opportunity. The alternative is to use algorithms and mental arithmetic to work them out.

'OK, up you come,' I said.

Jon and his team took the submarine from safe depth to PD. This is always quite a risky procedure because sometimes shipping may be stopped in the water. Sonar won't pick them up because sonar needs some form of noise to detect. We'd only find out when the periscope was raised, and that's despite the fact modern sonars are amazing pieces of kit.

'Mast going up, one sweep, no contacts close,' the tactical supervisor ops confirmed.

It was always reassuring to hear that, so I left and went to wander around the boat.

The next complex task was to surface the submarine, which meant getting all the right people in the right place and ensuring that all systems were ready to go. I had trained John, the OOW, to lead his team, so unless he needed me, I wasn't going to interfere. The only difference with this surfacing, compared to surfacing in friendly waters, was that we needed to get ready with weapons, ensure that the overt self-protection policy was correct, and ensure that the team stayed focused.

STROG is an amazing place, and I went up on the bridge for this part of the transit. It's the gateway between the Atlantic and Mediterranean and two continents with only a few miles between them yet with two totally different cultures dominated by opposing religions. As we made our way through, we were surrounded by all types of merchant vessels all going to and from similar places. Most of the merchantmen leaving the Mediterranean had come from the Suez Canal. The sea's surface heaved with transport carriers, gas carriers, oil tankers, and container carriers, all bound for nations worldwide, bringing us an infinite variety of goods so that we can drive to and from work, cook our nutritious and varied meals, and then relax in front of high-tech LCD TVs. As I watched the scene unfold in front of me, I mused that it was amazing how complacent we are about all this. We have become used to having all the things that these vessels bring to our doorsteps. I doubt many people realise how vulnerable it all is.

Five members of my crew, in addition to the OOW and the lookout, joined me on the bridge. Everyone always welcomes the opportunity to come up there. They can enjoy the fresh air, see the continents slip by, perhaps enjoy the antics of the dolphins swimming alongside us, and grab a cigarette or cigar before we dived again. I always enjoyed my time on the bridge in good weather. I'd be safe in the knowledge that the OOW was driving the submarine while I took in the situation and the scenery and enjoyed chatting about nothing yet everything with others that came up to join me. Conversation in these situations almost always followed the same pattern.

Someone would kick things off by saying 'I wonder what Gibraltar's like as a run ashore' or 'I've never been to Morocco, I wonder what it's like'.

Inevitably, someone on the bridge has been to the place in question, and they'll tell stories of their visit there, which are always amusing. On this occasion, having been to Gibraltar, it seemed appropriate for me to tell my story.

'The first time I went to Gibraltar was as a midshipman on the frigate HMS *Sheffield* in 1990,' I began. 'I partied a great deal, but I was also the sports officer on board, so I was responsible for organising the traditional Rock Race. As you all know, Gibraltar Rock is in excess of 350 metres high and hard work to run up even if you are fit and sober. Doing it while hung-over wasn't nice. I can vividly remember the captain showing some real disappointment that his sports officer had ended up so far back in the field.'

Out of the corner of my eye, I could see grins being exchanged and heads nodding in approval at my candid disclosure.

'I walked back down with a fellow midshipman,' I went on. 'As we arrived at the place where most of the apes loiter, he decided for some unknown reason to push one of them. I couldn't believe it. At first, the ape looked disgusted, then angry, and then he clearly communicated with the other apes. I knew then this was going to end badly, but I wasn't going to hang around and see what they did next. I started running and shouted to my mate to run too. I found my pace and actually moved pretty fast then, hangover or no hangover, with the apes close behind. Luckily, they gave up eventually, but we didn't, until we got to the bottom.'

The men laughed and squinted at Gibraltar, as though hoping to catch sight of the vengeful apes. Various quips were made about them looking out for me to exact their revenge, but the famous rock was already receding in the distance.

Some of the men on the bridge hurriedly made calls home. It was rare to be in signal range for mobile phones, so they always took advantage of any opportunities to talk with their loved ones. Obviously, now that we had deployed, we had to have one eye on the operational risk of allowing people to call home. The men knew the score though. They didn't talk about where we were or what we were doing. They'd feel good about making contact though. It is good to reset the clock, and we all always felt better for it.

Once we were properly through, it was time to get going at speed again. We dived as quickly as we could because we were really vulnerable on the surface. Not only is it difficult to manoeuvre, it is really difficult for other shipping to see us since only a third of the submarine is above the waterline. A tanker, if careless, could easily administer quite a dent to our hull. Once we had dived, we could better control our situation. It was our natural environment, and it was good to get back into it.

We'd picked up some communication from HQ on our passage through STROG, but at this point, we still had no real direction as to what we might be doing. I anticipated we would remain off Libya for about two weeks, allowing HMS *Triumph* to reload and return. This was going to be quite a challenge as I already knew that most of the anti-air targets had been removed, and therefore, there was little trade left for Tomahawk land-attack missiles (TLAM). Since most of the targets had already been taken out during the initial salvo of attacks, it would be difficult to determine what would be left to be targeted. Even warfare has economics associated to it, and you don't use a very expensive TLAM if there are cheaper alternatives available.

The handful of news reports I had seen strongly implied that the navy and the air force were tussling for dominance and relevance in theatre. In my opinion, the latter would do anything to prevent the former from contributing when they could. Whatever the truth to these stories, they added to my sense of unease. In my mind, there were two pressing issues, both of which were out of my control but which would need careful internal management. The first was tasking. If we were not provided any useful tasking within the constraints of Tomahawk, it was likely that we would find it difficult to maintain our war-fighting skills. All the OST we had received prepared us for the worst-case scenario and the most complex war situation we could face. However, as the enemy had been largely obliterated, we were focusing our skills in one particular area of warfare. Where we were going, we needed to be able to do everything: surveillance, reconnaissance, intelligence gathering and analysis, special forces operations, anti-submarine warfare, anti-surface warfare, strike operations, and more. We would need to up our game rapidly as we deployed to the next theatre of operations.

We had already formulated a plan for this tasking. The team had used 'seven questions', the standard planning process which I'd introduced when I had first taken command. A warning order (the articulated plan as to how we would achieve success, what success looked like, and the boundaries within which the team had freedom to operate) was in place. The plan had taken into account our tasking, what the enemy was doing, and how we could achieve the best results. Bearing all that in mind, we also considered the geographical areas opening up to us. Submarines operate in areas known by friendly forces. It's a way of avoiding what is known as mutual interference.

As we arrived in theatre, there were many NATO submarines operating there. This enabled us to close the coast. There was, of course, a degree of risk from our own forces, but it was great training for when we came up against a more challenging enemy later in the year.

The possibility of using our Tomahawks was a constant subject for discussion among the men. Opinion seemed fairly united on the subject; we were there to deliver hostility to the enemy, so that was what we should do. Some of the less-experienced submariners were predictably quite gung-ho about it.

'It's what the boat should be doing, we can't just go around patrolling,' said one. 'We should be firing.'

Others though had obviously given the moral implications of using our weapons some deep thought and sought out my opinion.

'We just need to get on and do it,' I reassured them. 'When the time comes, it will be my call and my responsibility. You just need to deliver.'

In the meantime, I had plenty of other pressing issues on my mind. Indeed, even as I looked ahead at potential stumbling blocks down the line, we were presented with the first of what was to be a clutch of challenges presented by my aging vessel.

The initial setback was when the handle for reactor control rod drive motors control came off. I found this particularly annoying because we had been instructed to change the old handle prior to sailing from the UK (despite objections on our part), and the new one didn't work.

The second and more pressing problem for Tomahawk was that the port-side weapon discharge system kept failing, which meant we only had three out of five tubes available. It was crucial to sort this out to ensure that we could fire our weapons. Aside from adding a new concern to my growing list about the operation ahead, this also presented a short-term problem for my crew. The men living in the WSC were now forced to hot-bunk in the forward bunk space while the team affected the repairs. I hated it when my men were put out by anything other than what is necessary. I needed them to contribute effectively, and they had to be rested to be able to do that. This was not helping.

To cap it all, two more defects occurred in quick succession. I was in my cabin, reading a book on the Middle East, when Dan Seager, the assistant marine engineering officer, came in to see me.

'Sir, the garbo [garbage ejector] is not functioning,' he said.

'OK, be more specific,' I replied. This was frustrating, but they were always watching my behaviour so I kept my voice even.

'The garbo is blocked by a piece of string and will not shut properly to drain down,' he replied.

We both knew without saying that someone's unilateral 'good idea', probably trying to recover from an earlier mistake, resulted in a loss of capability. People had been taking shortcuts and trying to dispose of items which clearly shouldn't have gone into these receptacles.

Problems like these sound so innocuous, but they are serious. I could waste time trying to find out who it was and sanction them, but there was nothing to be gained from that. The best thing we could do was to accept it and move on. They would know who they were.

Then, in a matter of moments, Dan was in to brief me about another defect that had come to light. The slop pipework had a blockage in it. It was the worst-possible-case scenario. Individually, all these defects were serious, but in combination, they were a disaster. When there is a blockage in the slop pipework, the GE serves as the secondary method of getting rid of waste. My team needed to fix the blockage and the GE fast. We could not live with a situation like this on a submarine with 130 men on board. We were unable to use the galley. The sinks were out, no washing facilities were available, and there was no ability to get rid of our waste. In a matter of hours, our situation would become impossible.

Complacency had caused this, and I was not happy with this. We could not afford to be complacent. I called the HODs in.

'This is not acceptable,' I began. 'We've got ourselves into this situation, and it smacks of complacency. We've become comfortable, and we all know the moment you get comfortable, you get caught out. Our boat is delicate and needs looking after. We need to make sure we focus towards that. I am not happy. We all shouldn't be. Filter this down through your teams.'

It took more than twelve hours to fix the GE and slop system. During that time, there was slop sloshing around everywhere, including my cabin. The engineering team had to painstakingly check metres and metres of pipework, drilling into them to check on their condition and then repairing them. It took a team of five to do the job, which equates to sixty man hours wasted because of someone's carelessness.

Defeat on board Turbs was never an option, and it certainly wasn't in this case, but it wasn't very nice to live in for that long. The focus of my encouragement to Dan and his team was to get on with it and try something different. We can spend too much time thinking about how to give the problem to someone else when in fact it is in our realms to fix or mitigate it ourselves.

'If everybody is thinking alike, someone is not thinking' is a common phrase, and it is spot on. On submarines, most teams have a 'red cell', whose aim is to think out of the box as the enemy might. The best-operated submarines choose people that can think like that. The ones that don't succeed don't consider who is going to provide that role and, therefore, never overcome group thinking.

I was always keen that my crew challenged decisions before I even made them and especially so at the planning stage. Obviously, this had to be constructive, and for it to work, there needed to be a symbiotic relationship established between follower and leader. I made it clear that we were a democracy right up until I made a decision, and thereafter, we need to go together as one. However, I also encouraged my HODs to challenge thereafter, albeit subtly. I needed that to continually evaluate the decision I had made. It became an important part of our psyche because change never fails when it is done early, with a plan and reason, but it always does when it is done late and with no plan.

Leading a submarine, or indeed any organisation, requires a common goal that inspires a group of people to work hard together. In addition, they need to feel they could make a difference. Of course, it didn't help that the scope of our operation was changing almost daily. Aside from dealing with our internal challenges, we also needed to provide options both internally and externally to our HQ. After all, we were the 'eyes' of NATO.

We received a signal from our commander of task force (CTF). A CTF is usually admiral or general level. In this case, our CTF was a two-star admiral in charge of all maritime operations. The signal stated that there was not much left to attack with TLAM in Libya. However, we were to remain at two-hour notice to fire. We had to remain in constant communications, which meant we couldn't really do anything else except wait in case we needed to be used. I was disappointed that our superiors no longer wished to use our Tomahawk and wanted to preserve them for East of Suez, which was where we were now headed. I knew the crew would feel the same way. Everyone would be acutely aware that HMS *Triumph* would come back out and use hers again. She was even now sprinting back to the Mediterranean.

It seemed that for now this jaunt had resulted in nothing. On the plus side, I now had a chance to deal with our flaws that needed addressing rapidly to ensure long-term success. I sent a response to HQ, offering a programme proposal to get us back towards where we were supposed to be going.

Maintenance still needed to be conducted to ensure that we were ready on arrival East of Suez. The weapon storage teams needed to withdraw all weapons and make ready while we awaited direction from the Cruise Missile Support Agency (CMSA) on our potential tasking. I kept a weathered eye on the Intelligence, surveillance, and reconnaissance (ISR) tasking in conjunction with the rod control lever defect, but I felt it was all manageable. The tasking was important. We couldn't be in a position where we could not execute something instantaneously when directed, yet we needed to conduct maintenance. This was a challenge because before we could arbitrarily take down a relevant piece of equipment, we needed to understand what the enemy was doing and then work that into the tasking. Plus, we had to consider any *potential* tasking we might yet be given. We also needed to build contingency into all that, just in case there were delays in the maintenance.

We were now two days into the mission and conducted our first strike rehearsal, which is a simulated coordinated attack using Tomahawk. Overseeing a Tomahawk attack is like conducting an orchestra to achieve the right tune. Unless all the missiles arrive at exactly the right position, at the right time, you won't achieve the effect you want. It requires a great deal of articulate planning and adept execution.

HQ did not deem the rehearsal absolutely necessary because they intended to conduct strikes for real soon, but they allowed it to happen because I specifically requested it. It was obvious they believed they'd achieved everything they needed from the first strikes. I was not convinced. None of this seemed to take into account the well-known will of Colonel Gaddafi. There is an old saying from Sun Tzu, the renowned Chinese military general, strategist, and philosopher, which says, 'When you do battle, even if you are winning, if you continue for a long time it will dull your forces and blunt your edge.' We were already seeing evidence of this now with NATO in charge. There were delays in decision-making. The UNSCR 1973 seemed to be breaking down. While the UNSCR was pretty clear as to what it was supposed to achieve, NATO appeared to be interpreting it differently. In my view, it was all down to the fact they hadn't structured the operation to achieve regime change.

As a front-stage player, it was interesting to watch this all unfold. It was amazing to see how many units were operating in our area, including two aircraft carriers, four frigates, maritime patrol aircraft, and so on. The sheer numbers were starting to concern me. I signalled NATO to let them know exactly where we were. I didn't want to be run over by our own forces.

Even at this early stage of the campaign, it appeared that despite the considerable kinetic attention of NATO, Gaddafi continued to make progress regaining territory. There was evidence that members of his government were defecting now, but he didn't seem bothered. It was very obvious he wanted to win or die trying and, therefore, become a martyr to the cause of Islam. If that happened, I expected the rhetoric would become more anti-Western.

With all this going on around us, the team settled down to operating in the area, dealing with the high levels of activity while remaining undetected from our own forces. I was really happy with my men despite the mistakes earlier. They ensured we sailed when we said we would and did everything that we were told to do. They seemed to have renewed vigour now too and were thirsty for more. Once again, I reminded myself we needed to concentrate on what we could change and forget what we could not. It had always been my biggest challenge.

A welcome distraction from these thoughts was the pleasure of promoting one of my chief petty officers to warrant officer. One of the great moments of command is promoting people. The trainee Coxswain was running the event, and it turned into a saluting festival. He saluted, the Coxswain told him to salute, I saluted, he saluted again, the MEO saluted, and at about that time, I gave up fighting it. The moment was not lost though as it is the words you say that matter. Everyone always remembers what was said to them on a day like that. It's quite a powerful and personal moment for them. It also prompted me to reflect on the intertwining of normal submarine life and operations. Although we knew what we had to do, concerns over the enemy didn't overly bother us. Our greatest challenge was understanding how we fitted into the broader plan (if it was evident) and avoiding the greatest enemy of all: complacency.

CHAPTER 5

Plan, Understand the Risk, Decide

One of the most memorable pieces of direction I received during my time in command was a signal that said 'MOVE NORTH AT MAX SPEED—DETAIL TO FOLLOW'. This happened during my first patrol in command and against a very capable enemy. While the submarine went deep, out of communications and at maximum speed, it was obvious to me and my team what we were going to have to do. While the HQ worked on the strategic plan, we needed to work on our internal plan to ensure that at the next communication window, we had any information that they might require, whether it was our understanding of the enemy, our weapon status, defects, personnel, endurance, or our assessment of the environment. We would have it ready to go and potential plans according to any further direction we were given. This was not to *outthink* the HQ but to *add* to their planning.

The Royal Navy, like most institutions, is steeped in standard operating procedure (SOP), tactical operating procedure (TOP), and doctrine. There is nothing wrong with SOPs and TOPs—they are safe, proven, and effective. For those worried about consequence, as long as you follow them, you will never get in trouble if it goes wrong. However, sometimes they are not always right for dynamic situations, and equally, you're unlikely to get outstanding results either. As warfare develops, TOPs and doctrines rarely keep up, and therefore, you end up using yesterday's techniques for today's issue. Broader still, innovation can be hampered by bureaucracy, and progress fails to flourish. For that reason, I insisted that we invest time in trying to enable my team to think broader. 'SOP and TOP are the baseline.

You can always go back to them but find new ways and justify them,' I would say to the team. 'We must plan for the unexpected, no matter how radical you think it might be, to remove the need for intellectual analysis at the moment critique.' That can open up Pandora's box, but it's worth it.

Submarine captains have a difficult task to ensure they are fully prepared because once they have sailed and once they are radio-silent, everything they have . . . is all they have. Those who are really effective at this skill realise that time is short and, therefore, start their research and planning as early as possible. Attention to detail is key.

During any long-term strategic operations, there will be the requirement to conduct more than one mission or phase. The key to success in this process is to ensure that each section is prepared separately but incorporates as many common aspects as possible so there is no duplication of effort. The simpler the process, the better. The time before an operation is the only time it is possible to concentrate completely without distraction, allowing you to plan with certainty and avoid hesitation later on. The more information you find in advance, the more you will know your enemy, the environments to be operated in, and the tasks involved. Get this right, and you will inevitably be more decisive and successful. The reason it is important is that your team members need to have trust in your plan. They can only have that if there is information to back up the assumptions and conclusions. An example of a plan we used during our pre-deployment training is included at the end of this book.

I always follow a broadly similar process in planning because the steps are effective in virtually any situation. I have adapted them to corporate life because they are equally pertinent there. The 'enemy' is different, but the approach is largely the same.

The questions you need to ask are the following:

What are the enemy doing and why?
This is all about threat evaluation. We are trying to assess capability and potential. It is possible to spend too much time thinking about this, but the person who doesn't spend enough time on it *will* fail. To understand a potential enemy, you must understand the environment in which you will both operate. In some cases, the enemy is not always

who you think they are, and therefore, you need to do this capability piece for a variety of 'actors'.

The *enemy's intent* is probably the most important factor. Determining a potential adversary's intent gives a fuller picture of their overall capability. In basic terms, 'capability + intent = effect'. Working out their purpose, or reason for being, should not be confused with a *statement of intent* (although this does have an input). Differing between rhetoric and potential action helps to focus your own plan. For example, in the submarine world, the least-capable submarine operated by someone with intent to defend (or attack) at all cost may actually prove a more difficult target to engage effectively, particularly when you are constrained by your own rules of engagement. Capability without intent is impotent. In basic terms, you could put a well-run old diesel submarine against a capable nuclear submarine operator, and he might win, particularly if he was in his own environment and better motivated. I know this for a fact because I've been in that exact position in my early years. I've never forgot that lesson and have always treated everyone with respect ever since. That attitude has given me an advantage without doubt.

Finally, understanding their *patterns of life* is a key element to success. Gathering information about where the enemy operates is equally important. Operating inside enemy territory is a challenge. To do this successfully, anywhere where you may be constrained should be avoided, and it is only possible to do this by understanding the patterns of life. *Patterns of life* is a military term which involves interpreting routines. If you adapt this to HUMINT (say you were a particular kind of office worker and my contact of interest), I'd want to know which company you work for, your motivation, and your family background. I'd find out that you get up at 06.00, go to work for 8.30, meet other company workers in the same bar at 17.00 two nights a week. You go home at 19.00 to your family, except on Fridays, when you always drink at the bar and then go on clubbing until 01.00 the following morning before going home. Your spouse doesn't like it but accepts it, so life goes on ad infinitum. The true test is when this pattern changes, when for the second time (not the first, because that's an anomaly) you go to some meetings on a Wednesday and then one on a Friday as well. Something has changed, and therefore, I need to watch closely

because the decision I've been making regarding your threat level has
been based on a particular standard course of action. Understanding
patterns of life can be an exceptional challenge, particularly if it is
assumed that the enemy operates as you do. Understanding the norm
and establishing a baseline should be a priority. Real-time analysis is
a priority to adjust your plan and decide correctly.

What have you been told to do and why?
Before you determine this, you need to know your team's doctrine,
tactics, and historical analysis of previous operations. You also need to
consider your own resupply, intelligence provision, support network,
etc. This is very important in shaping your decision-making process
and avoiding complacency or overreaction.

I like really broad and vague direction because it allows a wide
range of courses of action. However, whatever the mission provided,
you must determine how best to employ your team to maximise
strength and minimise weakness. Sometimes it can appear almost
too difficult, but with the assessment you have made of the enemy
and yourself, you can plan. To make the most of any effective plan,
you need to contain it within three dimensions to any operating
environment:

Physical. An understanding of the physical environment means
it is possible to operate despite it. You should invest serious time
understanding it and should, at best, be able to exploit the physical
to your advantage or, at worst, be able to avoid, in both time and space,
anything that might detract from the plan.
Legal. You must know the law, or at least the salient points that will
affect decision-making. Everyone has rules of engagement (although
they might not know it), and people must engage within those if they
are to fight legally. Any unlawful action adds to the problems the
broader team has to face. You must be able to justify every decision.
Moral. What you do must be morally right, and the context in
which you are charged with executing missions should be as sound as
can be. Decision-making may become impaired by moral and ethical
influences, so if solutions to these questions are found during the
planning phase, it takes away the pressure of the moral component

of the environment. You should also make efforts to understand your enemy's moral stance. If there is a difference, ensure there are safeguards in place to operate within your own moral boundaries.

This all sounds like a lot, but actually, when it's natural behaviour, it is simple. Once you have these in place, you are able to plan with confidence. Importantly, you must plan—there is a fine line between the right amount of planning and procrastination! Good teams do a lot of planning, particularly when they are trained well. Good captains also do their own planning, not because the team can't but because there must always be a wide range of options. As I said before, if we all think alike, we're not thinking. Once the plan is in place, decisions made, it must be briefed. In fact, unless you are able to communicate what it is you and your team need to do, it is likely to fail. I've always understood that communication is about the recipient, and therefore, one form does not fit all audiences. You need to work out who needs to know what and then deliver the message accordingly. That takes time and intellectual effort to brief effectively both upwards (to your HQ) and to your team.

Then get on and do stuff! Execute the plan. I had said to my team at the beginning of our journey together, 'We are a democracy during planning, right up until we have made a decision. Thereafter, we all go in the same direction,' and that was true throughout my time in command. When you execute the plan, you need to be dynamically unpredictable; you must set no patterns, particularly when you are gathering intelligence.

Finally, you need some *control measures* in place. You need to understand whether you are achieving success or not, and if you are not, you must be willing to go back into the plan, change, adapt, do what is necessary to adjust it to achieve success.

All of the planning gives you and your team intellectual space, the ability to anticipate, the ability to think out of the box, which can eventually become potentially life-saving. The likelihood is that things will go wrong; however, so long as you are able to regain the initiative, you gain strength from that.

In the case of this ever-challenging deployment, a near-constant supply of innovative thinking was required both in planning for future action and in knowing how to deal with unexpected day-to-day problems. For a while, it seemed that no sooner had we recovered from one crisis, another one popped up to take its place, either externally or internally. All these challenges aside, we were proceeding in accordance with our plan.

Back off the coast of Tripoli, we weren't far from the Colonel, as Gaddafi was now routinely called aboard Turbs. We had spent so long studying his actions, we now knew so much about his regime, his forces, his tactics. This inevitably provoked some discussion about the man himself. In the control room, during a moment of quiet, the banter was coming thick and fast.

'Apparently, he is surrounded by a personal guard of 40 Amazonian virgins,' announced Wingnut, a chief petty officer, who was always presenting himself as an authority on this subject or that.

'You're just getting that off *Wikipedia*!' shot back the coxswain, who invariably adopted the contrary position to just about anything for 'sport' alone.

'Yeah, well, it says he is colour-blind, and he definitely must be or he wouldn't wear all those gaudy clothes, that's for sure,' said Wingnut, undaunted.

The lively exchange was broken up by the general alarm.

'Emergency stations, emergency stations, hydraulic burst, hydraulic burst, hydraulic burst in the control room. Stand by to operate ship's systems and watertight doors in hand control.'

People moved rapidly but calmly to their emergency stations. Firefighting teams readied themselves, and attack breathing apparatus (ABA) teams moved to the control room at speed. The wardroom became damage control HQ. We had suffered a major loss hydraulic failure of the systems that managed masts.

Surprisingly, submarines spend a great deal of time at PD, watching and passing back intelligence, which means masts are vitally important. In fact, you can't stay long at PD without them. When you are deep, you may not detect a stopped contact on sonar, but the risk of collision is reduced significantly because you are separated by depth. At PD, with the mast lowered, there is no depth separation. There are a mass of calculations used to keep us safe by allowing us to raise the mast occasionally. No mast, no baseline, no safety.

The over-arching aim is to keep safe but keep the mast down as much as possible. To conduct a full all-round look (ARL), it takes 30 seconds, which affords 360 degree coverage to the range of visibility. One of these ARLs is required every three minutes. If a contact is detected, then we need to deal with that separately.

The maths involved in detecting a contact and calculating, whether or not to go deep in case you collide, is quite simple. However, the stress of what might happen means it takes real discipline to keep control. Plus, add to this the series of calculations required for five other ships all closing around the sub at different speeds and ranges, and the challenge intensifies. The mental arithmetic that command-qualified submarine warfare requires is considerable.

The safest place to be is always deep. Once we determined there was no risk of fire, we returned to standard manning and took the submarine deep to repair the system.

We couldn't communicate with HQ, and anyway, we knew all we needed to know about the tactical situation. We calculated that the probability of a strike in the next couple of hours was less than 40 per cent, so the best option was to get on and repair the fault. I would let HQ know the decision I had made afterwards, but it felt very uncomfortable for a couple of hours. What if things did change rapidly?

Once again, the men met the mark and managed to repair the defect within 1.5 hours, and we returned to PD as soon as we could. The radio supervisor (RS) brought in the daily intent signal that instructed us to remain in position and conduct intelligence collection. I gave it back to him, and he passed it on to the team to refine their plan. This had become a pretty smooth process now; information came in, and the team assessed it, added it into the planning process, understood how we fitted in, briefed it well, and then executed it. All this came from a mixture of understanding of how to plan operationally and constant practice. Now the crew were seeing the results of their endeavours. Importantly, it gave me spare capacity to think ahead. I was still focusing on the long-term deployment. We heard that HMS *Triumph* had arrived back in Devonport with all the fanfare and recognition they deserved. It was gratifying to see that the crew from *Triumph* got the recognition they deserved at the end of their patrol.

In the late twentieth and twenty-first centuries, particularly during the Cold War/post–Cold War period, the sensitivity of submarine operations meant that they were rarely recognised for what they had done. Within the submarine community, we all know what we do, but when you compare the risk and rigour that submarines take compared to others in the military, it is a real surprise there wasn't more recognition for the general submarine community. As *Triumph's* welcome showed, finally a small part of our story was being shared with the general public. Perhaps others would now begin to better understand the role we played.

I have always taken huge pride in being a submariner. We are a brotherhood of less than 3,000 in a country of 60 million. We fight and win together. If we don't do it effectively, it has severe consequences for us and the country. That was something I constantly reminded my men and myself. We were an elite force, with a technical and warfare knowledge that is better than any other armed service in the UK. What we take for granted as standard is completely the opposite in the wider world. People often say to me I have chosen a strange way of life, but I am certain it generates some of the best people out there.

Submariners are a group of people who believe in elitism and look to provide heroic leadership. Today, heroes and inspiration of the nations' youth are footballers and film stars. Military heroes are all short-lived; very few endure for very long nowadays, and that is a shame.

If *Triumph* was basking in its moment in the spotlight, it was far from over for us though. My team needed to stay ready to strike without warning and without remorse.

A signal was received decreasing our NTF to twelve hours, which would give us more of a leash to do what we were really good at. The Colonel was still making progress, and NATO now had some tough decisions to make. The problem from my perspective was, they couldn't condone removal of the Colonel by NATO force—that would only assist the rebels. However, even with the removal of the air threat, they weren't making much progress, and this was supposed to have been a swift operation. The intentions from CTF were evident within the direction given. It was time for us to close the coast of Tripoli. Ironically, although our mission would be too short for recognition by NATO, we would be closer than any NATO ground or maritime forces to the man himself, and we would be there continuously. I was quite looking forward to this. Most importantly, the men were happy, which was crucial for me.

We closed into the coast at speed because there was no anti-submarine warfare (ASW) threat. The main danger at this stage was operating in a very busy shipping environment. I decided we could take the risk, working on the principle that we were actually out of the standard merchant vessel transit routes and there had been very little reported fishing-vessel activity of late for obvious reasons.

Close to the coast, there was little, in fact nothing, of interest at the naval base at Al Khum, but I had expected this. The only military activity we detected was an Italian helicopter and a Spanish ship, which randomly transmitted on her active sonar for reasons that none of us understood.

As we became confident with the environment, I decided it was a good time to delegate more. It would be good training for Gareth, my XO, to give him some of the fun of command. He was a very capable officer, and I had every confidence that he would make the most of this. Besides, I would be there to back him up if he needed it.

'Gareth, are you happy with the plan?' I asked as we sat in my cabin.

'Yes, I am,' he replied with a nod. 'The team is focused, and both watch leaders are dealing with the tempo. I'll call you if there is any major activity or change in activity.'

I knew he would. When we were undergoing OST earlier, the FOST team had 'killed' me off with one day to go. This was the external team's strategy to see how well Gareth dealt with command if anything happened to me. I had a rather dramatic heart attack and collapsed in the control room. The performance resulted in me actually really hurting myself as I fell from my seat on to the deck around the periscope. According to the crew, Gareth's face was quite the picture, but he immediately stepped up and dealt with the enemy contacts and the internal challenges well. The FOST team was happy with what they had seen, and we both had a story to dine out on later in our careers.

We had been set off the coast of Tripoli for a few days before we started receiving the intelligence we requested. To our surprise and slight consternation, we were informed there were two known minefields less than 5 nautical miles (nm) from our position. Even more worryingly, we had already powered through one without knowing it was there. I might have changed our route had I known that earlier.

That morning, we intercepted our first embargo runner.

'Captain, sir, at green 30 at a range of 12,000 yards, I have a merchant vessel, classified as target of interest 12,'said Tom, the OOW. 'Intend going deep, closing the target remaining outside of territorial waters.'

'OK, crack on,'I responded. 'Make sure we get some intel and feed it into the decision-making of NATO, noting that they are doing this within their own territorial waters.'

The XO and tactics and sonar officer (TASO) dealt with it well, got control, and took the upper hand. I left them to it.

The merchant vessel was undoubtedly running arms down to Benghazi, but she was doing so within territorial waters, so there was little we could do about it except report. Later, in the same watch, we were flown over by a P-3 Orion maritime patrol aircraft, which forced us to dive deep. The Mediterranean seawater was very clear, and if we had remained where we were, the likelihood was that they would have seen us.

Our second contact of interest (COI), another maritime vessel, made a run for it. They didn't know we were there but knew NATO had a presence, and we reported back to the CTF. Just after it had exited territorial waters, an incredible explosion from the direction of Tripoli was heard on sonar. It was a definite indication of some degree of action.

For our vantage point, we could observe other daily activity which all seemed to indicate that life of sorts was continuing in Tripoli. The buildings looked untouched, people were going about their daily lives, and the fishermen continued to do what they do. The battle was now concentrated in the east of the country, so things could carry on pretty much as normal elsewhere.

I sensed that NATO's resolve was beginning to wane. Despite a couple of sucker punches, the Colonel had survived all that had been thrown his way. Perhaps the West had underestimated the resilience his presence created and his powerful use of 'the world is against us' approach to leadership. By now, all the US forces had left. The only services left in the area were European Union ones, and that only added to the problem. If NATO wanted regime change, which they did, they needed to act more quickly and decisively, and that needed strength in numbers. The constant delays only served to allow the Colonel to get stronger.

As the days wore on, there seemed to be even less appetite from HQ to use Tomahawk. The suspicion was that since an RAF man was in charge, he had a natural tendency to look after RAF interests first. Every opportunity to fly a mission was used over and above any other means, which is typical of the politics that always go with war. I am pleased to believe the Royal Navy has always played the 'straight man' in internal politics even though it is sometimes to our disadvantage.

As bad as the Colonel was, you had to give it to him; he had achieved the first principle of war admirably. The first of the ten principles taught to all officers of the British Army, Royal Navy, and Royal Air Force is 'selection and maintenance of the aim'. A single, unambiguous aim is the keystone of successful military operations, and he had this off to a tee. His singular aim was to stay in power, and in everything he did, he ruthlessly pursued this goal. His ability to motivate his team to achieve what he wanted was impressive. He had stood up to the first punch from the coalition, knowing that division would occur among the allies. As long as he continued to move on the ground, he would stay on track.

Although apprehensive, I looked upon the positive, in particular from Turbs's viewpoint. This assignment was the ideal opportunity to refine our skills prior to arriving in the more complicated theatre, East of Suez.

Meanwhile, the usual suspects continued to do the usual things. The embargo runners persisted in running the embargo, and as far as I could see, there were very few boarding operations happening from our end. The Spanish warship was still transmitting continually on active sonar and all radars, which indicated that the crew was not concentrating at all. If this was the case, it would prove interesting in a couple of days when I intended to find out what they'd do if they gained contact. It would be a useful exercise to see how far we could press with capable people in a semi-safe environment. I suspected they wouldn't even realise we were there.

We'd been there ten days when we heard HMS *Triumph* was on her way back out to relieve us, allowing us to return to our primary tasking. It was now time to start turning back to the Middle East. We had only been out a short time, but it felt like months since I had seen my family, and I was missing them a great deal. When I turned in that night at eleven o'clock, my last thought was how much I was looking forward to a reunion in our next port visit, which was to be Fujairah, one of the seven emirates that make up the United Arab Emirates.

I was woken at 00.30.

'Next on propulsion watch lay aft,' sounded over the main broadcast system.

That didn't sound good. I got out of my bunk and headed straight to the control room. Already, people were going back aft, hurrying past the outside of my cabin, traversing through the airlocks.

'Officer of the Watch, how are we doing?' I said.

'Sir, they're lining up for single-sided operations. We're reduced to thirty revs while that's happening. Surface contact density is fine.'

This action would severely reduce propulsion availability, so something was definitely up.

When I reached the control room, I sat in the chair, grabbed the phone, and rang the manoeuvring room.

'Manoeuvring' came the single-word greeting from the other end.

'It's the captain. How are we doing?'

'Stand by, sir, the MEO is here.'

'Sir, it's Ben, the feed flexibles have failed. We're single-sided and in control. I can't give you an estimate on the repair yet, but we're limited in propulsion.'

'OK, fight the problem through. I'll be back shortly.'

A flexible hose that was supposed to last ten years had failed catastrophically and resulted in ten tonnes of water flooding into the bilge. The hose was only three years old. We had a major problem on our hands. The only saving grace was that this sub had a two-sided system and one side was still OK. If the other side went though, we would have to shut off the reactor. It just wouldn't function.

Aft was a mess when I arrived. In fact, it felt like a really bad dream. Down on the lower level of the engine room, there was water everywhere. I could see the men trying to work on the problem, and they were wet, dirty, and tired. They were as conscious as I was that if they didn't find a solution and the other side failed, we would be left 12 miles from the Libyan coast, with no reactor power available, relying on our emergency systems alone. That was not a great place to be. The political implications of failing to get this under control were significant, but then again, when weren't they with a nuclear-powered submarine?

I decided that the best strategy was to withdraw while we had the chance, request new hoses, and then do the repair. Other than the large quantity of water in the bilge, the main problem we faced was we didn't have any hoses on board. Plus, since any hoses we had brought in would inevitably be from the same batch that had failed us, there was every chance they would be defective too.

The HODs and I had a discussion.

'Sir, we need the hoses, but I know that we can generate some bungs which will block the system and allow us to get full capability back,' Ben said.

'The problem with that is it will be difficult to justify that to HQ,' interposed Ian, the weapon engineering officer (WEO).

Gareth chipped in, 'There are two potential sources to get the vital parts. We could either go to Souda Bay in Crete, some 400 miles away, to rendezvous with our supply people, or we could make use of the variety of NATO assets around our present position to bring us what we needed.'

The second option was by far the more attractive for us all. Indeed, it struck me it would be a great use of the logistics system.

'Good discussion,' I concluded. 'Right, let's let HQ know both options. Tell them we're going to pursue our own repair while awaiting stores via the NATO route. Ben, keep your team focused on working the problem through. They've done well containing this. Now we need to recover from it.'

Later that same day, the answer came in from HQ. It was not the one I was hoping for. Our preferred option, using NATO assets, was judged to be too arduous. In their opinion, it was easier for us to conduct a very slow transit to Souda Bay. The journey would take at least two days, and for much of that time, we would still be within the launch area. It was far from ideal, not to mention unnecessary and frustrating.

I found this decision so difficult. The least informed members of the crew would not be able to understand why with so many ships, aircraft, and well-established supply routes, this could not be achieved right where we were. That an organisation can achieve precision strike but could not provide some flexible pipes to a submarine with so many units around would be incomprehensible to them.

I could only surmise politics at play; however, there was no point in discussing my views on the matter with the whole crew—it would only fuel speculation. I did have a private word with my officers though, instructing them how to deal with it and play down any criticism. They can't learn unless you share some of this stuff.

As we headed towards Souda Bay, the team knuckled down and used the time to carry on making the bung. I was proud of their resilience and persistence. They were convinced this option was going to work and reasoned that, whatever happened, it was worth having in our back pocket.

Although progress was slow, we arrived at Souda Bay two days later. We surfaced early in the morning and motored in slowly. This was my first time to Crete, and I was quite taken with the place as I observed it from sea. The huge snow-covered mountains dominated the horizon and were in striking contrast to the picturesque and colourful Mediterranean coastline below. We were scheduled to come back to the area soon, and I was already looking forward to seeing some more of the surroundings.

As we approached the bay, I went to the bridge to await the arrival of the boat which was carrying the stores we needed to enable the repair. Although the weather was lovely and the sea perfectly calm, the operators of the small rigid inflatable radioed ahead to insist that we closed to within one mile of the shore. I couldn't really understand the logic behind the request, but we were guests, and therefore, we did what were asked.

The boxes of stores arrived on board, and the crew immediately began going through them to pick out the pieces they needed. Then Keith, one of the assistant marine engineers (AME), came to the bridge with some very thin hoses.

'Can you believe it, sir, they're not in the consignment,' he said, looking incredulous. 'These look like hoses for something else.'

Unbelievably, the hoses we really needed, the sole reason for this diversion, were not there. I was pretty calm when I was told this. I have learned over the years to rely on no one but my own team. I always prepare for contingency just in case we are let down. My strategy is to find an alternative, and if one is not immediately available, work the problem through.

Ben wrote a signal to HQ to tell them of the oversight, and we were told to hang fire while they tried to locate the elusive supplies. All we could do was wait, so I immediately opened up the casing to visitors. Everyone was allowed to get up, enjoy the fresh air (which is quite a commodity after weeks in a steel tube), call home, smoke, or do all the above. The men welcomed the opportunity, but the atmosphere on board was strained too. We couldn't help but be aware that, more than likely, we had had a wasted journey and we were still in the same poor situation too. We waited for an hour while the logisticians attempted to locate the hoses. After Ben had spent a brief time on the casing with the rest of the men, he took his team down below to carry on with the bung. As time went on, it seemed increasingly likely we were on our own on this one. Sure enough, an hour later, I received a call to say the vital parts had not, in fact, left the UK. It was unbelievable.

'OK, men, we are unable to get the supplies from HQ,' I said, doing my utmost not to betray any sign of frustration. 'There is little point hanging around, waiting for the parts because they certainly won't be here today. We need to use our own initiative, and right now, my money is on the marine engineering department's solution.'

By dinner time, the men had repaired it, and I was full of pride and admiration for what they had achieved. Once again, working with limited resources in a difficult situation, they had proved themselves.

As we got underway to return to our original position off Tripoli, I had a lot on my mind. While off the Crete coast, I had caught up with British and American newspapers, which talked extensively about the

Libyan situation. The RAF seemed to be in the thick of the action, conducting lots of strikes, but virtually nothing was being said about the navy, in particular the submarine service and its role. A deeply felt rivalry among the British services is a tradition that stretches back far into history—the army, navy, and RAF always trying to outdo one another at every conflict. It seemed to me that on this occasion, the RAF was flying high (if you'll excuse the pun) and the navy was well out of the loop.

Times like this can be a real test of leadership. While I was beset by personal misgivings about our tasking, I could not let the men know this. I had to show them it was business as usual even though we had yet to make an impact and seemed increasingly less likely to do so. I also had to look to the future and manage their expectations, although I had been at pains to be realistic with them throughout the engagement. When NATO took over, I made it clear that our chance of conducting strike was minimal. Thus far, I had been proved correct too to my intense frustration. NATO is an interesting organisation. The problem with any coalition is that power becomes consuming, politics plays out, and the effect is always on those at the front line of operations. Others way more strategically astute than I have commented and written on it. Clausewitz eloquently summed it up with the term *friction* in 1832. Sun Tzu said something similar circa 500 BC, yet here we were today experiencing it again.

As I continued to muse on the issue, my attention was suddenly diverted to a plethora of bizarre emails and signals. The news was patchy at first, but it appeared that something terrible had happened on board HMS *Astute*. Tragically, while the submarine had been berthed at Southampton docks, Lieutenant Commander Ian Molyneux, the *Astute*'s WEO, had been shot dead, and Petty Officer Christopher Brown was wounded. The shooter was AB Ryan Donovan, who had drunk heavily for forty-eight hours before going on guard duty. The quick thinking of two Southampton city councillors who were on board at the time had prevented further bloodshed. Council leader Royston Smith, a former RAF flight engineer, and Chief Executive Alistair Neill wrestled Donovan to the ground and were subsequently awarded the George Medal for gallantry.

Learning details of the incident was quite shocking for everyone on board Turbs. Many of us knew one or all of those involved. Our thoughts also went to their families. I thought of Iain Breckenridge, the captain of *Astute*, whom I knew well. Iain had also been the captain of HMS *Tireless* when it had suffered an explosion in the North Pole in 2007. It had been under the ice cap when the incident occurred, apparently caused by an oxygen generator candle in the forward section. Two *Tireless* crew members were killed: Leading Operator Mechanic Paul McCann and Operator Maintainer Anthony Huntrod. During that incident, I happened to be directly underneath, on board the submarine USS *Alexandria* on a planned exercise. I knew Iain to be an excellent leader, so I was sure that he would deal with the challenge.

As I learned more of the *Astute* incident, my thoughts turned closer to home. I wondered one of my ABs who was not really suited for the military environment might see this. He was not a follower or a leader and possibly a little psychotic. In fact, it was difficult to understand why he had joined. He was already on my warning for discharge shore (which meant ending his career with the Royal Navy). The fact was, it was difficult to understand how he had been selected for the submarine service at all. He had joined the crew in March. Actually, that's not true; he had been scheduled to join us in March, and he didn't manage to join us at all. He was late by seventeen hours, and we sailed without him! When he did eventually come aboard, I could see straight away he had no team interpersonal skills whatsoever and did not like authority. While he was new to the navy, he wasn't new to life. He was a mature entry. Everything he did seemed chaotic and, in some cases, a little psychopathic. In April, when we set off to Libya, he had been at the captain's table, where disciplinary incidents are heard and dealt with, and I had admonished him before giving him another chance. The fact he decided that he was cool with doing the whole process in front of the cameras which were filming *Royal Navy Submarine Mission* was astounding. It made good TV though. I later learned that this was not the first time he'd been in a similar situation on previous postings, but right then, I hadn't had his full report. The more time I spent with him, the more obvious it became that he really wasn't suited to a naval career. I wasn't certain how I was going to deal with him in the long run, but I hoped that the tragedy on board *Astute* didn't provide him with ideas.

After the three-day return journey from Souda Bay to the firing area, I received instructions that we should return to . . . Souda Bay. It seemed that, for us at least, this operation was over. Our new instructions meant we needed to quickly refocus on getting East of Suez, which was the focal point for the long-term mission. It was a blow and proved to me that my earlier suspicions were well founded. Still, a run ashore was in the offing, so I was able to quickly quell the men's disappointment at not firing by talking up the upcoming port visit.

We arrived alongside Souda Bay in mid April in very windy conditions. In foreign ports, we always employ the services of a pilot with local knowledge of the area to guide us, although all the planning and execution is still done by my team. The theory behind this is that a local will deal with the tugs in the indigenous language, which is the most efficient way to ensure everyone does as needed to get the boat alongside. The final stages of getting a submarine alongside are exceptionally difficult. She doesn't do very well on the surface anyway, but astern propulsion is used. There is no telling which way the stern is going to go.

I felt uneasy from the moment the pilot arrived on the bridge, transferring from the oldest tug I had ever seen. The wind was continuing to pick up, so the conditions were already fairly challenging, but the first thing the pilot asked was what my plan was. He didn't just ask once either. He asked several times as we were closing into the jetty.

'I'm not sure the tugs are going to be much help now,' he suddenly announced. 'You might be better off guiding her in yourself.'

I didn't have any time to argue though. Using the wind on the rudder at very slow speed, we made the approach and managed to get the lines across. There were lots of people on the jetty, watching our progress, but as I quickly discovered, none of them appeared in the least bit interested in grabbing the ropes. I didn't relax until we were safely secured.

Once alongside, I caught up with the captain of HMS *Cornwall*, and we managed to enable one of my petty officers to catch up with his fiancée. I also bumped into one of the dads from my son's football team, which was quite bizarre. He was returning from the gulf. Here we were, thousands of miles from the UK, yet we were discussing our children's football team as though we were on the touchline back at home.

The run ashore was enjoyed by all. It was good to drink beer and relax with the men (although only briefly as they needed space from me). The hotel bed did not do my back any good as it was particularly uncomfortable, but then they always are after weeks at sea. We spent three days in Souda, where we also did all the pre–Suez Canal maintenance, repaired many things that had broken, including the flexibles and the rod control lever, and left in good spirits, heading towards the Suez Canal.

CHAPTER 6

See Simplicity in the Complicated

HMS *Turbulent* was the second 5,200-tonne nuclear-powered Trafalgar-class hunter-killer submarine built by the United Kingdom—HMS *Trafalgar* being the first. The difference between *Turbulent* and all other submarines was the *spirit* of the mighty Turbs. The team aboard often changed, but those who served upon *Turbulent* were proud to rigidly follow her motto, 'Turbulenta Hostibus Fiat'. There was something about that sub that meant we all wanted to live up to the high standards of our predecessors and not let them down.

Taking a submarine to sea is not a simple evolution, and bringing it back is harder still. There are three aspects to the successful execution of this endeavour—serving your people, managing the platform, and dealing with the operation. Of those three elements, it was the team that took up the most of my time and rightly so. An effective team is driven by the fact that they buy into their leader's vision and understand where they fit in. Every time a new crew member joined, I would take time to understand them, explain my vision and how we as a team worked. Of course, life on board a submarine is not for everyone, and it is very easy to spot those who are going to take up a disproportionate amount of your time for all the wrong reasons.

You either love being a submariner or hate it. I had fallen into the first category right from the start. My first time on board a submarine was in 1988 on board HMS *Splendid* during an acquaint visit from Britannia Royal Naval College. To begin with, the overwhelming feeling of being in a completely alien environment, with absolutely no understanding of anything that was going on around me, was almost frightening. The exceptionally early-morning boat transfer probably didn't help. My first experience of the control room is an exceptionally vivid memory. The control room is the operational nerve centre of a submarine. It is a complicated, cramped area, with computers everywhere and a unique sight, particularly in dimmed red lighting. Crew members are generally in stationary positions, making reports in a language you can hear but don't understand. Meanwhile, at the centre of this orchestra of simulated chaos is one man, and it is obvious that he is in charge.

Observing the relationship between the *Otus* captain and his team on the occasion when I first decided to become a submariner shaped much of my subsequent philosophy as a captain. I have given much thought to kinship, which is the creation of the bond between a leader and his team. On board submarines and ships, a captain must be absolutely devoted to their crew because they have a responsibility for their lives, their well-being, and their survival. It is a delicate and symbiotic relationship, and there is an art to maintaining equilibrium. You rely on them to provide, while they rely on you entirely. Any leader that forgets they are the arbiter of standards and the provider of discipline or who are unwilling to make those difficult decisions will quickly lose the understanding of their men, and ultimately, their command will fail.

Effective military leaders never lose sight of the fact that command has always been, and will always be, about people. It should be about making sure that, as a team, success is achieved. Men and women should be given the opportunity to learn their individual limits and learn to depend on one another as a team because they *want* to and not because they *have* to.

Captain Fell, who was the Perisher teacher between the two world wars, summarised it better than I.[1]

'The submariner must be a navigator, an electrician, a torpedo man, a gunnery type, and even a bit of a plumber. He must know men and get on with them. He must use initiative and tact and learn how to enjoy hard living. He must accept responsibility young and not misuse it. There is every reason why he should join and delight in

---

[1] Martin McPherson, 'Perisher: The Making of a Submarine Commander', in *100 Years of the Trade* (CDISS, 2001).

joining submarines, but the greatest joy of all is the companionship, unity, and feeling that he is one of a team which only he as CO can let down. The supreme moment, the moment of truth for the CO, is in his attack. Then, his judgement and actions alone can bring success, failure, or death. He has no one to hold his hand, advise, or correct a fatal move. His eye alone can see, and his instincts sense the correct and only tactic to pursue. On him rests all responsibility. When he feels the faith of his ship's company behind him, he knows that they trust him and will carry out or even anticipate his slightest command, then indeed, he is a proud man.'

A team is nothing without followers though. Yet while followership is rarely taught, it is invariably expected without hesitation. There is an art to followership. It is not about blindly following what the leader has decided to do or about learning to knuckle-down and accept decisions without question. It is about contributing to the team to the maximum of one's ability.

Team followers should *add value* to the team. In a submarine, the initial value comes from wearing a submarine badge. Anyone who wears the badge is qualified, which means although they may not be a subject matter expert in a particular field, they know what needs to be known about the complex platform. If something goes wrong, they'll be able to confidently deal with it until specialists arrive. It is not possible for an individual to be an effective member of a submarine team until they can deal with this. The second part of value comes from contributing to the final outcome. Specialist, general, and personal capabilities are vital components of achieving success as a team. Ensuring that each person offers up everything they have, accepting that even if it is not used on a particular occasion they will not stop offering, is a key part of followership.

Most organisations, both in the services and outside, make the mistake of believing everyone must have ambitions to be a leader. They don't. Besides, it is an entirely impractical starting point because if everyone is leading, no one will follow. To function as an effective unit, there needs to be a mixture of leaders and followers. What is most important is that the followers have the ability to buy into what the leadership is trying to achieve. If they can't or won't buy into the vision, they will have a negative impact. This negative impact manifests itself in one of two ways. Firstly, they will mar the reputation of an organisation because they are its representatives, and therefore, if they do things ineffectively, it makes the organisation appear ineffective. Secondly, it results in destructive behaviour. If there are those who don't like being there, they disrupt others, and that can become a cancer within any group. This second behaviour is among the most difficult pillars of risk to manage on a submarine.

As we headed towards the Suez Canal, the team's behaviour occupied my thoughts. Once we had negotiated the iconic canal, we would be only about ten days from our first experience of a run ashore on the Arabian Peninsula. The prospect really concerned me because although my men worked really hard and delivered, some members of the crew had no ability whatsoever to control themselves ashore. Many people enjoy a drink. In fact, they might even enjoy getting drunk on occasion. However, the difference between good and bad is how people perform when their inhibitions are removed. In Souda Bay, we had got away without attracting attention by some careful leadership from my senior ratings and leading hands and with some skilled negotiations with the local police. We would not be so lucky in a country where alcohol is frowned upon.

The real threat of trouble only ever rested with a few. On board our submarine, that few numbered five. It was the same people time after time after time. There is always the odd bad apple in any organisation. The services are actually quite lenient with their people even when there are incidents of bad behaviour; the preference is always to rehabilitate. It is not my place to say why they do this. Perhaps there is a fear of litigation, but the upshot is that individual leaders have to have a strategy to prevent incidents as far as possible and then deal with the fallout when things do go wrong. I needed to talk to my crew to ensure they understood their part, and we would have to begin establishing relationships with hotel managers, police, and others at our next port of call to ensure that if anything went wrong, there were methods of containing it locally.

We were still in the early days of the Arab Spring, and tensions were running high all over the Middle East. Thousands of people were turning out to protest against leadership regimes that had stood unopposed for decades. They were having an effect too. Ahmed

Shafiq, the Egyptian prime minister, had resigned in March after an uprising in Cairo, which saw millions of protesters rise up against police brutality, lack of freedom of speech, corruption, and economic issues such as high unemployment, food price inflation, and low wages. This pattern was being repeated extensively elsewhere too. The last thing we should be doing was drawing attention to ourselves by displaying the worst aspect of 'Western behaviour' when we visited these volatile countries.

However, before this could receive my full focus, we had to get through the Suez Canal.

The Suez Canal is a defining moment during any deployment. It is the transition between West and East, the gateway between warfare theatres of operations and the final detachment from HQ. Once through, we'd be on our own. There is no easy method to return to a NATO base or the UK if there is a problem.

We arrived at the canal late in the evening of the day before we were due to transit. My first overwhelming impression was one of organised chaos. There were just so many large ships, all waiting to go south through the canal. The submarine seemed so small compared to these ships. It was powerful in military terms, a machine of war, yet in other ways, it was so insignificant. If one LPG (gas) tanker did not turn up because it couldn't transit the canal, that would have far more of an impact on our country, certainly in economic terms.

I've always approached anyone and everything as though they are more important than me, being permissive as far as I can be, and this philosophy would probably really help us here in this chaos.

It was hot and humid on the bridge as we carefully manoeuvred around ships to get into an anchorage position. It was a tense moment. Submarines were never really built to anchor, and there are huge risks with doing so. The greatest danger is that we would be unable to recover the anchor on completion. Having no anchor makes it extremely difficult to operate at all dived, although it has been done before, and actually, anchors compromise operational position because of the noise that can be put into the water. If you are no longer quiet, you can be detected and will therefore probably not be able to achieve your mission. However, if we lost the anchor, we would not be permitted to transit through the canal.

The last time I had been through the Suez was in 1996 when I was the navigator on HMS *Spartan*. Although it was a long time ago, it gave me some experience to draw upon. I noted with some satisfaction that my navigator had planned this transit with exacting detail, indeed far more so than when I had been in the same position.

The team rigged all the necessary equipment to be ready to commence the transit at about 2 a.m. the following morning. I tried to get some sleep because I was going to be on the bridge for a considerable amount of time. I didn't sleep well. My what-if mind was spinning, trying to go over every possible eventuality and reaction, worrying about our vulnerable state. Some comments made by the film director during dinner played on my mind. TV Geoff had been musing aloud about the Arab Spring and the potential risk to us. 'Maybe it's not the canal and navigation that are going to be the problem at all. What if the RPG attack is mid channel? There's nowhere to go, nowhere to dive. If we take damage, what do we do the other side? If we go to Aqaba, will there be assistance there?'

I must have fallen asleep because I woke at 4 a.m. still in my clothes. I was still on my 'bench' because I hadn't pulled the bed part of it down. I shaved, brushed my teeth, drank a coffee, brushed my teeth again, and then went to the bridge, feeling both apprehensive and excited. If we were going to be attacked by opportunist fundamentalists, it would be tonight. This was the most dangerous part of the mission so far.

It was still dark and really difficult to get our bearings when we were eventually called forward to the approach of the canal. We were on schedule. It wasn't until the sun began to rise that we became more aware of our surroundings, and it began to feel more comfortable. We were surrounded by dozens of ships large and small. In the near distance, we could see the thin, lush green strip that indicated the edge of the canal and, after that, golden sands stretching as far as the eyes could see. There was a reassuring military presence, with armoured vehicles patrolling the canal bank and the whir of helicopters overhead. These were just some of the 1,800 troops provided by the Egyptian authorities to protect us along the entire 100-mile stretch of the canal. There were three helicopters, four patrol boats, and the troops ranged every 200 yards on the shore, all facing away from the canal. Our hosts were aware of the potential disastrous consequences of an attack on a British vessel in their waters and clearly weren't taking any chances. I just wished they could have done something about the plague of tiny insects that swarmed all over us at first light!

Entering the canal was far more difficult than I remembered it. There was a tidal stream and lots of contacts, making it difficult to pick up the entrance immediately. It was time to embark the first of what was to be many Suez Canal expert pilots. He was a really average-looking gentleman (although I don't really know what I expected) and had a distinctly grumpy demeanour. To be fair though, his mood was probably understandable, thanks to the earliness of the hour and the fact that there are no creature comforts on the bridge of a submarine.

'Go left, go left,' he shouted, gesticulating wildly with his arms.

All right, mate, calm down, I thought.

Fortunately, the entry into the canal didn't take too long; therefore, he was rapidly exchanged for a second pilot who was to be the guide for the first part of the transit. The second expert was very quiet indeed, and we did what we needed to without interference. The third pilot who joined us refused to come to the bridge at all. He decided he was perfectly content with giving conning orders from below. This did not suit me at all as we were not in control from the best vantage point, which was the bridge, and we had a somewhat lively discussion on the phone before he eventually turned up on the bridge. To begin with, he was not happy at all and was very sullen, but after some good food, a bit of lively conversation, and plenty of diplomacy, we managed to get him fully onside. Indeed, before long, he was visibly starting to enjoy himself, so much so that he cancelled the following two pilots and stayed on for the remainder of the trip through the Suez Canal. After the shaky start, he turned out to be quite entertaining company. He made some very interesting observations and seemed to have an opinion on just about everything. It was interesting hearing about his lifestyle at his home in Port Said, which seemed so different from ours, although I was not entirely sure I bought into the 'two to four wives' rule that he was so passionate in advocating.

As we passed through the canal, we occasionally glimpsed the odd ancient monument looming in the distance, but most of the time, our attention was drawn to the constant forbidding presence of the force protection all around us. The number of troops was immense. Each of the small towns we passed was heavily policed by the military. It was clear that they did not want anything to happen.

Inside the submarine, life continued as normal as we made our way down the Suez Canal. That is with the exception of water consumption being reduced to a minimum as we could not 'make water' in the canal. Our distillers were exceptionally effective pieces of equipment, but we needed reasonable quality saltwater to start with and riverine or canal water will not work. During the transit, we 'rowed the canal' for charity using one of the Ergo rowing machines in the WSC. Over seventy of us volunteered for rowing slots of 2,000 metres to match the 163-kilometre length of the canal. The goal was to do it as fast as we could. When it was my turn to do my 2,000 metres, I had been on the bridge for over fourteen hours and really didn't feel like it. Still, it was important to join in, and I managed 7.24 for 2,000, which I was happy with. More importantly, the team managed to row the full distance quicker than we transited, raising over £3,000 for charity, and all done without the ability to shower.

It took sixteen hours to get Turbs clear of the Suez, and all in all, it went very smoothly. The boat transfers were all well conducted, and each of the junior officers drove the boat through the canal, which was vital for their experience. I couldn't help reflect on what things might be like on the way back, whether there would be any changes or whether it would be business as usual. Despite the Arab Spring, there didn't seem to be much change to those who looked on from the sidelines. People waited on the banks to cross the canal, the military had the same massive hold they always had, and the place looked the same as when I last went through. I started to wonder what real changes would come about as a result of the Arab Spring. Change is great as long as it results in something better; however, that is not always the case. There were already signs that some countries were beginning to regret uprising. In Tunisia, for example, the middle class were now becoming vocal that they had not stood up to one regime simply to succumb to another form of tyranny. Meanwhile, always at stake were the massive revenues from those transiting the canal. No regime, new or old, wanted to begin messing around with that.

As soon as we were through and disembarked the last pilot, it was time for the crew to start cleaning the boat for the captain's rounds. These are the most thorough set of rounds to ensure the boat is immaculate prior to arrival in our first port. While many of the men moaned about it, it was an excellent exercise in focus. With the right degree of encouragement and application, they would overcome their reticence and, in turn, feel achievement and pride that our old submarine looked as new as it could.

Pride in the unit you sail in is crucial. Most submarines look pretty good; they need to because dirt causes havoc with machinery and equipment. However, there are a few that look amazing. Turbs was one of those because we as a crew owned and were *Turbulent*. When visitors came on board, even in the darkest days of deep maintenance, we wanted to make the right impression, and part of that was via a clean submarine. Where we were about to go, it was vital that we took this pride on, and we made sure that anyone who visited the submarine took the message away that this was an awesome piece of military hardware in excellent condition, with a crew that clearly know what they are doing. This scrutiny was going to be later in the trip though. Firstly, the Red Sea was approaching.

I have always found the Red Sea to be a truly bizarre place. There is a huge amount of traffic to deal with, and the water temperature is *really* warm. It is 30 degrees at the surface, and even at 250 metres, it is still at 28 degrees. This presents all sort of problems to a submarine, not least that it makes it hard to create the necessary vacuum to achieve faster speed. To give a degree of comparison, in the Atlantic, the water temperature may reach 14 degrees at the surface and drop to about 3 or 4 degrees at 250 metres. Even in the Indian Ocean, where the surface temperature is 30–35 degrees, it drops to 15 degrees at 250 metres. Here in the Red Sea, the whole boat became exceptionally warm, and the air-conditioning plants had to work hard to reduce the internal temperature below 25 degrees. It was only April too. I wondered what it was going to be like in July.

We were heading south towards the Bab el-Mandeb, or BAM as we knew it in the military. The team and I had to prepare for the challenge of yet another choke point. This one had a very serious threat—Somali pirates. Historically, they have boarded a variety of merchant vessels in this area, and they were quite brazen in what they would attempt to take over. It was amazing really—young Somali pirates armed with little more than RPGs and AK-47s were boarding huge ships and taking them over, with no experience of the ships they were boarding.

NATO submarines are routed using a system called SUBNOTES. They work much the same as when aeroplanes log their flight paths. Submarines will declare their routes, the depth zones they wish to travel, speed, and destinations. The intention is that all those forces with submarines are able to avoid mutual interference and potential collisions. Although the BAM is quite shallow at this time, no NATO submarine had been through there dived, although in my view they could have done so. We were about to transit 200 nautical miles of the most pirated waters in the world on the surface when we were in our most vulnerable condition. Not surprisingly, this concerned me. I discussed the situation with Gareth and the team at a previous planning meeting to work out the safest way forward once we were through the Suez.

'So how are we going to deal with this, knowing that we are a little limited with options?' I asked.

'Sir, we've been looking into it, and we've got a couple of courses of action available to us,' said Gareth. 'Firstly, we go at the exact routing speed of the SUBNOTE, which has us passing the narrowest part of the choke point before sunset. We'll attract attention, but in our favour is the fact that the all the merchant vessels that exited the Suez the same time as us will be ahead of us. The pirates might have no interest. The second option is to delay as long as we can and enter the choke point after dark.'

The scanty intelligence we had on the pirates indicated that their night-time capability was not good. Our low freeboard silence (we make no noise because we are nuclear-powered) meant that they probably wouldn't detect us. The biggest risk was that they loosed off an RPG or AK-47 at the bridge, aiming to make us stop.

'As long as our people are below, the biggest risk to them of boarding at any time is that they will fall in and go through the propulsor!' concluded Gareth.

'There's some good stuff there,' I said. 'What if they do come for us with a swarm attack?'

'We head towards Yemen as rapidly as possible,' Gareth countered. 'It's the better of the two options and closest to our navigation track.'

'Or we dive,' I said. 'I know it's not in accordance with the SUBNOTE, but our safety is paramount, and we need as many options available as possible.'

I gave the options some thought.

'OK, I like the second option, and we should go in after dark,' I concluded. 'It will feel uncomfortable, timing-wise, and we will get spooked. We need to be able to make considered decisions after deliberation and justify everything we do.'

Twelve hours ahead of passing through the BAM, I met with the two watch leaders. In planning and briefing, my priority was to assure the crew that the decision to take targets was mine.

'Fellas, are you happy with the plan?' I asked.

'Yes, sir,' they both said.

'What's the what-if?' I asked. 'You know this isn't a test. We just need to make sure we've got everything covered.'

They'd thought about that already.

'Sir, we're confident we understand the rules of engagement, and the team know as well,' Jon replied. 'We've table-topped them, we've practised, and we're ready to deal with any encounters.'

He then added, 'Although the intelligence is a little vague, we know the full range of vessels they are using. We also know when we will be in proper range of their bases too. If we get the timing right, we might not see any.'

'I think you're right, but we should anticipate that we will be in contact,' I agreed. 'I'm keen to avoid antagonising them. We're unusual, and you know how that can play with people's minds. They might see it as a huge prize. OK, just make sure you note every decision you make with legal justification. The XO or I will never be far from the control room, but if you take action under self-defence, do what you have to do.'

We all looked at one another. They nodded, and I left.

They had to be prepared to fully engage with whatever required engaging with, in the knowledge that the legal ramifications that went with their actions were my responsibility and mine alone. I had spent considerable time thinking this problem through. My men and

I would come under scrutiny, massive scrutiny, for any actions we took, yet it was imperative I took the focus off any potential comeback. It was not right for the young men charged with firing the weapon on my order to come under any pressure. My men understood that I would do that for them because as long as they did what I asked of them, they had done the right thing.

Before we could tackle BAM, there was the monthly requirement to conduct what is known as weapons quarters. This complex evaluation is required to test the weapon discharge system that, while loaded with weapons, cannot be exercised. I've often likened the challenge to a version of Tetris, but with weapons. There are five tubes, a load of weapon storage racks, and sixteen of them have weapons in them. The other four have equipment and racks for the specialist riders to sleep on. (Riders can be anyone from maintenance personnel to linguists, sonar experts, or special forces.) Even when you remove all that, the four are not in the right place to extract the weapons and test the discharge system. Also, on occasions, there is a need to spin up, which means powering up the weapons so they spin the gyros and align the navigation systems in preparation for targeting of the TLAM weapons, and they need to be in the tubes to do that. It can take up to thirty weapon movements to achieve the aim. At this point in the trip, in the midst of Operation Ellamy, the men conducted a total of seventy-seven weapon movements, which is a considerable feat. Believe me, it is easier to load and fire them than it is conducting weapon quarters. I was impressed by their efforts. The more times they did this exercise, the more efficient they became, and the quicker the WSC returned to become the training/sleeping environment it usually acted as. Weapon quarters were completed with twenty-four hours to spare before we set off to BAM. We were ready.

As we surfaced and approached BAM, tension was once again palpable. The GPMGs were rigged on the bridge, and the aimers prepared their personal weapons and checked that the GPMGs were working correctly. Our intelligence was pretty good about what to expect; whether or not the pirates knew we were there was another issue. Our main problem was identification. A fast craft manned by pirates looks much like fast fishing vessel, so trying to differentiate between any would-be threats is difficult.

BAM itself was interesting, if not slightly unnerving. It was a really strange place, large enough that you felt you were at sea, but you could see land on both sides, which narrowed up ahead. It certainly wasn't time for sightseeing though. The GPMG was manned. All personnel on the bridge were wearing body armour, and support teams were in the junior rates' mess, fully armed and ready to go.

I wanted everything to feel as normal as possible, but in reality, I wasn't going far away from the control room. If and when anything began, it would happen fast, and rapid decisions would be needed that might result in life or death. We had to get this right.

'Quick draw bearing 240' came over the intercom from the bridge. (When we are on the surface, we send a very small team of usually two or three to con the submarine from the bridge on top of the fin.)

The ship control officer of the watch made the pipe, and suddenly people swung into action.

'Officer of the Watch, Captain, what have you got?' I said.

'Sir, two skiffs, laden, eight personnel in each, possibly armed, closing at speed,' said Ollie, the OOW.

'Gareth, we can't take any risk, let's get ready to engage,' I said to the XO calmly.

This was business. We were trained and had practised these procedures many times, and I had gone through all the legal considerations long before we reached this point. I'd studied previous encounters and refreshed my memory on what hostile intent, hostile act, and self-defence meant. In essence, I would be able to justify everything we might have to do.

'TASO, read warning 1 and then 2,' I commanded.

The warnings were the legal process that has to be undertaken prior to engagement to give oncoming craft every opportunity to stand down. Whether they understood what was being said over the radio in English could not be known. At this point though, I was the only one who should be thinking about this or, indeed, considering the implications of what was about to happen. Everyone else was reacting automatically and rightly so. My eyes took another quick sweep of the immediate surrounds, and I saw the medics were standing too and the submarine had been shut down to the safest state. Then I looked at TV Geoff, who was in the control room, overseeing the filming of the unfolding drama. They'd been with us since we deployed, so I was quite used to having them around. I barely noticed them some days. Then suddenly, I realised I had forgotten about one person—the other cameraman. He was still on the bridge.

Reaching out, I grabbed the intercom. 'Officer of the Watch, this is the captain. Is the photographer on the bridge?'

'Yes, sir, he is' came the confirmation.

'Let's get him down for his own safety,' I replied, keeping my voice steady. I couldn't believe I'd forgotten about him.

Both periscopes were now trained on the vessels, with Gareth and me urgently attempting to assess their intentions. As always, things were happening very quickly, but it was crucial not to make any knee-jerk reaction. Our response had to be well thought through and measured.

To add to the sense of urgency, we started receiving messages from a merchant vessel which up until a few moments ago had been happily travelling alongside. It is not uncommon for vessels to do this at choke points like this. The thinking is that there is safety in numbers, and tagging along with a nuclear submarine is possibly one of the safest options there is. However, the captain had heard our two warnings and wrongly assumed that they were directed at him. For a few moments, there was some confusion before we realised the misunderstanding. As soon as we did, the TASO called the captain and clarified the situation, much to his evident relief.

Meanwhile, the two craft had closed sufficiently that we could now see them with the naked eye. They were small well-powered white vessels, with men in them, armed and clearly discussing among themselves what they needed to do. For an agonising few moments, they stared at us, and we stared back, weighing up the next move. Finally, they clearly decided to turn their attention elsewhere, abruptly turned and sped off. Relieved, we stood down, but we already felt this was only the first flashpoint in what would undoubtedly be a long night. Still, now we had this experience under our belt, we would be better prepared for the next potential engagement.

That night, we made sure the sonar team manned sonar sets, which we usually only do dived or during fog. Sonar is a good aid for detection and classification.

I went to the bridge as we transited the strait itself, but since it was night-time, there was little to see. It was interesting to see the merchant vessels hastening past at maximum speed. They had all switched off their navigation lights as a precaution, and water was being continually poured over their sterns to prevent anyone from attempting to board them.

'Bridge, Sonar, new contact at red 10, bearing moving left, initial classification is a high-revving vessel' came a voice over the intercom.

I was still on the bridge at this moment, and all of us were looking in that direction. There was nothing to be seen. Our night-vision goggles showed nothing, although to be fair, they rely on some form of light to enhance the picture. The contact was, however, definitely moving down the side.

'Nothing visual down the bearing,' said the armed lookout as he trained his SA80 rifle in that direction.

'Ask the sonar to report,' I said to the OOW.

Just then sonar lost the contact. Bewildered, but safe, we carried on. We couldn't see anything, but equally, it hadn't engaged us. We passed like ships in the night!

Once clear of all traffic, we dived and continued with our exceptionally slow speed of advance. As soon as things were back to normal, the team continued preps for my rounds. The boat was already looking very clean indeed, which was encouraging. I wanted to ensure that the team was proud and ready to present the boat to any VIPs that came on board in Fujairah. Even so, now we had navigated BAM, I was still anxious about the run ashore. The behaviour of a few of the men was troubling me, and I had to put my mind to a better way of dealing with potential problems. However, before that, an even more pressing personnel concern emerged.

The first moment I became aware of an issue was during the morning Operations Group meeting. One of the officers (whom I shall call Officer A) started his standard brief on the geopolitical situation with the following statement: 'I was unable to get any information about the current system, so I have emailed my family to ask them to send stuff, so here goes . . .' The TV cameras were filming.

I let him continue even though the other thirteen personnel present were clearly all as surprised and alert as I was. This didn't bode well. I passed a note to Gareth, asking him to investigate further. I didn't want to inspect his emails. I already sensed this would go further and could well turn out to be something that I needed to adjudicate on. There was no room for error with this; protocols needed to be followed. We needed to play this by the book.

When the briefing had finished, Gareth stepped forward and quietly asked him if he could see his email account. A little while later, Gareth came to see me in my cabin. He looked shocked.

'Well, he willingly showed me messages where he'd asked his family to send him details about the UAE, Yemen, and other countries in the region,' he said, sitting down with an exasperated sigh. 'I hardly dared look further back, but I did, and his sent box was unbelievable. Since we've been out, he has been emailing with extensive details on a variety of things. While it's probably naivety, it beggars belief.'

I shook my head slowly. I was struggling to believe what was happening. My team had always been really good about communications security (COMSEC), and here, an officer in a privileged position had abused it. All this had happened in the view of the embarked film crew too. I would not be able to contain this event because his family knew, his fiancée knew, and the film crew knew. I needed to inform HQ.

I reflected back to the first time I had met Officer A when he joined Turbs back in the UK. I'd noticed him, nursing his pint, and sensed pretty much straight away he was probably a submarine officer even though he was out of uniform, and I introduced myself.

'Hi there,' I said. 'Are you part of the submarine crew?'

He greeted me back and told me he was about to deploy with us, and then he rapidly told me how this wasn't quite what he was expecting and how he wasn't looking forward to the deployment. I understood the sentiment, at least in part. We all miss our families, but it is the job we signed up for and one that most of the people on the crew loved. When we set off on this deployment, I misguidedly assumed, or perhaps hoped, that he would buy into being in the team. He had enough previous experience to understand the challenge, and while he didn't do anything wrong initially, I instinctively knew he would need support. Now he had given me a big problem to deal with. I had to maintain the delicate balancing act of demonstrating fairness on board while maintaining our excellent reputation.

'There's more,' Gareth said, looking at me directly. 'You're not going to like it.'

'Go on,' I said, steeling myself.

Then Gareth went into some of the detail. While it was probably innocent in intent, this was not in control. Internally and externally, I now faced a number of challenges, one of which was the TV crew. I tackled this first.

'I need a favour,' I said to TV Geoff. 'Could you not focus on Officer A for a while?'

'Mate, he's one of the main characters of the series,' he said, looking a bit taken aback. 'I can't stop with him now, and anyway, the MOD agreement is there.'

He had a point.

However, this was a major compounding factor; if proven that one of my leaders could have broken the law, this would make his position on board untenable as an example to others. In addition, he clearly didn't want to be here. He had lost his focus for the environment or those around him, and his actions could put him and us in real danger. However, I knew that this would be a difficult process at this early stage, and removal from post for his and our safety would not be sanctioned. Process had to take its course. I would, however, start the long and thorough administrative process of collecting evidence to present a reasoned explanation and assessment of this situation.

The best I could do for now would be to explain the severity of the situation to Officer A, the potential consequences, and the implications of any actions he might want to take, and hope that he would think about it logically. However, whatever was on his mind was affecting him, and his approach was already having a negative effect on the management of his department. He had inherited a well-run team, who were now becoming dysfunctional and losing motivation. The root cause of his issues was difficult to determine, but it could not affect our delivery.

Turbulent diving off the South Coast

Close surveillance during PDT

Diving the submarine

O Group

Turbulent on surfaced transit

Tomahawk missile

Conducting close warship engagement training

CHAPTER 7

Unlock Team Potential— Always Do the Right Thing

In the early stages of my command, I had a watch leader who was really struggling with the job of OOW. His attitude was right, he was a good man, but he simply couldn't lead his team. He was visibly overwhelmed with the amount of information presented to him, the decisions that needed to be made, and the potential consequences. I made every attempt to assist him, but whenever he was not being overseen, he crumbled. In a world where the smallest wrong decision can have fatal consequences, this was serious. This state of affairs couldn't continue.

Time was of the essence. This man's previous captain had recommended him for Perisher, and as far as I was concerned, there was no way he could make the grade. It would be setting him up for a very big fall to even try to peruse this track, not to mention the enormous waste of money from pushing him down a career path he clearly wasn't suited for.

I wrote a report and brought him into my cabin to discuss it.

'How do you think it's going?' I asked.

'I could be doing a lot better than I am,' he replied honestly.

'You're right,' I agreed. 'I want the best for you and the team, but what I've seen so far tells me that you are not going to go to Perisher. I'm not going to recommend you, although I know your previous captain did. It's not fair on you. You know the pressure, and it would break you.'

He looked devastated yet relieved. It was obvious he was almost waiting for someone to tell him this, whereas nobody had.

'You know, you're good with your people, and I think you're attitude is great, but actually you need to be looking elsewhere,' I went on. 'Your future career in the submarine service will not involve submarine command. I know the next few weeks will be difficult because we are still at sea, but I'll be there to support you. You just need to keep safe throughout.'

'As you leave the cabin, smile. You, me, and the XO are the only ones that know anything about what I have just said.'

'That's understood, sir.' He nodded and left my cabin, walking confidently past the control room and down the ladder to 2 deck with a smile.

He was a different guy during his next watch. The pressure had been removed, and he worked well. I had unlocked the problem of self-pressure generated by the expectation that he *must* get selected for Perisher when he knew as well as I did it was never going to work out well.

I didn't leave it at that. I then spent considerable time with Dan, the then XO, moulding this young man's next career steps. After I'd done what needed to be done, by telling him Perisher wasn't an option, I needed to look after the man. I had to show him and others there was no stigma attached to this 'failure' and that I was committed to seeing this through. I was more than happy to do this because, although he couldn't make the grade as a submarine commander, he had a fantastic attitude and well deserved my loyalty. It was as much down to him as to me that this worked out so well for all concerned. Sometimes failure can be a great enabler, and it was good to see him achieve success in the surface fleet. Situations like the one I have just described happened more than once during my command. I resolved that it didn't matter who I was given or what skills were lacking; I would give everyone who came to me every opportunity to learn, train, and prove themselves. If they couldn't though, despite effective coaching and mentoring, then I would be direct and tell them how it was and where they should actually focus. However, if they did not demonstrate the right attitude (and attitude was key to me), then I would do what was necessary to remove them. By this, I don't mean simply removing them from our submarine to someone else's to simply offload the problem but out of the submarine service altogether. Taking someone out of the service is often a very lengthy and comprehensive process, but this didn't mean I shied away from it.

As I continued to reflect on Officer A's future, I couldn't help but wonder what the factors were that were affecting him. Was this personal or the product of someone offloading a personnel challenge because we had had success with others in the past? He had gone from vessel to vessel. He must have been given every opportunity to succeed, but this was not for him, or he never really wanted to. Whatever it was, he was not responding to anything we could do for him here.

TV Geoff came to see me.

'Captain,' he began (he always called me that—he found it amusing). 'Can we do an interview?'

'Sure, when and where?' I said brightly. Meanwhile, I was thinking, *What is he up to here?*

Five minutes later, he was back, fixing my microphone and framing the shot. He asked me a few generic questions, and I gave him a few bland generic responses. Then he came right out with it.

'Captain, if someone had done something they shouldn't have, how would you deal with it?'

He already knew full well how I dealt with discipline—by the book. Now it was obvious this was about Officer A.

'The Royal Navy has standards and protocols which must be adhered to,' I answered. 'I deal with any disciplinary issue fairly and appropriately.'

Not a bad answer, but where is he going with this?

The director lowered the camera, and I switched off the microphone.

'Stay and have a chat please,' I asked.

'He told me everything, Ryan, and on camera too,' he said.

'What?' I said, unable any longer to contain my frustration about how this was developing. 'How could you do that? I did ask you not to.'

'I asked him one question: "How's it going?" He spoke for a long time about everything.'

'Well, now you know the challenge,' I said, shaking my head. 'I've got to protect my team and to protect him. It's not going to be easy.'

Nothing about this situation was easy or straightforward. Command is a privileged position, one that you have to earn, not only by selection and successful completion of courses but most importantly once you are on board and lead your team. Your team, their families, half a billion pounds' worth of military hardware, a nuclear reactor, weapons, operating alone in a void less explored than space, mission orders that are broad but allow you to plan and execute without recourse to others, making decisions with political consequence, decisions with consequence to life—that is the responsibility of submarine command in the twenty-first century. Our culture works hard to prevent change. Not everyone is cut out to be a submarine commander, or indeed any sort of leader, but having the right attitude is crucial. Teams are made up of leaders and followers; as long as you are one or the other, that's fine. If you're not willing, then there is a problem. That attitude has to be apparent from the moment a raw recruit first signs to the services.

The reason why the submarine service needs to choose the right people is that every single member of the crew has a crucial part to play. If just one person does not pull their weight, or worst still is obstructive, it infects the whole team. In such a close dynamic, it's intolerable. This was why the issue of the actions of one of my officers was not one I could just live with. I had to find a resolution and fast for him and us. Situations like this test one to the limits because the way one reacts as a leader has an impact on a large number of people.

We were now through BAM and arrived in the Gulf of Aden, near the International Transit Corridor Zone, where merchant vessels are protected from pirates by a variety of warships from all over the world. As planned, we met up with other Royal Navy units, including RFA *Argus*, a helicopter carrier, and her Merlin helicopters from 820 Naval Air Squadron. We had arranged a couple of submarine-versus-helicopter exercises, which was a great opportunity to practise evasion.

I asked a friend of mine, the commander of the 820 Naval Air Squadron, if the camera crew could go up with them to film the exercise, and he readily agreed. However, in perhaps an omen of things to come, it all rather fell apart when we tried to transfer the cameraman to the helicopter. The helicopter came in far too low, and I was amazed that he didn't actually touch us. It was the lowest I had ever seen one go and rightly aborted the transfer. The incident also abruptly ended the training package because the helicopter crew went away to 'learn from their experience'.

There was no point dwelling on the close call, so I turned to my attention to the inspection. The men had worked hard for some days now, and it was important to put in as much effort inspecting as they had put into cleaning. I was not disappointed. The level of detail in their efforts was quite incredible. The engine room in particular was the best I had seen in my command even though it is the most difficult compartment to clean. Indeed, I was certain it looked better then, than when others held the submarine. I told the crew exactly that, and the men were rightly proud and happy about what they had achieved. With only a few days until we were alongside, when it was certain that people would visit, we could be confident that our submarine looked the best and represented the UK well.

Elsewhere, the Arab Spring continued a pace, but now our focus was on the situation within the gulf and Iran. Iran had the ability to shut the Straits of Hormuz, yet even open-source information mooted that they were posturing. They were, without doubt, a proud nation, and I had the upmost respect for them. We discussed the situation at the O Group daily meeting.

'You're right about the political situation, but their history is incredible,' Gareth said. 'They are a warrior race. Misunderstood in some cases, understood well in others. No one has ever conquered them though. They have withstood Western pressure well.'

'You're right, Gareth, and we needed to treat them carefully,' I agreed. 'One mistake in posture in the wrong place and we could cause a diplomatic challenge for our governments. In addition, we were entering their backyard, the Gulf of Oman, their home waters. We have to treat them with respect.'

I felt like adding *and honour*, but that sounded too much like a line from a Hollywood film.

As we entered the Gulf of Oman, not far from the territorial waters of our future host nation, we surfaced so the film crew could film some generic linking sequences. We 'shut off from diving' in order to prepare for harbour in a couple of days. In basic terms, this meant we put the submarine in a state whereby no inadvertent operation of any equipment could start the diving process. It was always a clear signal we were going to go alongside soon. Men went to the bridge to taste the air, smoke, and relax before the inevitably difficult entry into a port that was new to us.

'Watch stand too—warship in sight'came over the main broadcast. 'Captain, sir, Officer of the Watch, at red 10, 12,000 yards, I have one Iranian frigate, probable Kilo-class submarine and a support vessel.'

This hadn't shown up in any of our intelligence briefings—need to check the quality of the intelligence we are receiving, I thought.

'We can stay here and interact when they call us up, but our standard responses might have an adverse effect, or we can remove ourselves from the problem totally,'I said in the control room. 'There's no time for discussion, team. Let's get ready to dive rapidly. XO, Coxswain, get set up, clear the bridge, let's get going. I'll talk to HQ.'

We were still at the height of the Arab Spring. Having the wrong interaction now could make the already tense atmosphere in the region worse still. As we rapidly prepared to dive, it became obvious the frigate had seen us because it changed course and had begun to close in rapidly.

'Is that everyone below?'I asked.

'Yes, sir, all accounted for, air in the groups is good,'the paddy said.

'Navigator, depth of water?'I asked.

'200 metres.'

'XO, range to the warship?'

'Sir, 4,500 yards, ATB of 5 starboard, closing at speed.'

'Make a pipe. Diving now, open all main vents, revolutions five-zero.'

We started diving rapidly. If we had followed the process handed down from submariner to submariner, it would take eight minutes to get underwater. However, because we knew our platform and had practised, we were underwater in two. With one last look at the frigate through the periscope, we disappeared. She would never find us, and we had already seen some of their tactics in action. They'd look around for a while and then continue with whatever it was they were doing. I was pleased with the team, who had acted quickly and efficiently. The incident was great training for my officers too because it showed they needed to be ready for anything and couldn't switch off, ever.

Eventually, the Iranians continued transiting towards the Gulf of Aden. They were part of a well-publicised Iranian counter-piracy task group and probably part of strategic messaging for the Iranians in the region. I couldn't help but think of the captain of the Kilo, someone like me who was focused on contributing to his nation's security yet at this stage perceived by the West as a potential enemy. At our evening review, I spoke to the team.

'That was well dealt with. Our control of the situation was good. That's what they look like, just like us. We're going to be here for a while, so we need to get used to this. Things can change so rapidly, and we deal with it by always de-escalating right up until HQ tells us to escalate.'

We returned to PD and surfaced on 2 May. Soon after, the radio supervisor knocked on my cabin door.

'Here is the out-of-routine immediate signal that's just come in, sir,' he said as he handed a slip to me.

I already knew what it said. I could hear the team in the WT shack talking: Osama bin Laden had been killed in a US raid into Pakistan. The founder and head of al-Qaeda had been in his Abbottabad compound that was around 100 kilometres from the Afghanistan border. As I surveyed the news, which was being intensively reported and analysed by every single media channel, I reflected that the problem with having killed bin Laden was that it wouldn't stop the threat from Islamic militants. Al-Qaeda is an idea, not an organisation, and when one head is cut off, another grows. However, as everyone recognised, it was a major victory for the United States and achieved at least some degree of closure for the nation. The attacks of 9/11 caused the deaths of over 2,000 people. Whether they were for a higher purpose or not, they were wrong; innocent people died who had nothing to do with bin Laden's fight. Maybe justice had been served by this revenge killing almost a decade later; however, this event was going to add to our security issues. In an already fluid environment where we were not fully established, this had the potential to change the dynamics again. His people might want to retaliate anywhere and against anything. We needed to be ready.

At least we had a few days to relax and prepare for what was in store. We were scheduled to spend five days in Fujairah for some much needed R & R. The hotels we were all booked into were pretty amazing. If anyone outside the service ever questions the level of luxury we get alongside, I always invite them to consider the rather-tight conditions we usually live in. On board Turbs, we have no personal space, work in cramped conditions harder and for longer hours than any prisoner is used to, and don't see daylight for most of the time. I would be prepared to argue quite forcibly that it is quite right the military looks after us in harbour. Before we arrived alongside, it was time to talk to the team over the main broadcast.

'Men, this is the captain, listen up. Well done. We've done some amazing things to get here, contributed in a variety of areas, and now we're about to go to Fujairah. You'll be aware by now that bin Laden has been killed. Be sensitive about this fact where we are going. Some of you have been there before. Remember, we are guests. We will establish our reputation now, and we all have a part to play. Abide by their rules, respect their culture, and have a good time.'

It was time to make our first of many entries into the port of Fujairah and go alongside our support vessel RFA *Diligence,* or Dil as we knew it. As I sat on the bridge, conning the submarine alongside Dil, I was really struck by the dry heat and the sparse scenery. My head was buzzing with what I would say to all the key people I needed to build relationships with while I was in port.

Once we were safely alongside, I went down below into the air-conditioned submarine. It afforded real relief from the heat and was very refreshing. I returned my binoculars to my cabin, drank lots of water, and then waited for all the people that we needed to meet to arrive—the chandler, the Royal Navy liaison officer, the local police, and so on. It was also time to say goodbye to the TV crew, 'Geoff, our legacy is in your hands,' I said as they departed, feeling sure they would do us proud.

Once they had left, it was time to deal with my own people. Officer A's progress or recovery was becoming increasingly troublesome, and I was finding it difficult to balance what he needed, we needed, and what HQ was telling us to do with him. Beyond all, I hoped training would take over for him. *You're a trained leader. You need to lead, and if you can't lead, follow, but don't do this,* I thought.

I couldn't talk to anyone on board about it because I had to maintain my impartiality. I spoke to HQ about the problem again, but they continued to insist that the situation was recoverable even though I was certain this would never be the case. Officer A plainly didn't enjoy being on board and was doing everything he could to demonstrate this. He was not quite obstructive but was certainly never constructive in his approach, unsurprising in his unhappy state. His small team was beginning to fray at the edges, and one of them had already been to see me about the problem. I listened but did not provide opinion. My greatest fear was starting to be realised—the rest of the crew who couldn't help but be aware of what was going on might conclude that my inaction was preferential treatment and my lack of comment on him was consent of his actions. In reality, I was simply managing him on board while waiting for HQ direction, although this waiting and lack of acceptance of my judgement on this issue was disheartening. Officer A's well-being was still my responsibility, although I was breaking one of my own rules and should have sent him home against their direction.

At least there was one glimmer of hope. The crew seemed to be working things out pretty well for themselves. The team dynamics around Officer A were interesting. The others were automatically isolating him, and he was quite happy to be left out of activity.

During the port visit, we established a good affiliation between Dil, the US support protection force, and ourselves, as well as with the locals. This was probably just as well because within a matter of hours of coming alongside, two of my men got into a fight between themselves at the hotel. We dealt with it locally, made profuse apologies to the hotel manager, and reported it up the chain just in case any complaints reached them. The UK maritime component commander was rightly unhappy, and so was I. The fracas was between two of the usual five offenders, fuelled by copious amounts of alcohol. I just couldn't understand what went through their heads when they did these things. Why, after all the briefs the XO and I gave, did they still make these ridiculous mistakes? Once again, I was left dealing with the consequences, and the men were staring another disciplinary investigation in the face. Despite every control possible being put in place, still the odd event will happen. For me, it wasn't what the issue was; it was how we dealt with it that counted, internally and externally. Externally, people would want to see corporate and personal remorse. Internally, I needed to demonstrate resolve, and I would within the laws of the Armed Forces Act and the summary trial. It is without doubt a daunting process for the accused, but I was always fair, and the team knew that. Equally, I always made a point of speaking to the subject a little later.

'You know, it's nothing personal, it's business,' I'd tell them. 'You've accepted the sanction but make change. It can't carry on like this.'

This approach seemed to work.

Meanwhile, Officer A's issues had become progressively worse while alongside. He wanted to go home and was willing to attempt anything to do it. He had now threatened to go AWOL, which I reported back to HQ even though I suspected it was just an empty threat. Inexplicably, despite all the information, the order came back to 'manage the risk'. The management of this risk in my eyes was to send him home, but that was not an acceptable outcome at this stage from the HQ. I highlighted to Officer A that if he tried to get out of the country, he would be arrested at the airport by the authorities because he did not have an entry visa. Officer A was to continue to sail with us even though privately I thought this was ridiculous. It was not fair to him or us. He wanted to go, and I wanted him to leave too.

For the next ten days, we were to be on an independent exercise period (INDEX) to get used to the area. After sailing, Gareth and I decided to make one of the watch leaders duty captain for the duration of the exercise period. We also moved everyone else up one level so that they would have the opportunity to discover the challenges of the next stage and tailor their education, training, and focus accordingly. Initially, this seemed like a step too far. Our first damage control training scenario was appalling. There were too many people out of place, and there was a complete lack of focus. Gareth and I had deliberately stepped back to give them this chance, and then we had to rapidly intervene.

'Men, this is the captain,' I said on the main broadcast. 'You'll know that that did not go well. I sell our capability as a top fighting elite unit to the HQ based on the fact we can do it. We need to focus rapidly. R & R has made us weaker than we were. Redress the balance rapidly. Anything can happen in this area. Our interaction with the Iranians should have told you that. Focus. That is all.'

My words and adopted stance of a 'disappointed dad' had some effect because the trainees stepped up after that and things started to run as they should. It had been a nerve-wracking time letting things go wrong, but it was important for them to find their own limits, and the only way to do this was to let them make mistakes. As long as any situation was recoverable, then there would not be an issue.

Although I was exhausted by the intensive period of training, I decided to make one last appeal to HQ regarding Officer A. We were due back in Fujairah in a few days to conduct maintenance and a crew change, and this seemed a perfect opportunity to send Officer A back to the UK. More than twenty-four man hours of work written by myself and Gareth were sent in and approved. My commodore had got involved and supported the assessment that it was not in our interest or his, and we prepared to land him. The reality was that Officer A wasn't cut out for the navy and especially not the submarine service. My failure was that I knew this a long time previously yet I had reluctantly followed the guidance of my contemporaries to comply. I should have sent him home so much earlier. I could probably have avoided so much of the latter stages of that destructive cycle by resisting the administrative cycle and just getting on with it. *Always learning–must share that with all when this is over,* I thought.

As soon as the INDEX was completed, we returned to Fujairah for maintenance and a crew change. Corrie and the kids flew out to spend some time with me, and I was very excited about seeing them all even though I didn't have an enormous amount of free time because I still needed to ensure we were ready for the next patrol in six days.

Officer A returned to the UK, and I was informed that they had taken direct control of him. He would need to deal with the discipline element that came with his behaviour on board; however, in the long run, this would be the start of a new journey for him.

Our second visit in Fujairah felt a little better than the first. We were more familiar with the personalities, such as the owners of the hotels and some of those associated with the crown prince. It is a lively place, with most of the entertainment for Westerners centred on the hotels, which are among the few places where alcohol is allowed to be consumed. I warned the crew once again that this was to be our home, on and off, for the next seven months, so they needed to watch their behaviour. I also immediately increased our get-to-know-you initiatives with local dignitaries to ease our integration into the community. The first of these was a reception, which we held on board the submarine. My senior team and I put in a lot of effort to make sure our guests all had a good time. Building these foundations was essential so that we could call in favours in the future if the need arose.

It wasn't all about socialising though. We still had to keep a close eye on Turbs, and there was a need for some urgent maintenance. We had discovered a defect with one of the saltwater pumps some weeks earlier and ordered a replacement to be flown out to Fujairah so we could fit it when we arrived. Unfortunately, in a repeat of our experience in the Med with the elusive flexible hose, we found out the stores hadn't left the UK. This was hugely frustrating because if we hung around waiting for too long, it would throw us completely off schedule. I immediately got in touch with HQ to urge them to get the parts to us quickly. Although they reacted almost straight away, inexplicably they put them on a plane that was headed for Bahrain, more than 360 miles away.

'What about the RAF base here in the UAE?' I said to Gareth when I heard the news. 'They've got to get them to us, and everyone knows the delays associated with the dogmatic customs process. That could all have been avoided.'

Gareth gave me a what-can-you-do shrug and shake of the head.

A few hours later, we received some more news.

'The good news is, the pump has arrived at Fujairah Airport,' Ben reported. 'Unfortunately, it's been impounded.'

Sometimes you just couldn't make this stuff up. The next twenty-four hours was spent in frantic attempts to get the pump out. In the end, I had to draw on all the contacts we had so carefully cultivated at our reception. I couldn't help reflect that we had already used up all our favours even though we had months to go in the area. There wasn't time to dwell on the failure of our logistical system, again. Time was marching on, and we were under huge pressure to fit the pump in the shortest possible time frame. Fortunately, the marine engineers, along with some support staff that had flown out especially, managed to fix it in record time. We were ready to go once again.

The last piece of the puzzle was to change over 50 per cent of the crew and to completely prepare for the next patrol. Among the new faces we welcomed on board was Officer A's replacement. There was a noticeable sense of relief among the crew when Phil came aboard and took charge of his department. One man in a position of responsibility can have huge effect on subordinates and peers alike. It is his choice as to how he wants to do that. Some leaders do what's right naturally, and some don't know exactly what to do and take time to learn. Watching Phil greet his subordinates, I could already see that, to my relief, he was committed to his team and was taking it seriously.

I went with my family to the airport to say goodbye, which, as always, was exceptionally difficult. We had had a great time together, but I was very conscious that the next time I would see them was six months away. I didn't show it, but I was quite emotional as we exchanged our final words. Luckily, they were strong because they are well equipped to deal with any challenge thrown their way. It did feel quite final for me though. At that point, I didn't realise how close to final it might be.

CHAPTER 8

Lead in Defeat—It's the True Test

It was time to sail and conduct an indication surveillance tracking and reconnaissance (ISTAR) patrol. These patrols are demanding because you are dealing with both potential enemies and friendly forces yet working hard to avoid them all. If our vessel was detected by anyone, the game was up. We would have failed, and without doubt, there would be political consequence.

If somebody had told me that that day might well be the last one for me, I might have said different things to my family when we'd said goodbye at the airport the night before. However, the submarine service is really bad at normalising what is quite frankly a dangerous business. Other services do the same. We take for granted that the machinery and training we receive is there to keep us safe, and we wish to be assured that the leaders who take us off to do what we do do so with confidence that we will return. I was that leader, and this was about to become the worst day of my command and the best.

I hadn't really slept very well. As always, my mind was preoccupied with what lay ahead as I visualised the challenges one by one. One of the issues that particularly troubled me was the number of new faces on the crew. I had discussed it with Gareth the previous evening.

'That's quite a change of crew,' I began. 'We need to make sure we're ready and the reality is, we don't have much time before we'll be in the thick of it. We've really got to focus the first four days or so.'

'A couple of damage control exercises will focus the team,' he suggested.

'Should be enough,' I concurred. 'But we need to stay focused on the political situation as well.'

Gareth nodded. 'Yes, you can almost feel the tension, and we're in a friendly country!'

'It was busy out at sea last time, and we know that it's really difficult to determine friend from potential foe. I haven't been down the submarine in the last twelve hours, Gareth. Do we have all the intelligence updates we need?'

'Yes, sir, we've got it. I've checked with both the watch leaders. They know what the plan is, and even though they've not briefed their teams on the detail, I'm convinced they're on top of it.'

The following morning, as I left the hotel and headed to my hire car, I was struck by just how hot it was, and it was still only 7 a.m. The drive from the hotel to the port of Fujairah was not a remotely interesting one, with the exception of the mountains in the distance. There was simply an expanse of anonymous-looking buildings. As I sped along, I mused that the mere fact they were building so much was in itself incredible.

When I arrived in port and crossed the gangway, I thought again how exceptionally hot it was. It was a really unforgiving, dry heat that doesn't quite make you sweat but does make you feel really breathless and uncomfortable. I couldn't believe I was stupid enough to go running in those conditions a few days earlier. Glancing over at the armed sentry, AB Bergen, I could see he was already looking pretty sorry for himself. I hurried towards the control room to take final reports from the HODs.

'Sir, the water temperature is 34 degrees Celsius, the hottest we've seen so far,' said Ben. 'The flash up [which starts the reactor] has been really difficult. We're there, but we're not running at maximum efficiency. We need cooler water.'

I'd been right about the extreme heat. The mercury held stubbornly at a sticky 45 degrees Celsius for air temperature, and the knock-on effect was that the water was a balmy 34 degrees. Turbs had been alongside in Fujairah for quite a while in these unforgiving conditions, which meant that, aside from the reactor, other systems might prove to be quite temperamental. Submarines like ours were designed to operate in the cold waters of the Atlantic, not in the exceptionally warm waters where we found ourselves now.

'If it's a local heating issue, then we should get that as soon as we're out of the harbour,' I replied. 'How are the rest of the systems?'

'Everything else is holding up fine' was the reassuring answer.

'OK, if we're not going to be able to do this here, let's get going. We'll sort this out once we're out in cooler water.'

With that, I went to the bridge as we started our departure.

The thought that continued to niggle away at me was that when we eventually got underway, our coolant plants would inevitably function at a lower capacity, possibly as low as 50 per cent of their usual output. At least everyone knew to expect this. Our best option was to get out to sea, where the water was cooler than in the harbour, blow down the coolers, and then the systems would operate effectively once again. Even if we did manage to achieve this though, we still faced the more immediate problem that, without sufficient coolant plants, we would be putting undue pressure on all the other equipment on board until we sorted out the original problem.

The tugs pulled us off Dil. Normally, I'm really excited about driving out, but this time, I wasn't at all. Intuition is a great thing; you get it from years of experience and perhaps some other source we don't truly understand, which most people call gut feeling. I couldn't work out why, but I had a deep sense of foreboding. Something just didn't feel right. I had plenty of other things to do and think about though. I needed to get out of harbour, which is always difficult wherever you are, get dived, get sorted, and get on patrol.

While we collected our towed sonar array from the support vessels, I looked around. My eyes settled on the plethora of support vessels and self-protection teams provided by the US Navy.

Why can't the Royal Navy do this without the help of the USN? I thought. There were some amazing-looking boats there. No one was going to mess with them. I was listening in to the chatter of the self-protection vessels on VHF when suddenly they sprang into action. Even though it turned out to be only a local fisherman who had come in too close in a high-speed boat, it was impressive to watch. There was certainly no need for a response from us. By now, the towed sonar array was fixed, and we were off.

In a short while, we were quite a long way off from Fujairah. Just the tops of the mountains on the coastline were still visible, and I prepared to leave the bridge to go below.

'Captain, sir, the DMEO is on the phone,' the OOW said, handing me the phone.

'Sir, it's Simmo, Ben's back aft. The water temperature hasn't changed yet, but we think there may be a blockage in one of the strainers to the combined cooler. We're going to line up and clear it.'

The knot that had been in my stomach all morning tightened. I already sensed this was serious. As I was preparing to go below, the phone rang again.

'Captain, sir, it's the DMEO again.' He handed back the phone.

'Sir, all the freons [air-conditioning plants] have failed. We can't get them back on.'

'OK, work the problem through, I'm on my way down,' I said.

Taking a deep breath, I took one last look out across the large expanse of still, glass-like water and then began the most challenging three hours of my life. I went down the tower ladder, carefully one step at a time, until I entered the control room.

Aside from the immense heat which hit me with, the first thing that struck me as I made my way to the middle of the control room was the overwhelming feeling of tension. The atmosphere everywhere was thick and heavy. We had all entered the unknown, and despite all the training and experience we had, this was about to test us to our limits.

It was surreal as I entered the control room. All the lights had been dimmed, and the equipment had been shut off, with the exception of that vital for life or driving the submarine. It felt even hotter in here. In fact, the compartment was like a furnace. Listening to the succession of messages coming through, it was clear things were worse elsewhere in the submarine, if that were possible. Back aft, humidity had apparently reached 100 per cent, and the temperature was now over 60 degrees in some parts. Personnel were overheating, and there were very clear signs the situation was rapidly becoming out of control.

We all respond differently to heat stress. Physiology, fitness, and to a lesser extent, genetics all play a part. In high temperatures, the main means of heat regulation is evaporation of sweat from the skin; however, when air temperature and humidity are high, as in this case, the capacity for evaporative cooling is significantly impaired. The cardiovascular system reacts by directing heat to the skin to help increase heat transfer, but this places a considerable burden on the heart. If you carry out any physical activity, which we had to do, it strains the cardiovascular system still further.

I had enough medical knowledge to know that when the body temperatures rises above 104 degrees Fahrenheit the risk of heat injury rises significantly and the function of organs such as the central nervous system, the kidneys, the heart, and the body's regulatory system will deteriorate. Regulatory failure can occur early on in a situation like this, and other symptoms will soon follow. Indeed, although many casualties develop mild symptoms first, there would be a rapid progression to severe illness among many of the crew. Some too would circumvent the mild symptoms and get very sick very quickly. The prognosis was, quite frankly, terrifying.

Decision-making in a situation like this, let alone *sound* decision-making, was a virtually impossible challenge, yet if I didn't make the right call, things would most certainly escalate to dangerous, potentially fatal, levels in a matter of moments.

'Sir, the fore planes won't extend at the moment, and we think there's a problem with the forward escape hatch,' said Wingnut, the chief stoker.

For a brief second, I wondered if things could possibly get worse, then they rapidly did.

'Casualty, casualty, casualty, casualty in the tunnel' came over the main broadcast system.

What's the situation? I thought. *There are already four major problems:*

- *We've lost air conditioning, uncontrollable condition, equipment fails.*
- *Fore planes don't work—shouldn't dive without them.*
- *Escape hatch isn't sealing—can't dive.*

One casualty, there'll be more to follow—how long have we got? We need to deal with each of these issues simultaneously.

My natural tendency is always to run towards any incident and attempt to resolve it, but now, more than any other time, I shouldn't do that. I was needed elsewhere. Steve was an extremely reliable navy petty officer medic (POMA) whom I trusted absolutely (there are levels of trust that build over time). He would lead, and his first-aiders would assist until we had this in control. I walked towards my cabin. When I arrived, I was shocked by what I saw.

The casualty, a petty officer marine engineer, was seated on my bench sofa bed, half-naked. His skin was pale, almost translucent, and he was rocking back and forth deliriously, crying. I looked over at the POMA who was busy, trying to rehydrate the man, and even though he was presenting a reassuring face to the casualty, I could read the concern in his eyes. He clearly had the matter in hand though. Right now, it was most important that I got my team around me so we could make a plan. Normally, if there's a damage control situation, we'd go to emergency stations, but this was different. It was nothing and everything, and going to emergency stations couldn't help.

I hurried back to the control room.

'What's the status of systems, Mr Brown?' I said to the warrant officer weapon engineer who was sitting on the ship control.

'Sir, hydraulics is really playing up. We can't extend the fore planes. The after planes are now failing in position control electric and now only operate in position control hydraulic. But as I said, hydraulics is not reliable. Temperatures are high throughout the submarine, freshwater levels are dropping—last reading was 4,000 litres. I haven't been in comms with back aft yet . . .'

The list didn't seem like it was going to end.

It was clear to me that unless we fixed the air conditioning, we couldn't bring this under control, but the hatch wasn't sealing, the fore planes weren't extending, and in addition, we were already shutting down a variety of systems. Yet with the fore planes not extending and the after planes failing in their primary operating mode, this was impossible. In addition, all our systems were switched off—no sonar, no fire-control system (needed for managing the tactical picture), no radio communications, nothing.

OK, I thought, *there are now seven major problems:*

- *Air conditioning has failed, uncontrollable condition, equipment fails.*
- *Fore planes don't work–shouldn't dive without them.*
- *Escape hatch isn't sealing–can't dive.*
- *One casualty.*

- *After planes are only working in secondary mode.*
- *Freshwater levels are dropping–need a minimum for firefighting and reactor cooling.*
- *All sensors are switched off–we're blind if we dive.*

I was adding risk on risk, and while I could manage the lack of sensors, all this added up to one thing—I could no longer guarantee the safety of my team. That was really concerning as I'm always able to regain control. Automatically, I was solutioneering—*we should get back to Fujairah and work out a repair strategy once we've found the problem. But that's over two hours away.* I thought *it's an option if we don't get control of this. Equally, we could dive, but I don't know how feasible that is. I've got fifteen minutes before I need to make a decision.*

The reality though was at that moment, we couldn't dive at all. I was very confident of my ability to dive the submarine in reserve modes. I was able to draw from my days as an XO on HMS *Torbay*, where I'd had to control the submarine using only the emergency control systems and had managed the problem fine. The fact was, we 'played'with the submarine a great deal to see what she could do and knew her dynamic handling well. I would put those skills to use here if I needed to, but they need to sort the hatch out. My train of thought was abruptly interrupted by another urgent message over the main broadcast system: 'Casualty, casualty, casualty, casualty on 2 deck.'It was followed by 'Casualty, casualty, casualty, casualty on 1 deck.'

I caught my breath. How much worse was this going to get?

'Casualty, casualty, casualty, casualty in manoeuvring,'blared another grim message over the broadcast system.

For a fraction of a second, I had an unnerving feeling like the world was spinning past me while I was standing stock-still. I had to summon up all my strength to stop myself from rushing to each of those casualties. Men everywhere were succumbing to severe heat exhaustion, and nearly everyone was displaying symptoms, suffering from dizziness, vomiting, headaches, and weakness. At the more extreme end, there were fainting and seizures. I had to force myself to accept that other people were better placed to deal with the most severe casualties. Teams and individuals were already dealing with incidents autonomously, but I had all the parts of the jigsaw, and I needed to formulate a plan rapidly. Although I was, by now, well used to being in charge, the weight of this losing battle was relentless. I felt very alone.

In a bid to begin to order the jumble of thoughts that threatened to cloud my heat-addled brain, I started to look through the electronic charts. We were 26 miles from Fujairah. That meant more like a three hour transit to get there, and then maybe a further hour to get alongside. Meanwhile, we must be exhausting our limited water supplies.

'What's the temperature in the WSC?' I asked the ship control.

'Stand by, sir.'

I didn't get the figure because the next moment another message came through: 'Casualty, casualty, casualty, casualty in the wardroom.'

This time I just had to go and see for myself. I headed down the ladder from 1 to 2 deck and then into the wardroom.

I was stunned at the sight that greeted me when I arrived. Ben was lying on the deck, drifting in and out of consciousness, with our POMA giving him air and the defibrillator unit by his side. Whenever his eyes fluttered open, glassy and clearly struggling to focus, he started trying to give orders to manoeuvring. His voice, usually so strong and positive, was low and rasping. I was shocked to my core, and I'm someone who is rarely shocked.

I looked around the wardroom. There wasn't just one casualty—there were four! Three more casualties were stretched out on the deck in a similar state to Ben—two marine engineers and one AMEO. One of the intelligence specialists was providing reassurance to them . . . and water.

'Ben, you're going to be OK,' I said, kneeling down beside him. I wasn't sure if he could hear me or even knew that I was there. Then I went around each of the other casualties to do the same thing. *This is my team. I'm responsible for their lives. I need to find a solution to this–rapidly.*

I turned to Simmo, the DMEO, whose face mirrored the shock and desperation I felt.

'You're in charge,' I said, keeping my voice even. 'Do what needs to be done, but make sure you look after yourself.'

That was a formal order and pretty broad direction, but Simmo had always been excellent at what he did, and I didn't need to give specifics. He knew that he had to stay forward and hydrated, only going back briefly.

'Sir, I've told the teams to cycle regularly. No one's spending more than about fifteen to twenty minutes in the engine room,' Simmo said. 'There's a couple of major issues,' Simmo continued. 'The first one is that automatic protection may scram the reactor, and the temperature in the diesel room is too high to even start the diesels.'

We both knew what the problem really was—the combined coolers (the water inlets to the cooling systems) were blocked. You can't cool anything without the flow of water in, and the fact that was all of our equipment needs cooling—basically, we were in a pressure cooker. We needed to blow them clear.

So what you're saying is if the reactor shuts down—no restart—abandonment, I thought.

OK, I thought, *there are now eleven major problems:*

- *Air conditioning has failed, uncontrollable condition, equipment fails.*
- *Fore planes don't work—shouldn't dive without them.*
- *Escape hatch isn't sealing—can't dive.*
- *Multiple casualties and some key personnel.*
- *After planes are only working in secondary mode.*
- *Freshwater levels continue to drop—need a minimum for firefighting and reactor cooling.*
- *All sensors are switched off—we're blind if we dive.*
- *Reactor might scram (automatically—safety design).*
- *Too hot to start the diesels (therefore, can't recover the reactor).*
- *Heat in the weapon storage compartment must be increasing.*
- *No one knows except us.*

'Simmo, can we override the automatic protection so the reactor doesn't scram spuriously?' I said.

'Yes we can, but just be aware that this relies on the reactor panel operator to monitor, and there is risk with that, considering the conditions.'

I decided to go to the engine room to check on the engineers. As I moved forward, it was a good opportunity to see what the conditions were like throughout the submarine. Even though it was dark, because lights and equipment had been switched off, the situation that greeted me was pretty frightening. Most of the crew had removed at least some items of their sodden, sweat-laden uniform, and the sense of order that usually existed was visibly beginning to deteriorate. It wouldn't take a genius to surmise this wasn't going to improve soon. As the temperature continued to rise, its negative effects became ever more pronounced. Some members of the crew were becoming very loud, and as I moved among them, I caught snatches of a number of noticeably bizarre conversations as each individual struggled to deal with all the things that were going wrong, as well as the extraordinary temperature. Meanwhile, other crew members went the other way, and usually, outgoing men began to withdraw into themselves and become very quiet. Nearly everyone was clutching a bottle of water from the supply that was usually stored back aft, and was chugging on it continuously. Unfortunately, the water was so warm it gave virtually no relief whatsoever, and now the supply was completely used up anyhow.

I continued past the manoeuvring room, which turned out to be as chaotic as everywhere else. A quick glance at the dials on the dashboard confirmed it was over 60 degrees Celsius in this area with 100 per cent humidity. The heat was stifling. I could feel my heart hammering in my chest with the sheer exertion of moving around, and it was increasingly hard to breathe. One of the worst symptoms was the overwhelming feeling of fatigue that made it virtually impossible to think straight. For a fleeting moment, making sensible decisions in an atmosphere like this seemed a virtually impossible challenge; I needed to make some very soon, particularly if the repairs were not effective.

Down in the lower level (the deepest part of the engine room), I spotted a couple of the engineers. They looked terrible.

'You OK?' I shouted over the noise and our ear defenders. *What a stupid question, but what more can I ask?*

'Yes, sir,' they replied. I expected they would probably answer in the affirmative, but I was listening as much to the way they said it as to what they actually said. They were clearly exhausted, but just about bearing up. Good, I needed them, and they were cycling through, not spending more than ten minutes at a time.

'Keep hydrated,' I said, leaving to go forward.

I went back up to manoeuvring and spoke to Simmo, who happened to be in their briefly, keeping control, watching his team manage the problem. 'Overrides?' I asked. 'In place,' he said, and I walked off, back to the airlocks to get forward again.

My brain was buzzing. Many elements of this problem came to the forefront as I made my laboured progress forward. The sight of the immense suffering of my crew constantly assaulted my eyes. Our situation was critical. It didn't help that the heat exhaustion left me with a permanent feeling that I had forgotten something really important. I had to focus, however difficult it might be.

I tried to contain all the issues into three groups. Firstly, people were falling. Secondly, equipment was failing. Thirdly, there was no 'out'. If everything aligned wrongly, we'd be plunged into a situation where, no matter how many more casualties piled up, there would be no real hope of success.

I had now worked out that the 'return to Fujairah' option was out. Turbs wouldn't make it; the crew wouldn't either. Even if we were successful at getting back (three hours), attempting a complex entry into any port would be virtually impossible because, at the current rate of temperature rise, all the problems mentioned above would be upon us. I could ask for help, and indeed, I fully intended to, but what could anyone do in the timescale where we needed action? It would take longer for HQ to get helicopters or a frigate out to us than it would take for us to resolve this issue ourselves. Abandonment would result in fatalities, especially with the outside conditions as they were, and waiting for rescue would take hours. Broader than just us, the political consequences would be catastrophic to the UK if we didn't deal with it effectively. More importantly though, the risk of losing life was increasing rapidly.

The supreme effort of working through the problems one by one had a positive effect. I finally had clarity in what we needed to do. To cool the boat, we needed to dive. The last bathythermograph we had taken before entering Fujairah during our dived transit had shown the water decrease temperature as you got deeper—obvious you would think, except in places like the Red Sea, where it doesn't decrease a lot in the depth range SSNs operate. However, in this case, it was about a two- to twelve-degree difference, maybe more now that the surface-water temperature was so high—that would give us time. I needed to talk to the team first. I spoke on the main broadcast.

'Men, this is the captain,' I began. 'The situation is that the freons have failed, and the combined coolers are blocked. The marine engineers are working on it. The only solution is to get underwater to cooler water and cool down. We've got a few other issues to sort before we dive. It is hot, so hydrate. Look after your shipmates. Further information will follow.'

As a priority, I needed to contact HQ, but that would mean switching on equipment, and that would add heat and might write off the equipment. I had to alert them to our situation, though, so that someone else knew. Thereafter, I needed to deliver to keep the trust my team had placed in me. I could at least count on the fact that I had led all of them at some time or another in the past, occasionally in some in extreme (although different) situations, and we had always succeeded. I was absolutely levering off that credibility now.

As a short-term measure, I ordered the main access hatch open so I could get people out on to the casing of the sub and into the open air. I was aware it wouldn't really offer much relief from the crippling temperatures, but it might at least deal with some of the psychological symptoms. A number of the crew staggered out, looking dazed and exhausted, and I went up on the casing to talk to them. A couple of them looked quite questionable, so I told one of the leading hands to watch them closely. I was particularly concerned about two ME warrant officers. Two of the ME leadership team were already casualties, which meant there were only two officers remaining. If we lost those two as well, we'd have even more of a problem to deal with.

Fighting the mounting feeling of frustration at this chaotic day, I left the casing to go back down below.

Taking a deep breath, I said, 'LRO, connect up SATCOM and try and get hold of Northwood [HQ].'

Within minutes, I was talking to a young lieutenant who was the duty officer in the HQ control room.

'Controller, it's Commander Ramsey,' I began. Traditionally, we never use our names for COMSEC, but right then, I really couldn't remember the correct code. 'We are 9 miles from the allocated dived water. All the air-con plants have failed, and we are in deep trouble with multiple casualties. I intend to dive the submarine, and I'll call you back in twelve hours.'

'Roger, sir,' he replied. No request for other information. I must have portrayed a situation under control, or I didn't explain the gravity of the situation well enough.

That's it then, I thought. *We really are on our own again.* Even though HQ was now aware of our predicament, there was nothing within any of our plans that involved anyone else. There could be no miraculous Hollywood-style rescue. We could rely on no one. The feeling of isolation was overwhelming because, although I've seen it and felt it a lot during my career, this time it was beyond any experience I had had.

'Gareth, we need to get the fore planes out,' I said. 'We can accept the after planes in any condition as long as they are semi-usable.' Gareth went off to investigate.

We need to move quicker than this, I thought as I looked around the control room. *The team is functional, although the operating in silos is no longer working, so there's little coordination, but that's fine. Everyone's looking at me and feeding me with information. It's white noise most of the time, but they're talking.*

My attention was drawn to the ship controller, who wasn't in the best condition.

'Mr Brown,' I said, 'Get the coxswain up to the control room so that we can get going with this. Concentrate your efforts on the WE teams and the weapons.'

'Roger, sir.'

We needed to get the bridge cleared and get underwater. The plan would be to get to 60 metres rapidly and then get as deep as possible. Because no sensors were working, we needed to be deep. Once deep, we could cycle the main vents, change the water, cool the boat, cool my team, and gradually recover people. We had operated in this area before, so I knew that there were no trawlers, a few dhows, and just a handful of merchant vessels. All submarines were accounted for, so I was content to dive—returning to periscope depth without sensors would be another risk to understand and take—but first we needed to deal with the most complex event a submarine does, dives.

While the engineers dealt with the fore planes, I focused on doing the best we could for the short term. I ordered the crew to change the ventilation state and purge the atmosphere in the boat. I spoke again to the ship's company over the main broadcast system and explained the situation so everyone understood the problem and what the plan was.

The problem with solutioneering, you suddenly feel more confident about the future, and that can be dangerous. I avoid it wherever possible, I think about the end state but only focus on the journey there—in this case, stage by stage. Although opening the hatches initially had an effect, it made very little difference to our overall situation. It was hardly surprising really, given the outside temperature. In fact, as I went back to the control room, I could see immediately that decision-making and my crew's reactions were becoming still more erratic. In a space of a few minutes, a further five more casualty pipes were made, and it wouldn't take a huge stretch of the imagination to guess at least some of them would be very serious indeed.

'Ship Control, how are we doing?' I asked when I got to the control room.

'Sir, issues with hydraulics persist. They're continuing with the forward escape hatch,' he replied.

'I'm going forward,' I said and went down the ladder to 2 deck.

I needed to get around my team again. As I made my way around the vessel, I was confronted with the increasingly alarming sight of crew members wandering around with a complete lack of focus rather than following the purposeful, regimented routine I was so used to seeing. They were very clearly just trying to survive as opposed to functioning effectively. It was really heart-wrenching to see them in such disarray. When I reached 2 deck, it was even worse. The area was littered with unclothed men lying down, sweating, and panting, propped up against walls in tiny spaces, seemingly wherever they dropped. Negotiating the tight corridors between spaces was even more difficult than usual. I passed the junior rates' bathroom, where the POMA was using a hose to spray people cool.

'POMA, what's the status of casualties—how many, what condition?'

'Sir, twenty-four so far, seven are serious. First-aiders are with them. The rest are resting. This seems to be working spraying water.'

We haven't been making any water as the distillers are off. I must check how much we have left. We need at least 2,000 litres to operate the weapon storage spray in the event the weapons 'cook off' [explode], I thought. 'Keep fighting the fight,' I said as I went to the forward escape compartment.

When I arrived there, one of the engineer junior rates came up to me. 'Sir, the electrolysers and CO_2 scrubbers are off. We haven't changed the atmosphere. Shall I run the emergency CO_2 scrubbers?' He was right; we hadn't been monitoring the status of the atmosphere. *This added to our problems*:

- *Air conditioning has failed, uncontrollable condition, equipment fails.*
- *Fore planes don't work—shouldn't dive without them.*
- *Escape hatch isn't sealing—can't dive.*
- *Multiple casualties and some key personnel.*
- *After planes are only working in secondary mode.*
- *Freshwater levels continue to drop—need a minimum for firefighting and reactor cooling.*
- *All sensors are switched off—we're blind if we dive.*
- *Reactor might scram.*
- *Too hot to start the diesels.*
- *Heat in the weapon storage compartment must be increasing.*
- *Not in allocated dived water.*
- *No ability to return to port.*
- *No support nearby.*
- *Building up CO_2.*

At least I had knocked one off the list by letting HQ know! I thought. They must be almost there with some of these now. Despite feeling lightheaded and even more out of breath, I ploughed back down 2 deck towards the galley. The chefs' day-to-day job already involved working in the most inhospitable conditions. Although the kitchen space is among the most generous on the sub, it is invariably hot and humid anyhow. This situation would surely be unbearable. Yet there was one chef still in there!

'Leading Chef, are you all right?'

'Well, sir'—there was a pause—'the meat is certainly done, but I can't be sure whether the potatoes are going to be all right,' said the indefatigable chef.

I smiled and nodded. I really didn't have a response to his comment. I was just pleased that in this chaotic and exceptionally dangerous situation, with medics being overworked and close to losing the submarine, submariner's humour was still there. I suspected, or at least hoped, there would be more of that resilience going on around the boat, despite the enormity of the situation.

'Make sure you drink lots of water, OK?' I said, patting him on the shoulder.

As I walked down 2 deck, I made a point of speaking quietly and individually to everyone I passed.

'We'll be all right. I've got a way out of this,' I repeated again and again.

I returned to the control room to find that at long last the chief stoker, Wingnut, and another chief petty officer had got the fore planes out and fixed the escape hatch, which meant we could finally get underwater, but I was still really concerned about the rising temperatures. By this time, a further four casualty pipes had been made in quick succession. Once again, the sensation I was losing control of the situation flooded into my heat-addled brain. It was an overwhelming feeling, and it was hard to fight against the tide of negative thoughts that threatened to engulf me. Battling the emotions, I decided the best short-term solution was to sit down. At least when I was safely in the confines of the captain's chair, I could concentrate my energies on directing us out of this mess. I consoled myself that, even though I felt like a wreck inside, the lads had seen me wandering around. I had encouraged them, consoled them, and reassured them. Now I needed to consolidate all that by being decisive and moving things forward. *Temperature's the key thing now. The reactor needs to keep going, and the weapons need to stay safe.*

Now that I had sat down, I summoned up reserves of energy and thought the problem through again—the fact was this was complete confusion. There was still no sequence to this, too many variables, and in the confines of our steel home and potential steel coffin, it was difficult to see a robust successful solution. Blinking hard to clear my brain from the cloud of muddled thoughts, I concentrated on what I needed to solve this thing and get rid of the unnecessary noise while appearing to listen to every piece of information. Where were my people? We needed to be able to account for everyone, and since no one was in the right place, that might be difficult. I needed someone whom I could rely on to do this and knew instinctively Ollie Lea, one of the JOs, was the man for the job. While I instructed Ollie to do this, I sent Gareth off to check the rest of the boat so we were completely on top of the situation.

Even as I was communicating this, yet another casualty pipe was made. This time the trouble came from the fin where one of the lookouts had collapsed. The shouting of instructions up and down the 'tower' indicated that the team was all over the issue.

I cast my eyes around the control room to check the team was bearing up OK. I had seen too many cases of delirium already today. The memory of looking into so many glazed eyes and hearing countless loudly spoken, bizarre conversations would inevitably stay with me for some years to come. Fortunately, those in the immediate area seemed to be holding up OK.

'Navigator, report position, depth of water.'

The navigator reported, 'We were still 10 nautical miles from allocated dived water in 150 metres of water, sir. Safe depth is 60 metres.'

'Bridge—Captain, report any shipping.'

'Sir, nothing visible out to 10 nautical miles.'

'Search report contacts'

'No contacts visible.'

That gives us time once deep to sort stuff out. Need to get sonar back in some form.

'WEO, report the state of the WSC.'

'Sir, air temperature is 42 degrees Celsius and rising.'

'Ship Control, are we ready to go?'

'Sir, materially, the submarine's ready to dive, but I've had no reports on any manning anywhere, and I haven't had reports on the hatches.'

I made another pipe, saying we were nearly ready and that the crew needed to man compartments and hatches. Then, once all people were accounted for and all hatches were shut, it was time to get going. I was sodden; however, as I looked around the dark and eerie control room, I was one of few who had shirts on!

'XO, dive the submarine.' I left Gareth in charge of the dive while I concentrated on overseeing the rest of the whole process. It was like conducting an orchestra, but in this case, my players weren't in a good way.

The main vents opened, and I watched as the angle began to develop, and the depth gauge began to change 9.8 metres, 10 metres, 10.5 metres. The noise in the control room was getting louder and louder as people were becoming more concerned as to what was going to happen next. Normally, there is little talk except a few reports, but in this case, many were just shouting random bits of information. The fact was this was a way for individuals to release tension. I mean, there was no way out of this now. The submarine continued to descend and quite rapidly. I wasn't too concerned about the rate of descent, but I really wanted to see some change to our conditions. The temperature had still not changed. We dived directly to 60 metres and, avoiding normal process of stopping there and checking the 'trim' of the submarine, carried straight on to 120 metres. The depth of 60 metres made no immediate difference, nor did I expect it to, but that didn't stop me from making a main broadcast announcement to appeal to the hearts and minds of the crew.

'Team, we're at 60 metres on our way to 120. We will be going deeper when the depth of water allows. The temperature will cool, and we will soon start to feel the benefits,' I assured them.

I couldn't verify the veracity of this even if I had wanted to. I had no real information because everything was still switched off. More importantly, people were looking really concerned as to whether this would work.

A short time later, as the submarine was passing through 110 metres depth, the voice of Dan, the engineering officer of the watch, came over the main broadcast.

'All compartments, this is manoeuvring, seawater temperature indicates 27 degrees and is falling,' he said.

At this news that the temperature had reduced 10 degrees, the tension visibly reduced in the control room. Looking around, the massive psychological effect was palpable. I could read the relief on my crew's faces. They clearly believed they were coming back from the brink of a disaster, and they were not wrong—I had been true to my word.

'Are you all right, Captain?'

Stress has interesting effects on people, but I'd barely been conscious of the command rider standing at my shoulder. I'd been so focused on making sure my team felt reassured we'd be getting out of this, I had not considered the impact of this situation on my own physical well-being—in fact, it was clearly evident that my visible focus had reduced because I hadn't even noticed him there. When he asked the question, it really was the first time I had considered it.

'I'm good,' I replied with a nod to emphasise my reply.

Taking a deep breath to steady myself, I got out of my chair and headed down to the wardroom. I needed to check on the serious casualties. 'Gareth, when we're steady at depth, change all the water in the ballast tanks and internal tanks,' I said. 'I'm going to 2 deck to see the men.' Once there, I discovered there were now three men who were suffering from severe heat exhaustion, and they were being ably attended to by the POMA. The rest were walking wounded and returning to duty.

From there, I moved on to the wardroom, where I found the HODs. They looked exhausted and almost beaten by our situation. While it was understandable to feel fed up with the hand we'd been dealt that day, it didn't make any sense to me to dwell on it, especially not at this point in time.

'This is not the time to look backwards,' I said, somewhat abruptly. 'We all need to get out and lead our men. They need—no, they deserve—to see positive action from us. It is time to show them we are in control. The time to reflect on who did what and why comes much later.'

As I went purposely from compartment to compartment, it still looked bad. Some people were recovering; others were not, and they gave me the most concern. The Sunday roast had been turned into sandwiches, which were being gratefully received by the healthier crew members, not least because it was, by now, mid-afternoon, and this incident had been going on for many hours without respite. As I went around, I was relieved to find that many of the crew simply needed a few words of reassurance, while others were happy with just a few humorous comments. Mostly, all that anyone wanted was to know that someone was looking after them and that we would recover.

We changed all the water in the tanks as rapidly as possible and then started to bring on an air-conditioning plant. It was a huge relief once the first one was online. It was then followed in rapid succession by a second and then a third. We still couldn't turn on any other equipment to avoid overloading everything we had switched on and sending ourselves back to square one. The temperature throughout the boat was reducing, and now we needed to go after each of the issues in turn. Even though we were heading back to normality, albeit slowly, the atmosphere on board was still very surreal. Most of the crew was still half dressed, and strangely, this created issues in working out who was who and what they did. Most pressing was to find out who were the nominated firefighters, but fortunately, that was quickly resolved. Our next challenge was to ensure that the air purification equipment was working correctly. If it wasn't, we would be in the awful position of triumphing against the heat, then falling victim to the effects of too much CO and CO_2. At this stage, the emergency CO_2 absorbers were running, but we needed the proper equipment to do its job.

The boat was an absolute mess. Everywhere I looked, there were piles of sweaty clothing, abandoned seat covers, and other assorted detritus. Our washing machines would be working overtime for a long time to come!

I was still acutely aware that the real test would be whether or not the rest of the equipment worked and allowed us to continue on patrol. Or had we really damaged the submarine? We wouldn't know this for days to come, but that didn't mean we shouldn't plan for every eventuality straight away. Besides, getting the senior team to focus on this subject was exactly the thing I needed to reintroduce much-needed structure. As soon as Ben was well and able again, I directed the team to start planning.

To start with, the senior team's planning process for the challenges ahead didn't go well. It was obvious the whole discipline of planning had gone. It took two attempts to focus them properly, but eventually, they came up with a plan to return the submarine back to its original state. Then we 'clutched in' and got on with it.

Our starting point was that the extreme heat must have had an effect on equipment even though most of it had been switched off. We had been out of the design tolerances for almost everything, and our only possible saving grace was that we had sensibly shut most things down shortly after the calamitous failure had happened. Initial tests showed that, sure enough, there were issues keeping even minimal amounts of equipment functioning. On our first tentative return to PD, for example, the air-conditioning plants promptly shut themselves down again, thanks to the massive water temperature rise. It was obvious we couldn't stay up for long, or we would be back to square one, so we did what we needed to and quickly went deep again to the cooler depths. Then, as the boat cooled down once again, the engineers continued to work on bringing the system back to full functionality.

Although getting the equipment back in order was a priority, we couldn't lose focus on the individuals within the team. Nearly everyone on board needed some sort of attention, either physical or mental. At one end of the spectrum, there were some crew members who felt helpless because they believed they had failed both physically and mentally. Loyalty was strong on Turbs, and some submariners worried they'd let their shipmates down even though this was far from the case. At the other end of the scale were those who were massively gung-ho, making out it as all exciting and manageable. I couldn't help wondering what all this bluff and bluster was hiding and suspected there would be longer-term issues with post-traumatic stress. Our pre-planning and ensuring that we had personnel trained to deal with this would pay off.

For the next twenty-four hours, we spent considerable amounts of time deep in order to recover, interspersed with brief periods at PD. Once it was obvious that the situation had sufficiently improved, I gave the order that we should remain at PD. We needed to bring the focus back to our forthcoming tasking if we were to continue with operations.

Life began to recover to some form of normality. Systems were brought back online and tested to ensure sustainability. As predicted, the amount of washing that was needed was incredible. The team dynamics started to return to the status quo; however, it was obvious we had a way to go as I pointed out to Gareth when we chatted in my cabin.

'You know, there will be some longer-term consequences,' I said. 'Whether you are on the ground in Afghanistan or in a hot steel tube, stress and events of this magnitude have a real effect.'

'Yes, sir,' Gareth agreed. 'Mr Brown has already got the TRiM [trauma management] team up and running. They'll run trauma management sessions to deal with individual and group needs.'

I nodded in approval and added, 'This is going to take a little while for some. You know we said we were not going to let people exercise to force physical recovery? What are your thoughts?'

'People need something outside of watch-keeping,' Gareth said with a resigned shrug of the shoulders. 'For many on board, exercise is a lifeline. I would let them train again.'

'You're right, let's do that.'

It did feel the right thing to do. I was so glad that Warrant Officer Brown had taken time when we were back in the UK to train himself and people up. That was his initiative, and now it was paying off for our team.

'We need to be in a patrol posture soon,' I continued. 'Let's make sure we ready. We're only a few days away from being on station.'

Less than twenty-four hours later, I was taking a breather in my cabin for a few moments. I was beginning to reflect critically about the crisis and how we averted it when one final curve ball arrived.

'Sir, we've got a problem with one of the young ABs,' said Steve, the POMA who had sought me out in my cabin. Concern was etched all over his face.

'What do you think it is?' I asked.

'I'm not certain, but his legs are getting worse and worse,' he said.

'If he can move, let's bring him up here, and I'll see how he is.'

Drury was quickly brought to my cabin. I didn't take any medical training to realise this man was in a very bad way indeed. He looked absolutely dreadful and was clearly in a great deal of pain.

'Can I have a look at your legs?' I asked him. It was unlikely I would be able to diagnose the problem, but I needed to take a look.

He rolled up his trousers, wincing and labouring under the exertion. I leaned forward for a closer look, and in an instant, I recognised what was wrong. It looked to me like a clear case of cellulitis, which is a bacterial disease that is quite dangerous if untreated. I knew this because I had suffered from it many years earlier when I was on my Perisher command course. His symptoms looked far more severe than mine, and I was fearful about how it might develop.

'We can help you, but you'll need to rack out now for a while,' I said, sounding deliberately upbeat.

One of the medics helped him back to his bunk, and I turned to Steve.

'Is it cellulitis?' I said as soon as I knew he was out of earshot.

He nodded. 'Possibly. I looked it up, and it ties in with the symptoms, but it's way worse than that—I just don't know what it is.'

'We need to get him medevac. I'll get the XO and get going with that. In the meantime, what do you think—injected antibiotics?'

He nodded and hurriedly left my cabin.

Gareth prepared a suitably pithy P4 (personal for) signal, stating we were leaving our patrol area with one serious casualty. He informed HQ that Turbs would be in a very specific position at a set time for help medevac.

He signed off with 'No further contact should be expected.'

After breaking radio silence and risking counter-detection, we went deep and sprinted at maximum speed to the latitude and longitude outlined in Gareth's signal. Gareth informed the ship's company what we were doing.

By now, I was really worried about him. He was in a very poor state, and there was little we could do other than do our best to make him comfortable. I kept asking myself, 'What if we've left it too late?' My responsibility was to protect this young sailor, and if I failed in this duty, it would be very hard to live with.

The transit seemed to take an extraordinarily long time, but within twenty-four hours, we reached the exact position outlined in Gareth's signal. It was time.

'Captain, we're at the RV and ready to return to PD,' the OOW said. 'No contacts within 10,000 yards.'

'Up you go,' I replied.

The boat lurched upwards and gradually reached 17.5 metres.

'No contacts visual, stand by to surface,' said the OOW.

No contacts visual, that's strange, where's the help? I thought.

Then we surfaced. There, exactly where we said we would be was a Royal Navy Merlin helicopter. It was right by us. I felt a curious mixture of pure relief that he would now get the attention he so desperately needed and real pride that all sides had performed so well to make this rendezvous happen.

While the OOW talked to the team on board the helicopter to coordinate the transfer, the casing party hurried up to prepare for it. The sea was so calm, it looked like a sheet of dark-green glass. If we weren't distracted by the loud insistent whirr of helicopter blades, it would have been surreal. The Merlin lowered the doctor and a winch man on to the casing, and the POMA hurried down the hatch, clutching a paramedic's bag. After quickly and efficiently assessing the sailor's situation, they concurred with the diagnosis.

'Your medic got this absolutely right,' the RAF doctor said. 'There's no way you could have got on top of this. He needs hospitalisation rapidly. He's good enough to travel, and we'll suit him up now.'

'Thanks, Doc,' I replied, feeling a wave of relief wash over me. 'If you've got time before he's ready, one of the lads will take you and show you around. I'm assuming it's your first time on a submarine?'

'Yes, it is,' he replied, smiling broadly. Despite the gravity of the situation, it was obvious this was a real treat for the medical man.

While the team dealt with preparing the casualty, the doctor went off around the submarine. Soon though, it was time for them to leave us, and he was lifted off to begin his journey back to land, where he would make a full recovery. As soon as he had left, we prepared to get back underwater and return to our hunting ground.

This airlift concluded by far the most testing time I had ever had during my time with Turbs and probably in the Royal Navy (and I had a few). We had been tested physically and mentally. Some things had failed, and amazingly, others had not. People had amazed me by the way they had stepped up to look after their shipmates. I admired the ingenuity and resolve they had shown. They had followed and lead, despite the fact that the way out was not clear. They simply would not be beaten. The need to succeed had overpowered the need to avoid failure, and I was proud of their success. The POMA was by far the hero of the moment. Without him, we would have lost people, I was certain. I wrote in my notebook to remember to write him up for a commendation, not that I was going to forget! *Thank God that was over–back to fighting normal enemies!*

CHAPTER 9

Always Have an 'Exit'— Never Go Anywhere You Can't Get Out Of

Trauma management sessions were already well in hand by the time we started heading back into the 'hunt'. While I was fully prepared and expecting ongoing issues following the events of that Sunday, I was surprised at how far-reaching they were. Almost immediately, there was a noticeable change in the team dynamic. Many men were so shocked by the way they reacted to the mental and physical challenge they were consumed with guilt that they had let their shipmates down. They believed, albeit completely erroneously, that others were pointing the finger and judging their actions on the day.

What had happened was no one's fault, and we needed to demonstrate compassion to any perception it was. The fact that most of us felt some form of responsibility showed ownership, ownership that had been pursued through over a year of developing as a team. However, now was not the time to reflect on this. Now was the moment to tell everyone that they had done their best, acquitted themselves well, and that it was no one's fault. Indeed, I was also amazed at the resilience of my team. I was the only person responsible throughout. Taking that burden away from many of them seemed to help, but in reality, it would take a while to get over it. The quicker people could slip back into their daily routine, the better.

From my own point of view, I was still surprised at the speed at which the situation deteriorated on the day. It was incredible and overwhelming, and it made it difficult to ascertain any idea of the totality of the situation. We were rapidly running out of water (that could have had a cooling effect). Key players were being lost, yet the situation just kept on escalating. It was interesting who the casualties were too. Some were exceptionally fit people, and I hadn't expected that at all. Now I looked at it in retrospect, I understood better why some people had succumbed more rapidly. In one key individual's case, he was visibly stressed about the situation, which increased his breathing rate, which in turn increased his temperature. Unable to cool down, his body simply started shutting down. There were some examples of truly inspirational behaviour during all the chaos too. Steve, my medic, was incredible. The way he handled the pressure was extraordinary.

Despite doing everything we could, the legacy of what we now dubbed Sweaty Sunday was destined to live on aboard Turbs for many weeks and months to come and would play out again later in the deployment. Hours rolled into days; days rolled into weeks. On board, life continued as the crew worked at getting to grips with what had gone before while conducting a covert patrol. We trained, slept, and ate on a strict schedule. Meetings continued, planning was constant, education was sustained, and all the while, we watched, collected intelligence, and waited for the moment. In this intense, febrile atmosphere, I knew everything about the crew, their philosophy, and how they operated. Most importantly, I knew how to operate around and alongside them.

It is difficult to describe the feeling of being on board a submarine during a covert patrol, watching others in the ocean going about their business with no idea you are there. It is a bit like being a shark, watching and waiting for that perfect moment to go in and attack or, alternatively, to sneak in, grab what's needed, and get out again safely, swiftly, and undetected.

Covert patrols are always exceptional, whatever the situation. They either prepare you to take risk or teach you never to take risk at all. It all comes down to the CO and the example he sets. I have seen both operating styles in action, and I believe that if you are confident enough, you must take the risk.

Any organisation that wants to stay ahead of the game needs to know how to take risk, and risk does not equal recklessness. Risk is an overused axiom, talked about my many, but understood by few. It has become the buzzword of this decade. The fact that decision-makers are continually concerned about scrutiny by those who don't have to make decisions is having effect. I suspect those that determine how risk is to be taken in many organisations rarely have to take risk and, therefore, don't understand the personal element that is entwined within the process. You can formalise, mandate, regulate, scrutinise, and criticise risk-taking, but unless you have taken proper risk with proper consequence (and probably experienced the consequence), you can't *know* risk. Risk is never simplistic. From the outset, you need to accept you cannot remove it entirely.

There are many ways of dealing with the pressure, which accompanies any sort of risk-taking, but the priority is to avoid it becoming all-consuming; otherwise, it eats away at your confidence and distracts from the objective. By the same token, avoid any form of complacency because that too is equally destructive. The real challenge is translating this balance to the team, particularly when the make-up of that team can change by dozens of personnel at a time. I invested a lot of time and energy into helping my crew think for themselves. Every boss, from chief executive to navy commander, says they like their people to think for themselves. Many don't mean it, but I wanted to show my team I really meant it. So while the patrol was hectic on occasion and dull on others, my focus was ensuring that we were able to rise to the occasion when required.

The team did extremely well, particularly in the light of what had gone before, and before long, the patrol was over. Five weeks just disappeared into thin air, and it was time to transit, meet friendly forces from the UK and the US, and exercise with them.

A US submarine, a UK frigate, our support vessel, a variety of helicopters and maritime patrol aircraft were part of the forthcoming exercise. It was quite complex, perhaps even unnecessarily so, but I viewed it as great training for the team—in particular, my JOs who would plan and execute our role in it. If they could do it effectively, it would undoubtedly help them in their careers.

The submarine-versus-submarine exercise was by far the best part of our operation to date and definitely the most challenging. I always view anti-submarine warfare as the only real opportunity to try the art of warfare against someone equally capable. Even so, it is crucial to always look at the enemy as a capable opponent without overestimating his ability, while at the same time, letting him know we were in control even when we were not. Get this balance right, and the true joy of driving the submarine as it was meant to be driven, in a wartime scenario, is there to be taken.

As the successful exercise drew to a close, everyone was on a high, and thankfully, even Sweaty Sunday began to seem like a distant memory. The countdown began towards a well-deserved run ashore in the UAE. Many of the crew were flying their families or partners out, and there was a noticeable air of anticipation on board.

Then, as so often happens, our plans were thrown up in the air.

After managing to connect to email for the first time in a while, a flood of exceptionally strange messages arrived almost simultaneously, many of them discussing items of maintenance that needed to be urgently completed in Fujairah. No one had the complete picture, but the HODs and I swiftly surmised something was up.

I called HQ and spoke to the staff operations officer, who informed me that a P4 (personal for the captain only) signal should have been sent. Details were still sketchy, but we were to sail as quickly as possible. The run ashore was reduced from a week to between forty-eight and seventy-two hours maximum, and during this time, we were to repair eleven defects, bring on stores, and get ready to go. In addition, we were still expected to do some regional engagement alongside in Fujairah.

How do I tell the crew? I thought. It was terrible news after all we had been through. They would be bitterly disappointed.

Breaking any sort of unexpected news still ranked as my least favourite aspect of the job. Honesty at times like these is the best policy.

'Men, this is the captain. We've been given some emergent tasking.' I began a main broadcast address. 'You'll know the situation from the daily intelligence briefs. Now we need to go and save lives. I know this will be difficult for you to sell to your families, but you need to and, as always, without telling them why, what, where, or who. Let's get prepared, ready, and focused. It's time to make a difference.'

I wrote personal letters to each family to apologise and drafted a form letter so they could claim on their travel insurance policies. That was something I hadn't seen coming. With the exception of a few, majority of the crew were really buzzing once it all sank in. They focused on restoring supplies, fixing defects, and making sure we were fully prepared.

It is, of course, the captain's lot to convey news and especially so on a submarine. During a covert submarine patrol, there is no mail/email, which is exceptionally tough in this information age where people are always hungry for virtual information and contact. This occasionally presents me with some very difficult situations. The most difficult by far is what to do when I receive news that a close relative of a crew member dies. This was tragically just what transpired during the patrol a short while later.

News of this nature always takes me by surprise. It transports me straight back to the phone call from Corrinne in 1997 to tell me my mother had committed suicide. It was horrible news to receive, but it was undoubtedly absolutely awful to have had to break that to me. Now it was my responsibility to do this. During OST, I had to tell three people about bereavements in a week, but at least I was able to get them off the vessel almost immediately because we were close to Plymouth. Each one had a different reaction. I always expect people to vent their anger and am so conscious I'll always be remembered for being the one to tell them about their loved one passing away. On this occasion, the first man I told just looked at me, stony-faced.

'That's understood, sir, so you'll get me off today?' he said flatly.

'Yes, we will,' I confirmed. 'We've just surfaced. The coxswain will sort any onward travel. Concentrate only on your family.'

'OK, sir,' he said and left the cabin.

The second one burst into tears—not the odd, isolated tear but full-blown sobbing and wailing. Then he wanted consoling. After about five minutes, he sat up, said thank you, and left.

The third submariner talked at length about his mum and everything that she had done. We actually laughed at points in our conversation, and then he left to get ready to get into the helicopter.

The trickiest though was a DELTEX (delicate text), like the one which informed me that the father of one of my team (I will call him Luke) had died. To put it into context, I received the message after we set off our third patrol. We had managed two nights ashore in Fujairah, and for the leadership team, one of those evenings was spent engaged in diplomacy in the form of a volleyball match and barbecue in support of UNICEF. At least it was a winning mix of charity, sport, great food, and fine company.

We were headed to a totally different part of the world, where our enemy would throw us different challenges. We would be a very long way from anywhere friendly. In fact, we were heading a long way from anywhere at all. What we were trying to achieve was exceptionally important for national security, not least that it was going to save lives.

Even though it was early days in the patrol, we were already thousands of miles away from port when I received the DELTEX. As I held the piece of paper in my hand, I wondered how close Luke and his dad were. Did he look up to him like I hope my kids do to me? Did he hate him? I'd never know, and I couldn't ask the question because it would be unusual to start probing when I hadn't before. I had to hide the fact I knew until the end of the patrol. I couldn't discuss it with anyone, not even the RS who knew because he decoded the message. I would only be able to tell Luke of his loss days before we reached our next harbour.

Dilemmas like this all added to the overall challenge of our situation. We had spent over three months in this area during the Arab Spring, doing our best to understand the itinerant people, their views, religions, and dynamics. It had been extremely difficult to say the least. We had to take into account the fact that Islam does not accept infidels in charge of Muslims. Those that operate in Muslim states have to diplomatically negotiate their way around a system that is there to dominate them. This approach to life will always provide grievance. People will always feel bitter unless they are in charge, and actually, they can't be. I am constantly aware of this, and despite my military position, I would always pay deference to any Muslim while in their territory. I didn't have a problem with this; it was their country, their religion, and I was the guest. However, I found it difficult to accept that this approach can be exported worldwide.

We were immersing ourselves in a world where trying to discern good from bad was difficult. In fact, prior to arrival, it would be tough to distinguish enemy from friend or between neutrals and those that influence events. In some cases, we may never see the enemy but only witness the effect they could have. I couldn't help but reflect on when we encountered the Somali pirates the first time earlier in the deployment. I was very conscious that they were all sons of someone. Many must have had families, perhaps sons and daughters who I'm sure would think they were doing the right thing for them. Or did they know it was wrong but still do it anyway? I am sure that it could be argued that we did the same, but that is not quite the case. My team and I were there to prevent first and destroy second. This patrol would give me time to reflect on everything we had experienced since arriving in theatre.

There is little I can say about the patrol even now. However, I can say it was demanding for different reasons; it was difficult to establish clarity, and we felt the pain of that on many occasion. Balancing boredom and pure adrenaline was part of daily life, as well as the ever-present challenge of keeping the Old Girl going. Our days became a blur, and the aborted visit to Fujairah was quickly forgotten. Five weeks later, it was time to head back to reality. Strangely, it felt like a short period of time after no real contact with the outside, the patrol had been a real success, saved lives, and made a difference. While the results would only ever be visible to a few, everyone on board knew how they had contributed.

During the return journey, we were told that we would be visiting Bahrain instead of Fujairah. We had already predicted this might be a possibility, and thus, 80 per cent of a plan was already prepared. We would be the first British submarine to do this for a significant period of time and first ever to do it via a dived transit.

As we came closer to the point of re-establishing contact with the outside world, it was time to talk to Luke and give him the bad news. I had seen him every day, chatted with him, laughed, tried to be as normal as I could. He never had any idea of the awful news I was about to give him.

When the time came, I asked Gareth to send Luke up to my cabin. He arrived at the door and knocked, a broad smile on his face as always.

'Luke, come in and sit down,' I said.

He quickly sensed that this couldn't be good news and looked momentarily confused. He'd had a good patrol, and we'd got on well.

'Luke, there's no easy way to say this, but unfortunately, your father has passed away.' I saw tears starting to well up in his eyes as he attempted to maintain control.

'Will I get home for the funeral?' he asked. It was the question I had been dreading. I now had to tell him the worst piece of information.

'He passed away four weeks ago,' I said.

I had known four weeks, and now he understood that I hidden it from him for that whole period. Logically, he knew I could not have told him earlier. I hoped he also understood I would have done everything I could to have got him home if I could. Even so, it would still be raw. His father died four weeks before, and he learned of it only now.

There was little else I could say, so I kept it brief.

'I'm so sorry. I know what you're going through, and there is no easy path to comfort. What I can say is that as soon as we get into harbour, we'll get you flown off. Anything you need in the meantime, let me know, and I'll get it sorted.'

We sat in silence, with me wishing I could do something more to help him and him not knowing how to comprehend this shattering news. I felt drained. Breaking bad news never gets any easier.

My attention was quickly diverted by another piece of bad news. The Old Girl had decided to give us another major challenge. One of the two motor generators, vital to ensure our secondary power generation (the first being the reactor via turbo generators), was creating a lot of noise. The engineering team was convinced that unless they fixed it now, something catastrophic would happen. This was sound thinking as far as it went; however, it was a major repair and not one normally attempted at sea. They needed to change one of the bearings, and these bearings are big. This entailed cooling it down, opening up the huge machine to withdraw the bearing without damaging the housing, and then inserting a new bearing. As if this wasn't tough enough, the motor generator is in the diesel compartment, which is a pretty unsociable place at the best of times.

Finally, we didn't understand the heat dynamics of the two different metals involved.

'Sir, were running out of time to do the repair,' Ben said.

'I'm pretty certain that HQ would not want to take the risk of sending us through the Straits of Hormuz in an abnormal line up,' said Gareth.

'In addition, the current regulations say we should have both working if we're alongside,' Ben added.

This rule always struck me as overkill. It was a bizarre avoidance of an extreme event, but that is par for the course in the way we treat other issues in the nuclear world. We plan to deal with the most extraordinary of things, and therefore, the extraordinary eventually becomes ordinary.

'So what are the options?' I said.

'We can repair this at sea—we know what we need to do with this,' Ben said and then rapidly outlined a plan of how to do so.

The other HODs challenged and added to the plan as I sat passively listening. They were gradually all moving towards the same conclusion; they needed to get on with it.

'OK, let's get on with it,' I concluded. 'Make sure that Ben's team gets all the support they need. It's the command priority to get this fixed.'

The team started the repair, and it wasn't long before the first setback. This job was not going to be easy. I had allowed twice as much time as the team had estimated when I set out the plan for the repair, but even that didn't seem enough now. It felt very uncomfortable. *Had I taken too much of a gamble with this? Was fatigue getting to me?*

The men battled through, freezing components down to make the metal contract and heating areas up using oxyacetylene torches to make the different metals flex enough to release. They rapidly became very tired, yet the pressure continued to pile on. While that pressure was solely for me to manage, each time I went back to the heat and confinement of the diesel room, the team was noticeably beginning to lose their faith in themselves.

'How's it going, team?' I shouted over the din of the running machinery.

'Not too good, sir, we just can't get it aligned properly, and of course, it's getting more difficult to put it back in,' said one the engineers.

'Men, we've done harder than this and got though every time,' I said, keeping my voice upbeat. 'Hey, we recovered from Sweaty Sunday, and that was hard enough. Don't let the Old Girl beat you. You need to show her who is in control and keep fighting the fight.'

After a quick breather to refocus, they changed tack and found the answer of their own accord. By the morning, the system was back to normal, and we were ready to embark and pick up our commodore and a US Navy captain before the transit through the Straits of Hormuz.

The Straits of Hormuz is the busiest shipping route in the world, mainly because it is currently the only access point from the Arabian Gulf oilfields to the rest of the globe. Iran, with its potential dominance of the area, presents an ever-present threat of shutting down the straits. One of the duties of US and UK forces is to ensure that the international strait, the lifeline for many nations, stays open. How far we would go to achieve this aim remains to be seen. That is a political decision. Here we were, though, in an environment where just one wrong move could initiate a disproportionate reaction by any nation and set in train a series of events that would be difficult to stop.

This is what it is about, I thought. When we weren't preventing harm reaching our shores, we were building unique experiences to share throughout the flotilla.

The transit was going to be exciting, but the team was up for it. Despite the fact the straits include two nations' territorial waters, our standard method of transit is submerged, and therefore, by international law, we were allowed to transit through the straits in this manner. I couldn't help but remember a YouTube clip I had seen in which a US submarine doing the same thing had been harassed by Iranian patrol boats. Something like that would be a reputational issue, so on a personal note, I was determined to go in without detection by anybody.

The great advantage to submarines is their stealth, and this was yet another opportunity to prove that. Our plan was at variance with other nations' methods of doing this, but we had planned and rehearsed, and I was confident that we could do it. The team was focused and briefed and understood the challenge. We had gone through everything that could go wrong, and our responses were at the ready. Now all we needed to do was execute the plan with our guests on board.

The effect of having guests on board, particularly if they are high in the chain of command, cannot be underestimated. I always told my men to change nothing, but human nature is such that they all respond differently. Some become tongue-tied; others change their opinions and air them accordingly, while a few become quite loud. It is quite strange.

We dived, went deep, and immediately had to deal with an exceptionally busy shipping environment. I was pleased to see the team settled quickly into doing their jobs despite being unsettled by our visitors. The contact density increased steadily as we approached the straits. We returned to PD for the last time to take a navigational fix, let HQ know we were starting, and then it was time. The number of merchant vessels, mostly oil tankers, transiting out of the Arabian Gulf is great, and they have such a deep draught that we had to be careful operating around them in such confined waters. We couldn't just go under them. In addition, fishing dhows, warships, and powerboats (usually smuggling to and from Iran) added to an already complex picture. It was weird; we were in one of the world's flashpoints, operating with complete freedom to do whatever we needed within the bounds of international law. The only way out though, if we needed one, was back the way we came. If enemy forces did decide to take action, this was where they would do it, but only if they knew where we were.

The transit wasn't what I expected at all. Once again though, the team did fantastically and dealt with the alien environment professionally. As we continued further north-west toward Qatar, the waters fell eerily quiet. The silence was all the more bizarre after the frantic activity of the straits. We had gone from dealing with sonar overwhelmed by contacts to nothing in the space of 100 miles.

We passed north of the oil terminals that connect UAE and some of Saudi Arabia to the supply routes and headed towards Bahrain and the Northern Arabian Gulf. I began to feel quite tired, yet this was no time for rest. We would be entering Bahrain shortly, which would be a new port for us. None of us had been there on board a submarine before. It was time to surface and change focus. We were far enough away from Iranian territorial waters to avoid creating any incident. We didn't need to communicate with anyone until we were nearly in Bahrain, and therefore, with so few contacts, it was unlikely that any intelligence gathering units would realise who or where we were. We entered Bahrain, and following a complicated berthing, many of the crew were free to relax for a short while. I did need to talk to them first though.

'Men, this is the captain, listen up,' I began. 'We enter Bahrain today—the first British submarine for seven years. We enter in the middle of the Arab Spring, and you'll know there have been riots reported in the press. You'll also know that people will watch everything we do. We can make no mistakes. We can enjoy ourselves, and we must rest. Enjoy.'

Unfortunately, any form of relaxation was not to be for the engineers who went straight into a massive repair programme. Somewhat frustratingly, we were yet again hampered by a lack of stores. For the fourth time in this deployment, the organisation failed us spectacularly. The essential stores were stuck in a warehouse in Amsterdam!

Bahrain was an interesting stop for us even though there were constraints due to the widespread unrest. Possibly the most exciting and worrying experience came when we attempted to get to the embassy for a cocktail party. All of us got into the SUVs provided and headed in convoy to the embassy, except none of us knew where we were going and we didn't have GPS. Within ten minutes, we found ourselves in one of the off-limit areas where we definitely were not supposed to be, and of course, we were all in full uniform. We had a real problem. With the locals looking on, our amusement at our predicament rapidly turned to fear. We quickly found our way back to the main road, eventually arriving late and somewhat adrenaline-fuelled at the embassy.

What Bahrain did have that was most definitely in its favour was a US naval base with a massive naval exchange which was excellent for electronic and sports goods. The entire crew went on what can only be described as a shopping binge. The amount of protein powder, supplements, sports kit, and electronic gear that was bought was incredible.

On our third evening, there the crew really wound down and relaxed. The Royal Navy threw a show for us, which was fantastic, and the night culminated with a showing of the first episode of *our* TV programme *Royal Navy Submarine Mission*. It was an immediate hit with all of us and an engaging surprise to all the other guests there. Disappointingly, the night looked like it might degenerate later on, thanks to a few individuals that had too much to drink, but luckily, a few senior ratings stepped in and took those that were losing it home. We ended the night with no issues whatsoever. The team had learned to isolate the few to protect our reputation. We were always learning.

The maintenance package carried out in Bahrain was complex, and the teams had to meet real challenges to meet the sailing date. The two biggest ones were changing the radio mast (WT mast) and one of the many pumps in the engine room. The effort the team put in was incredible, but I was very conscious we needed to pull out all the stops to meet the declared sailing date.

Something else was playing on my mind too. Now our planned covert tasking was at an end; the focus was on a series of exercises with other nations in the region. HQ had clearly identified this as an excellent training opportunity and was sending out unqualified submariners by the batch load. The thinking was we could train them up over a six-week period and return them qualified. This would be the first time this had been done in any great numbers and understandably so. Our focus should clearly have been towards operations and sustainability. What HQ was asking us to do was feasible, but it was quite risky. Plus, the main crew had their jobs to do in addition to helping trainees.

The first batch of trainees arrived halfway through our Bahrain visit, contributing to a near 60 per cent change of personnel, with 15 per cent additional trainees. It transpired that most had been waiting nearly a year to go to sea. They were an interesting bunch. One was a qualified chartered accountant who had been advised to join the navy as logistical writer, while another was on his second year of a PhD in chemistry. At least they were all motivated to achieve, which was half the battle in my view.

Forty-eight hours before sailing, I received a phone call in my hotel.

'Sir, it's the RS, there's a P4 in for you,'said my caller. 'UKMCC are also on the addresses, so you could come down here or go to their HQ.'

'Thanks, I'll go there,'I replied. 'It's closer.'

UKMCC coordinated all forces in the region. We worked for them when we were exercising, but when on operations, we worked for the HQ in the UK. On arrival, UKMCC gave me a copy of the signal which instructed us to proceed on operations. We would pick up the remainder of our tasking at a later date.

I rang the hotel and got hold of Gareth.

'Gareth, P4's a mission change,'I began. 'I'll meet you at the boat soonest.'

'OK, sir, I'll get the rest of the team together, and we'll see you in twenty minutes.'

Because we planned for every eventuality, there was little more to do. All our strategies were in place, and we were ready for operations before transiting to India for an exceptionally important exercise with the Indian Navy. The mast had been changed and, although not 100 per cent, was functional. The pump had also been changed after the team worked twenty-four hours around the clock in conjunction with experts from the UK.

Before sailing, I got together with my HODs to discuss the impending operation.

'Shall we take a bit of risk and send more people home?'I asked. 'What do you think?'

'Sir, the next tasking is all about exercises and the transit home, and there are some real challenges,'Gareth responded. 'It would be good to get everyone some home time though, and we'd achieve our goal of getting everyone home at least once during the deployment, with the exception of you and John.'

'I agree,'said Ben. 'Ian's already at home and back shortly, so he would agree, I'm sure.'

'Yes, it's about time we clawed back some time, particularly for those who had their time off disrupted because of the patrol,'I said.

Families are crucial, and the men needed to spend time at home. The threat from the enemy was different, but the balance of risk was not based on having a full complement of qualified and experienced personnel, so I made the decision.

'OK, can you get the team to work the detail?' I finished. 'I've got to go up and meet UKMCC to let them know we're stored, armed, and ready to conduct operations.'

Once we sailed, I let the team know the plan for our next patrol. Discretion was key. There would be no communications with the outside world for a while, and the team understood why after they heard our brief. It is always easier to understand when you can see the difference you are making.

As soon as possible, we dived the submarine north of Qatar and started the exit off the Arabian Gulf. The challenge of navigating these waters was compounded by a massive change of crew, although most had been on board before and were able to adjust rapidly. They had to. We started the deep transit through the bizarre area of no activity heading towards the choke point. As night fell and activity started to increase, we began the return to PD, undetected, to communicate.

Once at PD, we raised the WT mast to send and receive vital messages. Then our problems began. The mast wouldn't lower back into place. The radio supervisor looked at me, and I looked at him.

'Did you say that it still indicates raised?' I asked.

'Yes, sir.'

I hurried to the control room.

'TASO, what's the state of the WT mast?'

'Indicates lowered, sir.'

'The RS says he's still got power on the mast, that doesn't make sense,' I countered.

'Search Periscope, can you see the mast?' TASO said.

'No, but it's really dark, I can't see much!' came the reply.

I began to get a sinking feeling in the pit of my stomach.

'TASO, can you get hold of the WEO, brief him, and ask him to come up to my cabin when he's ready, please? Keep working on the problem. You know how important the mission is. Let's fight to get going.'

'Roger, sir,' he said.

The mast is stuck up. I knew this would happen. I should have made a more forceful argument to keep the old one. I couldn't do anything about that now. We had to move on.

Ian came through the darkened control room to my cabin. It was in red lighting, with the addition of one small white light by my sofa bed and the glow from the sonar screen.

'Sir, Gareth and Ben are with me,'Ian announced.

They came in and sat down. We were now all cramped in a room smaller than an average bathroom. I always found this amusing—the senior leadership team of the submarine crammed into a tiny room. Those walking past probably thought the same thing. I certainly used to when I was a JO.

'Sir, it's not going to go down. We've evaluated the options, and here they are,'Ian began.

We worked through the options, which basically included returning to Bahrain, carrying on the surface to Fujairah, or destroying the mast. The group had already come to a decision in my view, but I challenged them with the opposite argument to check they could justify their decision.

'So you think destroy the mast and carry on with the mission?' I said. 'What if we need to fire Tomahawk? We need two separate communications paths, don't we?'

'We've got those. All we're losing here is redundancy,' Ben countered. 'We think we can live the rest of the deployment without it. We'll need to put measures in place to protect the SATCOM mast and make sure people know that.'

'OK, let's get on to HQ and let them know.' I nodded. 'Allow no room for discussion. Just say "We intend". Gareth, can you get them to surface the boat? Make sure we're fully aware and in the right force protection posture.'

In the meantime, we worked on getting the masts down by any means and get going. The team had four hours to do this.

The first attempt didn't work. The wire pulleys snapped from being over-tensioned during the rebuild. It was back to the drawing board. The hours dragged on as the engineers tried everything they could think of. The atmosphere in the control room was tense and was not helped by regular messages from HQ asking for updates. I was exhausted and really needed to sleep but doubted I would get any shut-eye even if I wanted to because the pressure was just too great. Before long, it would be daylight, and our location would be discovered almost immediately. Once our covert posture was blown, it would have a devastating effect on our exit and our future operations. We needed to save life.

'Men, this is the captain, although we're in international waters, there's a real issue here,' I said over the main broadcast system. 'We need to go where we must go, and it would be better if people didn't interact with us before we got there. You know people's lives are at stake. Do all you can to help the engineering teams to work on the problem.'

I knew that they understood how important this was, so I didn't labour my point.

One hour before sunrise, the team managed to release the hydraulic pressure on the mast, and using a block-and-tackle arrangement, they began 'pushing' it down. Time was now of the essence, so while the team dealing with the mast continued, we prepared the submarine to dive again, removing all the weapons from the bridge. The mast seemed to be going down achingly slowly, but eventually they reported that they had it as low as it could possibly go. Unfortunately, it was still protruding above the fairness of the fin.

'That was enough for me,' I declared, decisively. 'It is adequate for what we need, and we need to get going right now.'

I sent a message to the HQ, explaining we had lost half of our communications ability but we were good to go. There were just minutes to go before it got light. We dived rapidly with no messing around and immediately went deep before starting the transit out, far away from the last possible position we could have been in. If the enemy knew when we left from Bahrain, which they must have done, they would think we were further ahead than we were. That was to our advantage, and now we had to play that. The next time we would come to PD was in the dark hours or once we were through the straits, whichever came first.

We carried on at speed to get through, returning to PD and communicating with the HQ once we were out into the Gulf of Oman. We needed to get going as fast as possible and return to the cooler, deeper water, where we could gain more speed. Now the MEs needed to deliver; we had to get to the enemy quickly.

Although, yet again, we had been confronted by the unexpected, I was encouraged to see that the team had known what the 'out' was without prompting. They had proven their ability to get out of the situation and avoid unnecessary interaction, which could have compromised the future mission. Those skills would prove useful where we were going next.

CHAPTER 10

Know the Context—
It Drives How You Operate

There are many amazing things about the Indian Ocean; not least of all is the size. It is massive. On the chart, 3,000 nautical miles might look like nothing; however, when you are covering only 500–600 miles a day (and that is more than any other maritime unit can), the true scale of it is really brought home to you. It is best to use the time constructively, preparing and getting organised for whatever type of operation is about to be embarked upon next. Specialist equipment needs to be ready to go and operational plans examined again to make sure they are cohesive, stand up to scrutiny, and are fully understood by everyone. It is also a great opportunity to practise drills. The team did really well mainly because we all had a focus on the operation ahead. We knew what had to be done and hoped that we were going to be in time to achieve it. Turbs was armed and equipped, not only for strike or surveillance operations but also for special forces deployment or recovery.

The mission was time sensitive, the tasking was broad, but the team had worked out what success looked like and how to achieve it. We were the only ones with knowledge and experience in this area, so to enable decision-making thousands of miles away, we would need to communicate in the HQ decision-makers' language. Since we were a team that learned all the time and were chameleonic in approach to dealing with others, it enabled others to achieve success.

To pass the time, nearly everyone resumed their usual seagoing routines. These routines are really important, and I have always believed it best not to disrupt them unless absolutely necessary. The marine engineers have an 'honest hour'at 10 a.m. each morning when they all go back aft and clean. Those going off-watch make sure that everything is clean before it is handed over. While off watch, some crew members do physical training while others use their time to study towards professional qualifications. After food, some watch movies, others read, while many just go to sleep.

Recollections about the last run ashore are often the focus of conversations until the time nears for the next run ashore, so life goes on. Interestingly, nobody really mentions their time on fifth watch, on leave back in the UK. Doing so would seem disrespectful to those on board who haven't yet been home. It isn't mandated, far from it; it is just the natural cycle of things.

We were only a day away now from our designated destination. We would encounter some real challenges on this particular coastline, not least because we wouldn't be the only military people there. We had to ensure we weren't detected by anyone, which was, as ever, complicated at times. The team and I were prepared for this and focused on achieving success. We'd pushed to the back of our minds the knowledge that our future programme visiting India and the much-looked-forward-to exercises that went with this trip might well be lost because of this operation. Frankly though, none of that felt important any more.

I have spent my entire career learning about others and, in some cases, letting them know what I want them to know about me. I took great pride in the *Royal Navy Submarine Mission* TV series because for the first time it afforded the public an opportunity to understand a little about what we have to do, what we go through, and how we deal with it. Yet it did not show everything. That was not possible. There are so many things we do which will never ever be known.

Today was just one of those instances, I mused as we began to study our enemy in depth. They had no idea we were even there, but we were able to observe them sufficiently closely to understand their motives and expectations. I had no sympathy for them and no hesitation in engaging them should we have to. In my view, they deserved whatever they got and probably wouldn't care anyway. When the value of life is little, then death rarely matters. We can try as hard as we wish to 'convert' everyone to our way of thinking, but it won't ever work. Our only recourse is to communicate in a way they understand, and that way, unfortunately, is the delivery of violence.

We rehearsed drills, we observed the enemy, we closed as close as I would dare without risking counter-detection, and we reported their actions to CTF. Yet while we were increasing situational awareness and probably aiding other agencies to do what they needed to do, we did feel a little helpless. We had all these weapons available to enable us to preach the only language that others understood but were unable to use them. This is not to sound gung-ho. I am only aware that it is easy talking about taking life without having to do it face to face (that is the privilege of distanced warfare), but this was about protecting innocent people. The problem with such 'watch and wait' missions is the endless waiting and anticipating. Although HQ was good at letting us know what was happening, it was difficult to find a way through the fog of political pressures to find the direction that military people like to have. We like to know who the bad people are, what we can do to them, and when. The earlier we can get this information, the better we can prepare. And the better we prepare, the more likely we are to have success. Information like this was not a luxury we were going to get though, so it was extremely difficult to see how it was all going to play out. Meanwhile, the men continued with their routines and personal objectives, whether it was educational, physical, or rest. Life goes on in the steel tube no matter where you are or what you are doing.

As quickly as it started, the mission was over. As we left the area as silently and undetected as we had arrived, I mulled over the difficult set of emotions we'd all been left to deal with. Everything felt very fragmented as though we had achieved part success and part failure. There was also a feeling of happiness that we would still have the opportunity to continue with an excellent programme in India, tinged with sadness for not being able to contribute more in the area where we had just been. It was a difficult balance. I reminded myself that my personal emotion had nothing to do with it; it was important to ensure the team realised what they had achieved and refocus them towards the tasks ahead.

The next stage of operations was new to many of us, including me. We were on our way to India to exercise with the Indian Navy. The exercise was part of a bigger initiative to further enhance bilateral relationships, but we had a very important role to play.

I had already asked the MOD for information on anything that might be of importance and read as much as I could about India's history and their strategic relationships. I had a sixth sense this knowledge would prove important to someone while we were there.

My planning also focused on the ever-present problem of drunken bad behaviour among a handful of the crew whenever we went ashore. It had been a persistent issue on this assignment, and I had no reason to think it would be any different in India. It was so frustrating that these few idiots just couldn't seem to focus on the strategic implications of their actions. Following any of these incidents, I spent about four to five man hours on average, sorting out apologies to those who had been adversely affected, placating people and attempting to bring things back to normal. After that, there were disciplinary issues to deal with, which involved the coxswain, LO, and XO investing a further twenty-four man hours. In addition, there might be investigations by outside agencies, which only added to the number of hours expended on just one incident. Now that we are subject to the Armed Forces Act 2006, it takes a long time to process cases, and they may not come to a hearing for a month or so. Then, once it is all dealt with, there is the question of regaining our reputation, which is hard won but easily lost. The perpetrators rarely give it a second thought, but just one alcohol-fuelled incident results in a disproportionate effect, and it is always the same people. I'll never understand it.

We had done well in Bahrain but not so well in Fujairah, notching up one incident. We needed to recover our good form in Goa. I was conscious I had to be careful how I sold this on board. There was no use being threatening. Actions speak louder than words. I needed to get the ball rolling by getting them to agree with what I was trying to achieve and explaining the local consequences of getting it wrong.

'Men, this is the captain, listen up,' I began, addressing the entire crew. 'We've had some great success during the last patrol. The future is a different challenge. We're going to a noble and great country where we have a great reputation. You'll have seen the news and realise how important our relationship is with them. It is vital in the region. We need to do our best to protect that. Each one of us is a diplomat, and while we enjoy ourselves, we must respect their country. During the exercise with the Indian Navy, we will excel. Most of all, enjoy the visit. It's a unique experience by all accounts.'

Shortly after this, Gareth came in to discuss a personal issue. It was obvious he needed to go home straight away. His dilemma between loyalty to his family and loyalty to the submarine was absolutely commendable and also absolutely unnecessary. All those who had contributed to us making a difference deserved to be treated well, and I needed to send him home. The challenge was that the HQ likes to have two 'command (Perisher) qualified' officers on board so that if the Captain is not well, becomes incapacitated, or dies, the other can take over and carry on the mission or get the submarine to the next port. It does happen. On one occasion, a captain broke his leg and was dosed up with morphine and out of the game for weeks. Meanwhile, the XO brought the submarine off patrol and home. The XO in that scenario was my teacher Paul Abraham.

I told HQ I was happy to sail without an XO because I was convinced that my two watch leaders, who were both ready for Perisher, could step up to the mark, but they said no. They immediately announced they would send me a command-qualified officer.

I didn't have long to dwell on the decision. Right now, it was all about getting into Goa, setting ourselves up for success, and then participating well in the forthcoming exercise.

Something else was playing on my mind too. Even before we arrived in GOA, I was concerned about our entry into the port. There was no berthing alongside. We were going to have to berth alongside our support vessel and would be relying on tugs to bring us in. Every submarine that I had ever been in had problems with the management of the tugs because things are utterly removed from your control. I suspected my experience in Goa would be no different and was very quickly proved right. My first indication that there was going to be a problem was when the local pilot arrived on the bridge, looking utterly awestruck and nervous.

'This is my first time on a submarine,' he announced.

Oh, great, this does not bode well, I thought.

I began to patiently explain all the restrictions imposed by attempting to manoeuvre a submarine and the employment of the tugs.

'You want tugs?' he suddenly exclaimed, looking thunderstruck.

His reaction didn't fill me with confidence, and neither did the tugs when they arrived. One was used for berthing big container ships and, therefore, was not ready to push/pull a submarine with a very low freeboard. The second looked underpowered, old, and rather too much like a cartoon interpretation of a tug for my liking. I was incredulous that this was what the port had provided to assist a nuclear-powered submarine alongside our support ship. A rapid adjustment of the plan ensued, and we decided we would do everything ourselves until the last moment, introducing the tugs for the final piece of berthing. To begin with, the plan worked brilliantly. I even began to feel quite good about the approach, but my optimism was a little premature. As we closed towards the support vessel, I asked the pilot to attach the tugs and push very slowly. The pilot nodded, looking very serious and barked various orders while waving his arms about energetically. With the two tugs now attached, one began resolutely pushing, while the other pulled.

'No, no, stop!' I shouted. 'You're damaging the sub. One is pushing, and the other is pulling.'

The pilot looked mortified and barked more orders, waving his arms about even more hysterically now. In a matter of moments, the tugs switched. Now the one that was pushing was pulling, while the one that was pulling was pushing. We were just as badly off, and I was worried we were losing control. The next few minutes felt farcical.

Everything I ordered to bring things back on track was countered by the tugs. I would order to go astern and the forward tug would pull the bow out, but the after tug would do nothing. To avoid colliding with our support vessel, we needed to move ahead. Then I would order something else, and the tugs would do something equally counter-productive. I am generally pretty calm and fully understand the importance of diplomacy, but this had the potential for disaster.

'Please listen to me,' I said slowly and deliberately to the pilot, who was by now looking very pale indeed. 'If this situation continues, I will have no option to leave Goa, and you can explain why we weren't able to make it alongside. Please take charge of your team.'

He gulped hard and nodded emphatically. At about this point, I was able to take firm control of the tugs, and our second attempt was successful (just). Even as we were alongside, one of the tugs began diligently trying to pull us off. With everything finally safely secured, I thanked the pilot and apologised for my demeanour. He seemed to take it quite well (probably wouldn't invite me around for dinner though).

I said goodbye to Gareth, wished him luck, and then moved on to what needed to be done. Jon would pick up Gareth's duties until the fill-in XO, arrived. I'd work out how to deal with the potential change of key players once this day was over.

I already knew I wasn't going to see Goa at all during the first day. The programme was hectic. The first scheduled visit was to call upon the flag officer, a rear admiral, on board the Indian warship INS *Betwa*. After a small boat trip to the berth, a driver named Akash took me through the dusty, dirty, busy dockyard to the ship. I was dressed in my best white uniform and, on arrival, had to climb up a ridiculously steep ladder to get on to the ship. There was no way to make this look graceful, so imagine my joy that an Indian Navy photographer was on hand to capture the full glory of the moment. Mind you, I didn't have much time to consider it right then. All I was worrying about was not falling down the ladder!

After being met on the deck, I was taken to meet the admiral in the captain's cabin. The formal introductions were slightly surreal because my counterpart very obviously thought I was too young to be in a position of command.

'You don't look old enough,' he insisted more than once, despite my polite protestations.

Once we got through this, the ensuing discussion was all very neutral because neither of us was really in a position to offer anything concrete, save for reassurance of our continued relationships and reliance on each other.

As our slightly laboured conversation continued, a steward in a pristine uniform came out with drinks for the two of us. Almost immediately, he reappeared with a large chocolate cake set neatly on a

well-polished platter. I felt obliged to accept both. I had hardly begun
to consider taking a bite from the rich-looking cake before the steward
was back at my side, this time with a platter of vegetable samosas
decorated with little bowls of chilli sauce. Taking my barely perceptible
nod as a signal to load me up, the steward eagerly served me with a
samosa from his latest offering. Now I had a slice of chocolate cake
and a samosa on my plate. Deciding I should tackle the savoury first,
I took a bite out of the samosa. I'd barely had time to chew before
my nemesis was back at my side once more, this time brandishing
a platter of exotic-looking biscuits. I couldn't keep up and politely
refused the biscuit course, before finishing the samosa and subtly
jettisoning the plate with its barely touched chocolate cake on a nearby
table. I figured I would become quite overweight if I ate everything
that was offered. This short meeting was a sign of what was to come.
The people of Goa really did offer incredible hospitality.

After a polite farewell to my hosts on *Betwa*, I was ushered onwards
to attend a press conference. When this event was originally discussed,
I had imagined it would be a small affair. I couldn't have been more
wrong. Entering the large conference room, I was confronted by row
upon row of national and local press. I had no idea what they expected
from me and started to wonder if I had prepared well enough. Once
again, the initial conversational focus was that I was too young to be
a captain. I wondered if they felt a little short-changed by my youth.
The assembled hacks also seemed a little perplexed at my dark skin
colour. They were, however, achingly polite and curious about me and
the submarine.

'So, Captain, are you pleased to be in our country?' was one of the
opening questions.

'Your submarine has nuclear power. What do you contribute in
the Indian Ocean?' asked another journalist.

These first questions set the flow of the exchange.

'What are you looking forward to seeing in our country?'

'Are you good at warfare, and how do you compare with our navy?'

'What are your views on piracy, and how we are dealing with it?'

Finally, the question I'd been dreading. The direction that had
come out of my belated discussion with the HQ was there was one
subject I should distinctly 'avoid', and this was it: 'Do you think India's

approach to unilaterally and correctly dealing with piracy is right or wrong?'

My only option was to answer without actually answering, which is always quite a challenge. It was, however, one that I had perfected in other similar situations, and I achieved the aim.

That said, most of the time I found the line of questioning surprisingly easy and felt completely at ease. I suspect working alongside a TV crewman for sixteen weeks, with cameras watching our every move, had a part to play in this. Even so, by the time it was over and I thanked everyone for their time, I did feel quite tired. There was no time to rest though. I had a couple of hours of duty before a cocktail party. I had to go through incoming mail, prepare for briefings, speak to the HQ about some upcoming issues, and read some updates on the forthcoming exercise. At least I had some space away from all the activity to settle and prepare for hosting guests.

The cocktail party on board the *Betwa* was an interesting affair. The Indian Navy throws a good cocktail party. The admiral and his team were there, as were the *Betwa's* officers, a team from their maritime patrol aircraft squadron, and many local dignitaries.

While pre-prepared briefing notes can prepare you for some things, it is only by interacting with people that you can truly understand the right way to do things and what to expect. Reading people is a skill that cannot be taught; only experience and understanding of the cultures one operates in can really demonstrate whether our actions and words are having the desired effect.

Although the Indians were very welcoming and could not be more hospitable, I realised very quickly it would be difficult to fully immerse myself in their culture just like that. Gaining trust in any culture takes much more than one meeting. Anyone who thinks that is going to be enough is going to be disappointed. However, I did have one advantage that might get me closer, and that was my heritage.

In my early years with the Royal Navy, I deliberately didn't highlight my Sri Lankan roots. My father was from Sri Lanka, and although I had never lived there, I was conscious that at one time background was an issue in the services (it isn't any more). Now I realised my ancestry gave me a sense of commonality that others did not have. When I mentioned it, there was a noticeable change in how people dealt with me. Bizarrely, I began to feel quite at home, despite never having been to Goa before.

I talked with a variety of people about a range of topics, but the conversations always came back to my origins and in most cases pretty rapidly. Using language from my father's generation helped me, and soon we were relaxed and enjoying the company of my hosts.

Eventually, we reached the formal finale of the social engagement. The admiral, with whom I'd been discussing the interesting topic of how they were an emerging power with a long and amazing history and all the challenges that come with that, made his excuses and moved towards his aide. I continued chatting with the wives about life, my family, and in particular, the sacrifice that my wife had made during this deployment. I saw the admiral moving towards a podium and realised that I would have to speak. While I had no idea of what he was going to say, I planned to minimise my response to a few lines. I privately reasoned that way I could not make any mistakes.

When it was my turn to speak, I said, 'Thanks, Admiral, on behalf of HMS *Turbulent* and the Royal Navy for this incredible welcome to your great country. Others in my position might use this opportunity to talk to you all at length, but I have chosen to draw upon the words of the fourteenth-century poet Amir Khosrow: "How exhilarating is the atmosphere of India! / There cannot be a better teacher than the way of life of its people, / Of any foreigner comes by, he will have to ask for nothing, / Because they treat him as their own, / Play an excellent host and win his heart, / And show him how to smile like a flower." Thank you all for looking after us, and we look forward to working with you.'

Preparation, including all those hours of reading, had paid off!

I was tired but happy as we were driven through the darkened streets to our hotel. I felt a little frustrated because I really wanted to see the country. I had no idea what it was like in daylight, and all my expectations were based on films I had seen or books I'd read. I was impatient to experience it myself.

The following morning, I woke early and went down to the beach. I knew I had been right to be impatient when I was greeted by the truly breath-taking landscape. A vast expanse of smooth, bleached white sand stretched into the distance in either direction. Wooden fishing boats painted all the colours of a rainbow were stacked on blocks, waiting to be launched to gather the first catch of the day. Best of all, the entire area was virtually deserted. The locals hadn't yet arrived to start work, and the tourists wouldn't be up for an hour or so yet. For now, this patch of paradise was all mine. There was just me, this extraordinary beach, and the comfortingly familiar seascape in front of me. Feeling inspired, I set off for a run down the beach. I quickly realised after only about half a mile that it was actually quite hard work in the humid heat, and I reluctantly returned to the hotel. *How did Matt Damon do this in* The Bourne Supremacy*?* I thought as I walked back.

After breakfast, I waited for the transport to take me to the dock. At long last, I was about to see India properly for the first time. The initial stage of the journey to Vasco da Gama, where the submarine was berthed, was an entrancing mix of jungle interspersed with houses and shacks that were clearly influenced from the earlier era of Portuguese rule. Our driver had to be quite skilful to avoid the large number of cows and dogs wandering on the road. In this rich variety of life, what I enjoyed the most was the abundance of greenery everywhere. I hadn't realised how much I missed this colour after so long at sea. I certainly didn't see much of it on the Arabian Peninsula. Passing the multitudes of people going about their business was at first quite overwhelming. I had never seen so many people, but logically, I should have expected it in the second most populated country in the world.

Too soon, my trip was over, and I was back in port, on a boat taking me back to Turbs.

The men were doing well; no mistakes had been made, and everyone seemed to be enjoying themselves. They all agreed this was the best port visit yet. It was cheap enough to enjoy to the full, plus there were considerably less restrictions compared to the Arab countries we'd visited. Everyone felt relaxed.

On our final day, a group of us went to the pre-sailing conference to ensure that we were all fully aligned on what was to be achieved during the forthcoming exercise. My impression was that, although it would not be as busy as other exercises we had conducted in the past, there was still a lot to be gained from it. We were to have a number of additional passengers aboard for the exercise—a group from our flotilla was coming to sea with us to conduct an assurance visit and an Indian Navy rider from a Kilo-class submarine. A Kilo class fascinated the crew. That type of submarine was always the enemy, produced by the Russians and exported to anyone who could/would buy them. I had already met a captain of a Russian Kilo, Alexi, when Turbs represented the UK at the Norwegian's submarine centenary celebrations. He was an interesting character, and I had the utmost respect for him as I did for any captain of any submarine. Now this was the chance for many of the crew to meet someone who actually served on one and from a navy which we rarely interacted with.

I was exhausted after three days of rushing around, conducting all the diplomacy that needed to be done. We were shortly going to be sailing with a new XO, and that change in dynamic would have an effect.

'We don't have much time together, but I wanted you to understand our philosophy on board as it is different to other submarines,' I said while he and I were still in the hotel. 'We need to empower our team, give them room to do stuff, and learn. We drive the submarine differently to other SSNs. We dive differently, and our firing drill is different because they work and they are more efficient.'

'You will want to make your mark, but my advice is to be cautious. You are here for a short time, don't try to change too much.'

'I understand what you are saying, sir,' he responded.

The words were encouraging, but his body language didn't seem to match the comment. I tempered my misgivings with my positive assessment of his interaction with officers the night before.

After we had left shore and were out into open water, it was time to dive the submarine. I walked into the control room.

'Hi, sir,' Jon, the ops officer, said.

'Are we ready, John?'

'Yes, sir. Procedure alpha [slowly] or bravo [quicker]?' he asked.

'Happy with the trim?' I asked.

'Yes, sir.'

'OK, when you're ready, bravo.'

He briefed his team, but just as he started the process, the new XO jumped in.

'Sir, what are you doing?' he exclaimed loudly. 'We shouldn't be diving this way.'

'Thanks, XO, we've been doing this all deployment,'I responded calmly. 'I know that it's new to you, but we'll discuss it afterwards.'

I couldn't help but note the looks of alarm of the assembled crewmen's faces as they took in the stand in XO's intervention.

He broke in again, 'But, sir, we need—'

'Thanks, XO, I've got control of this, and your objection is noted. Now concentrate.'I cut him off.

The exchange completely changed the atmosphere in the control room, and it was totally unnecessarily.

We concentrated on diving the submarine, and afterwards, I went to my cabin. I was really annoyed with myself. Back in the hotel, I had to talk to the XO about his stand on how we dived the submarine, as well as the benefits of being a unified team. I asked him to come into my cabin.

'Sit down,'I began. 'Look, I may not have explained myself properly. We are a leadership team. We might have differences in opinion, and if that happens, we can air those in here. However, when we are conducting operations, we are unified in our approach unless we are about to make a mistake that results in catastrophe. If that's the case, step in.'

'OK, sir.'He nodded. Then he added, 'But I don't think that the procedure is fit.'

We were seriously in different places regarding unified leadership.

I concluded our conversation, 'You've only seen one way of skinning the cat, and you know I have seen many more.'

I wasn't making that up. I had observed how the Americans dived and adapted their approach. It was way more efficient.

'Anyway, as long as we're aligned,'I finished.

'Yes, sir.'

We carried on and readied for the exercise with the Indians.

The maritime exercise which involved us, our support vessel, an Indian frigate, an Indian submarine, helicopters, and maritime patrol aircraft demanded a delicate balance of leadership input. There were lots of opportunities to gain from this and lots to give for the whole crew, not just me. I deliberately delegated down to the lowest position to give everyone experience, but I was aware that by doing this, I was exposing the boat to the scrutiny of our additional riders. The men needed opportunities like these; after all, how would they learn otherwise? Yet there was always the possibility they might get it so wrong that it was reported back that we were not performing effectively. Preserving our reputation at this stage of the deployment was really important, but I had full faith the men were up to the challenge.

The change in dynamic within the officers was a problem, and a lot of that was down to Steve, although he did not intend this. Being XO is a position of power; sometimes whatever they say or do has a marked effect. I continued to coach him and hope he would take what he would from our style of leadership and followership. However, the experience made me very aware I had become very comfortable with *our* team dynamics. Sometimes that's a good thing, but accepting intervention is also important. We had a proven track record of accepting intervention, particularly from FOST and our flotilla staff. Therefore, my focus had to be on supporting my team while also visibly supporting the XO, and also subtly containing him where necessary. He had, after all, stepped up to the mark when HQ had asked. If, however, the effect threatened to become destructive, then I would intervene directly.

First up on the maritime exercise was a submarine-versus-submarine operation against one of the Indian Type 209 submarines. I found it interesting and a little disappointing listening to the briefings some of my men were putting across because the language was peppered with bravado. Some of this was definitely because flotilla staff was on board, but the enemy should never be underestimated. It's always a recipe for disaster. We were about to go in the ring with the equivalent of a guy who practises in this gym all the time, knows every kink in the deck and where to hide. I also expected our opponent would be better equipped than he made out. Most submariners are quick learners, so anything we did against him during the first exercise, he would certainly be ready to counter during the final exercise involving all the forces. We had two options: either roundly defeat him on first contact or wait and lull him into a false sense of security. There's a great saying I heard on advanced command and staff course: 'Warfare's about hearts and minds. It's about putting a cold hand on his heart and messing with his mind.' Nevertheless, I went with the team's preference and chose the first option. *There would be a lesson for all coming up*, I thought.

By this time, our Indian Navy rider had settled in and was asking questions and making comparisons with the way things worked with his own navy. According to protocol, he was supposed to offer his first name, yet he never did, and since most people struggled with his second name, it became difficult getting his attention. He became very used to being tapped on the shoulder and integrated very well with us. Submariners are submariners wherever they are.

When it came to the major exercise at the end, the captain of the Indian Type 209 did exceptionally well. We knew where he needed to be and how to manipulate the situation. He shrouded himself in the environment, rising above the thermal layer when he thought we were close.

'Submarine contact bearing 090' came over the main broadcast.

'Stand by Spearfish attack, select track 218 as target classified SSK,' the OOW said.

I stood beside him and waited to see what we did next. The rules of engagement were constraining in that we couldn't fire unless he demonstrated hostile intent, and that's difficult to prove. We only held him for less than a minute, and with no real range or demonstration of intent, the OOW chose not to fire. Then he disappeared.

'He's gone above the layer,' the sonar controller said.

We searched; the sonar team investigated every contact with vigour, but nothing. We held the friendly warships heading to the east, but we never held the Type 209 submarine again for the remaining part of the exercise (he never held us either). We learned subsequently that he had shot both ships successfully. *Good man*, I thought.

Our final adventure of the exercise was a photographic extravaganza involving some incredible helicopter flying. The helicopter seemed really vulnerable, an indigenously produced unit that was flown with real panache and zest, always feeling a little too close and desperately looking for the perfect shot. On one occasion that appeared to be from right next to us, it felt almost close enough to reach out and touch the crewman. We obliged our final contribution to this great exercise and to diplomacy.

After that, we said our goodbyes and headed back to Goa. As we got closer, I couldn't help but feel apprehensive about the same local pilot joining us and complicating what was already a constrained entry into harbour. Fortunately, my fears were not realised, and when a different and experienced pilot arrived, I was utterly relieved. It really is amazing the difference one individual can make. This time, coming alongside could not have been smoother.

We met up with all the many participants in the bilateral exercise and were exceptionally praiseworthy of all the achievements. Exercising with a warrior force, which we didn't do often, establishing relationships that would hopefully endure, and sharing commonality in a variety of areas were a privilege. It was all exceptionally positive. My team had known the context and delivered within it.

It was a shame to be leaving India; the whole visit was relaxing, and everyone had enjoyed it. We had things to do though, people to train, and places to go. Although sad, it was good to leave on a high. Runs ashore are often slightly too long, allowing complacency to creep in, blunders to happen, and reputations to be tarnished. This was not the case here. We were leaving at exactly the right time. I had been really impressed with my crew for enjoying it for the right reasons and for not making mistakes.

We had been privileged to visit a country that had clearly wholeheartedly bought into their own four principles of *artha* (world wealth and success), *kama* (pleasure and love), *dharma* (virtue), and *moksha* (knowledge). Despite the deep chasm between wealth and poverty in this nation, most accepted this and got on and enjoyed the life they had as opposed to dwelling upon what they didn't have. How we could all learn from that. The life experience had been incredible, but now it was time to go home.

CHAPTER 11

Celebrate Success—Theirs

The news came through that Gaddafi had been killed in his hometown of Sirte. All we could discern from the sporadic news sources on board was that the Colonel was brutally murdered and most of us were a little disgusted by that outcome. While we signed up to enable the Transitional Federal Council to enable democratic change, we expected democratic justice to follow. It would be disappointing to think we actually ended up endorsing tribal conflict, but it was easy to imagine this situation was now going to develop into exactly that. Fortunately most people on board were not too bothered about the development, and deep down, we were all united in the belief we had done the right thing throughout Operation Ellamy.

Privately, I wasn't convinced it was going to go the way that we in the West hoped. Egypt was still being run by the military, and Tunisia was awaiting elections. In Syria, there were widespread demonstrations, although it was unlikely anyone was going to intervene in that arena.

Religious passion and tribal feuds will always take over. There were few leaders in the region who were not guided by some extreme passion. Those that seek change always have a Machiavellian reason for it, yet they are charismatic enough to make it happen. It was exactly what the Colonel managed over forty years ago. There was no doubt religion would continue to dominate the argument, and I was convinced we were actually one step closer towards Osama bin Laden's vision of a world caliphate. Subsequent events have proved me right. Ironically, we may have played a role in pushing it in this direction.

We arrived near Fujairah and were ready for boat transfer to land personnel and pick up some new trainees as well as Gareth. I saw the temporary XO just before he left.

'Many thanks for stepping in like you did,' I said. 'I know that we had differences in approach, and I know we'll agree to disagree, but when you take command, keep the experiences to draw from.'

Prior to arriving, one of the chiefs during my daily trip back aft to the manoeuvring room mentioned having a barbecue on the casing, and I realised we hadn't done anything like that on the deployment. There was never time because we were always rushing from one operation to another and one exercise to another. Once all the transfers were complete, out came the BBQ, and there was a spate of feverish activity as the engineers on the casing set up half a steel drum. I couldn't help but reflect that the last time this many people were on the casing was Sweaty Sunday!

Gareth came up to the bridge, and we chatted. It was good to have him back. Then it began—our first and last deployment barbecue on the casing. The team looked happy and relaxed. Most were aware that our tasking was nearly over and it was time to go home. The trainees were slightly shocked by the event, but we all ate, relaxed in the sun, and chatted in what is possibly the most unique and sublime place to have a barbecue.

Once everyone had eaten, we cleared the barbecue away, and it was back to business.

'Jon, ready to go?' I asked.

'Yes, sir, casing and bridge are clear. All personnel checked, and trainees are crammed in the control room.'

'OK, I'll be there in a second.'

A short while later, I sat in the chair in the packed control room.

'All right, fella?' I said to one of the trainees.

'Yes, sir,' he said, sounding anything but.

'This is the best part of submarining—entering the world that so few know. What do you think's going to happen next?'

The trainee began to recite the process he had been taught at the submarine school while Jon and Gareth led the team through diving the submarine. Once dived, we looked for every opportunity to train the next generation.

While playing Uckers with Gareth, Ben, and Simmo that evening, we were chewing the fat as we always did when Ben piped up, 'Did you hear about the leading chef this afternoon? He told the trainees when we were in the galley that we had a barbecue every Saturday!'

We were all laughing as Ben threw the dice and plotted his next move with Simmo. My mind wandered as I begin to think about whether we got the right blend of relaxation and reward to go with all the team's hard work.

'I know the journey's not over, but I wonder if we got the balance right,' I said, raising the subject out loud so I could gauge my colleague's viewpoint. 'I mean we worked hard, we trained hard, and we fought well, but we should have probably relaxed a little.'

'Well, most of the crew went home at some stage, so there was some relaxation there, and we kept up that mantra of only working when necessary alongside,' Simmo said.

'And you [Simmo] led by example at the pool bar!' broke in Ben.

'I think we've recognised the team every time they've done something beyond the call, but they also know our standards are high,' said Gareth, bringing the discussion back on track. 'You can see it with the trainees when they come on board. They all want to stay here because the team is a good one to be with.'

Gareth had made a great point. The team had created a really positive environment by encouraging success, allowing those who can sprint to sprint, helping those who just wanted to get to the end, and isolating those whose attitude could not be changed. We had all created a great working environment. Now we just had to keep that going until we were back alongside.

We still had a week of training and minor exercises to do, and this became more of a challenge than operations. How do you keep your team focused when they have always had something to focus on and now they no longer do? We needed to maintain that hard operational edge, just in case, but it is impossible to sit on edge for prolonged periods.

I decided that the most effective way to deal with this issue was to get people to 'sell themselves'.

'Team, this is the last chance we will have this deployment to make sure that we've taught everything we know to others,' I announced the following day during O Group.

'This is actually going to be the most difficult phase of this deployment, and we've had some difficult phases! I know you'll make sure that people use the opportunity that this is.'

As I went around the boat afterwards, I kept pushing one point: *legacy*. This was our chance to make sure we left one. After all, leaders are only mentors for the next generation.

Fortunately, other issues also distracted the team. The chefs had come across a 'seam' of chocolate and were now happily doling out at a rate of about two bars per man per day. They were playing Christmas music in the galley too despite the fact we weren't even into November. The crew was noticeably unsettled though. Everyone had one eye on the fact we would soon be on our way home.

The first challenge of the return transit would be the numbers of new people. We had been ordered to take twenty-four trainees. I had formally objected to bringing in so many because I saw it as increased risk during what was going to be the hardest part of this journey.

Am I becoming more risk-averse as we head home? I thought. *If I start changing the way I promote considered risk, this could create other problems.*

My uneasiness was proven correct almost immediately during the first set of damage control drills. It was blatantly obvious the balance was not correct; team leaders were consumed with making sure that the trainees were being trained, but this was at the expense of achieving the collective goal. We weren't far from being in place to conduct the first dived transit of BAM, and we needed to be ready.

Gareth and I discussed it post a game of Uckers.

'Why's it more noticeable this time?' I began. 'I mean, there's a real difference in training groups here, and we need measures to make sure that we all integrate rapidly.'

'It's a focus thing,' suggested Gareth. 'Operations are over. It's that whole transit mentality creeping in.'

There was no choice other than to work through it and ensure that the team was ready for the challenges we were about to face, including the dived transit of BAM. By undertaking a dived transit, we would remove the threat from piracy completely. It was my suggestion that we did this, but this was before this massive change in personnel. While I was certain we would be able to do it successfully, I was now feeling the pressure to do this with aplomb.

I was sitting in my cabin, going through my notes for entering Aqaba, when one of the engineer ratings came to see me.

'Hello, how's it going?' I greeted him.

'Do you mind if we have a chat, sir?'

'Sure, come in, have a seat. What can I do for you?'

'I'm going to leave my wife,' he said, giving me a steady look. He was clearly serious, and I was a little taken back.

'That's a very personal decision, does she know?'

'No, sir,' he said.

'Are you sure that you've thought this through? I mean, you can always work things out if there's a problem.'

'There wasn't a problem, sir,' he said emphatically. Then, more quietly, he added, 'When Sweaty Sunday happened and I honestly thought that was it, it wasn't my wife I thought about. It was someone else.'

We sat in silence, looking at each other, knowing that many of us had thought that was it. Silence is a strange thing. You can ruin the moment by interrupting it. The moment seemed to stretch on for ages with me not wanting to say anything to guide him one way or the other, while he was perhaps waiting for some consensus that his decision was right.

'Look, you need to sleep on this before making any decision,' I said at last, breaking the silence. 'I can't tell you what is right or wrong but would advise you not to tell your wife until you can discuss it face to face. You might actually find out when you get home that this feeling was something else.'

He nodded, thanked me, and left. Sweaty Sunday was still having strange effects.

The next day at O group, the team discussed an intense training package to make sure we were ready to deal with standard submarine issues. We looked at numerous aspects, such as damage control and how to make sure everyone knew the particular skills required which were unique to our submarine or daily routines and how to make sure they knew how to operate a submerged signal ejector. The training package was hard, but the bigger challenge was ensuring that everyone bought into the vision of the way we did things on board and accepted it willingly. For some trainees, it was their first experience in this environment, but many others had been with other units who did things differently. We had a week to deal with this as we made our approach to the Internationally Recognised Transit Corridor, where a plethora of warships were operating, trying to contain the pirates, none of which would be expecting to detect a submarine. That was totally another challenge but great for the junior officers to cut their teeth on. They could learn to operate as if we weren't there and watch how others operated while blending in with the environment.

As we reached the west of the Gulf of Aden, about to make our dived transit of BAM, I was confident that the amount of preparation that had gone into this both back in HQ and on board would pay off. Combined team work done thousands of miles apart had produced an effective plan. The team had fully bought into the pathfinder mission. One wag aboard compared the tension around our situation to a scene from *The Hunt for Red October* movie when Sean Connery and his team transit the Neptune Massif. The idea was picked up and joked about by many on the crew.

Just as we were about to go deep, a 'casualty' pipe was made. One of the crew had suddenly developed breathing difficulties. The medics dealt with it rapidly, and the crewman recovered and then got on with his job. I admired his attitude. This was the selfless action of a man dedicated to the team above the individual, and this time, as always, I was humbled by it.

We were all excited and apprehensive about the dived transit. The width of available water was quite narrow, and we were going through deep. The large number of merchant vessels above meant we couldn't travel straight up if the seabed got too close. There wasn't much room for manoeuvre to the right or left either. Navigation had to be first class. I was reassured that, even though I had taken risk with landing one of my two navigators earlier, everyone else, including the new members of the team, was now stepping up to the mark.

'Gareth, it's looking good,' I said as we were sitting in my cabin.

'They're up for it, and the reality is we've got the timing right with this,' he agreed. 'The outbound Suez convoy won't be on us for a while, which should mean we can get pretty far north with the first part of the transit.'

'Good point. Let's just make sure we don't get overtired. We must capture everything from this so that we can feedback to *Triumph*, who's coming south.'

I went into the control room and had a look around through the periscope. I could see the coastlines of Yemen and Somalia. There were some go-fasts (the vessels that both pirates and fishermen use in the area) and definite chat on communication channels. They weren't waiting for us though; they were waiting for trade.

Then we went deep, and we were in the channel. I was impressed to see the team treating it all as normal business. The atmosphere around the vessel was supremely no nonsense and professional.

'WECDIS has us on track with 0.5 nautical miles of safe water to starboard and 1.5 nautical miles to port,' said the navigator. 'Tidal stream is as expected 141 at 0.4 knots. Four nautical miles to run to the wheel over to a new course 343.'

'Officer of Watch, roger.' Reports kept coming in at a standard pace, and people handed over succinctly when each watch was up. It felt like business as usual despite it being the first time a Royal Navy submarine had done this.

I didn't want to miss any of the twenty-eight-hour transit because for me it would be a once-in-a-lifetime opportunity, but I was torn. I couldn't let myself get overtired. Eventually, I succumbed and forced myself to grab a couple of hours' sleep.

It all went well, and when we finished the transit, we returned to PD in the vicinity of a set of islands to gain a navigational fix. We had an ulterior motive too: to enable the photographic team to take a picture of sunrise over the islands. It was an extraordinary sight. Hardly anyone else would ever have the privilege of capturing that moment. As soon as it was done, we had to get going as fast as we dared to ensure that we were in the right position to conduct our handover strike rehearsal. Our sister submarine, *Triumph*, was already in the Red Sea, transiting south, which meant we were not far off being released from being the UK strike platform in this region.

At 02.00, I was shaken awake in my cabin. The OOW informed me that we had a problem with the propulsor.

'There was a real jolt, sir, and the boat shook,' he said.

I must have been deeply asleep because I hadn't felt a thing. Now that my senses were fully alert, I became aware that the propulsor was indeed making an awful sound.

We had slowed down to four knots, and the noise was so loud that it was marking out all our flank sonar. Things do go through the propulsor from time to time. It is exceptionally strong and 'eats' anything, but clearly, whatever this was, was lodged. If this continued, we would be limited to very slow speed, but worse still, if this was part of the propulsor itself, we were going to be stuck. Fixing anything like this takes time, and it is rarely easy.

I immediately called together my HODs so we could scope out every possibility.

'The situation is this, we have clearly ingested something into the propulsor,' I began.

'The jolt would indicate that we may have gone through a drift net,' Gareth suggested.

'We're limited to 4 knots, and at that speed, we are three days from reaching Jordan and five days from Suez, for which the access date is fixed,' I went on.

'The MEs and WEs have been looking at cause and solutions,' Ben interjected. 'We've done the standard process of going ahead and astern, but nothing, and I have to say I'm concerned that we may be about to do serious damage to the propulsor.'

'When you say serious damage, are you talking about it not working or a massive increase in our noise signature which would write us off tactically?' I asked.

'Difficult to say,' Ben answered.

'OK, what are the options?'

'We could continue to Suez at 4 knots and attempt to transit through at 4 knots, or we could go to Jordan and attempt to fix it there.' Gareth said.

'I'm not certain that Jordan would let us stay indefinitely, and you know how long these repairs can take,' I said doubtfully. 'Equally, we can't go through the canal at 4 knots. It's still early in the UK, and there's nothing they can do in the next four hours, so continue with attempting to clear the propulsor, and we'll send a signal with options in a few hours. In effect, that will give the HQ days to sort out some options.'

Meanwhile, the crew continued with the standard procedure to try to shake debris out of the propulsor. Alarmingly, the noise was getting worse. In fact, we were now deeply concerned it might damage the internal workings of the shaft and we would lose propulsion altogether. We were still a long way from help.

For the first time, I allowed myself to consider whether Turbs's almost continual ailments were beginning to wear me down. The Old Girl was suffering some major problems, and it would be understandable if we all became tired of trying to fight them through. This latest one was even more unsettling because it was utterly out of our control. There was nothing we could do, yet the consequences were massive. Having no propulsion and drifting out of control in the Red Sea was not a desirable situation.

For the following two hours, we continued experimenting with ahead and astern revs to dislodge whatever it was. Still nothing. Feeling tense, I sat in the sound room, listening to the noise, hoping against hope that something would change, but nothing did. We were now close to the point where I would have to take the decision to return to PD, surface, and declare the problem to the HQ. We had no other choice. I left it as long as I could, and then, just as we had given up all hope, the sound disappeared. The propulsor spat out whatever it was, and the noise went away as rapidly and unexpectedly as it had arrived. We continued on our way towards Jordan with a sense of relief all round.

The transit towards Jordan through the Straits of Tiran was done at night, and we arrived just after sunrise at the naval base. Our arrival was well controlled. The base was very modern, and we were very well looked after.

Our arrival was timed to ensure it did not coincide with that of a French destroyer that was also visiting. Even so, when we were tied up, it became apparent that the French were not best pleased about us being in the base at all. We soon discovered why when we received an invitation to an air show that was being put on for the visiting crown prince of Jordan. Jordanian and French air display teams were jointly staging it. Both the French and British embassies had failed to talk to each other, and now we were stepping on their prized diplomacy piece.

There was little we could do about it. Leave was piped to ensure that most of the crew had gone ashore before the scheduled VIP visit to meet the crown prince aboard the French ship. We all went to the hotels, which were quite incredible, and after a brief period to chill out, we all regrouped to go back to the submarine and prepare for the official visit. After getting changed, we headed over as instructed. Then, incredibly, before we could get on board, a French officer came up, saluted me, and asked us to come back in three hours! I couldn't believe it. They had made the invitation and then turned the Royal Navy away in front of everyone.

As we walked back to the submarine, I called up the UK and told them what had happened. I had little choice. When I had originally been given the invite, I saw an opportunity to bring the crown prince on board our submarine and declared my intention to CTF. I informed HQ I had no intention of waiting for three hours to go back on board, and we would leave on completion of the air show to go back to the hotels. I added that I was pretty unhappy to have been 'mugged' by the French. We had been working on reinvigorating our military relationship, yet they had not thought twice about embarrassing us diplomatically.

I was still feeling a little out of sorts when suddenly the crown prince arrived and walked past towards the ship, along with his massive entourage. Once he was on the flight deck, the aircraft arrived and started the show. The air display was impressive.

Afterwards, to overcome the embarrassment of being so ungracefully turned away by our traditional enemy, we went ashore and found Irish bar called Rovers Return. It was good to see my team enjoying themselves and doing it well.

I was beginning to relax when Ben pulled me aside to tell me that there was a problem with the shore generators (they provide power to the submarine so that the reactor can be shut down). Among other things, it helps reduce the number of engineers on board so more people could enjoy the port visit.

'Sir, the shore generators are of the wrong power rating,' he said. 'They've given us two with half of the power output each. It's unsustainable at present, although we have tried. There's only one option because they can't get any generators here in a short time span: we'll have to start up again and supply power via the TGs [turbo generators].'

That means that the engineers will have to stay in sea watches, I thought.

The decision was made; the MEs returned on board. We had only been ashore for six hours. I returned to the hotel to ponder on what to do. The crew could get the diesels fixed, but it was Thursday and the start of the Islamic weekend. Our support was over 200 miles away in Amman and, therefore, unlikely to get to us for a while. Yet again, Turbs was struggling. It had become a frustrating pattern of events.

As soon as I awoke the next morning, I went back to the submarine to find out if any progress had been made. It hadn't. This presented many dilemmas. The first of which was there was no way my marine engineers could be left toiling away on board as though we were at sea while everyone else in the team enjoyed a run ashore. It simply wasn't right. There was also the question of just how long I gave them to sort the problem, particularly in the light of the fact they had made little progress so far. This showed that the likelihood of success was low.

It didn't take me long to make up my mind. We couldn't stay here like this. I called HQ and explained the situation.

'There's no way we're going to rectify this in the next forty-eight hours,' I said. 'Then we'll be getting ready to go to sea anyway. So we're going to go today. I know there's some reputational risk with both the Jordanians and the French, but I'll manage that.'

'Your choice, mate,' said Bob, my counterpart in HQ. 'Are you sure you don't want the run ashore?'

'It's a great place, but there's too much on this,' I answered. 'We need to get through Suez. The finishing line is in sight (well, 3,000 miles away), and we need to make sure we do this as one team.'

It wasn't even about diplomacy now. It was about getting home as one unit; whatever happens to one happens to us all. That was what had enabled us to overcome so many challenges thus far.

There was, of course, a diplomatic issue to overcome. I needed to go and see the local Jordanian commander and the French captain. They needed to know that we were enjoying the visit and their company but we were leaving for other reasons. I particularly enjoyed my visit with the French captain, where we sat drinking coffee, discussing leadership and the challenges of command. It was great to have learned from him and to have given back. They were on their way to the Middle East, touching upon many of the same ports we had visited, so there was much I could share.

The next afternoon, after a faultless departure, we started transiting to the Red Sea via the Straits of Tiran. After we were through the straits, I spoke to the crew.

'Men, this is the captain. I couldn't explain the reason for leaving before. However, you'll be well aware that the generators were not able to support our requirements, which meant staying flashed up,' I said. 'That would have been wholly unfair on the marine engineers because they would have had much less of a run ashore, if any. We are one team, and we do everything as one team. Therefore, we've sailed. It was the right thing to do.'

That was that—case closed. In some ways, it was though we hadn't really been in Jordan at all. There was no time to dwell on it now. There was more training to do and administration to finish off before we would return through Suez, back to the Mediterranean.

It felt surreal, waiting to transit the Suez Canal. Everything we had done in the last seven months in the Middle East and Near East was now history. We were no longer part of it. We were now about to be part of the European sector, something that had been so distant for so long. On a personal level, I was looking forward to talking to the Suez Canal pilots to discover what changes they had seen since we last saw them in April. We had learned from our earlier experience, and rather than staying in our anchorage position surrounded by other ships, we requested permission to be called forward from a position further south and remain underway (not anchored). They agreed, and I was able to sleep more soundly during the period before transit.

While we waited to be called forward, the team continued with their preparations for getting across the Mediterranean, which was not going to be easy. There was still a great deal to do. We were going to contribute to Operation Active Endeavour, and I welcomed this because it ensured we kept our operational edge until the very end. First though, we had the challenge of the canal to deal with.

It was very early in the morning when we received our notice to come forward to the constrained channel, prior to entering the canal. It was dark and just as chaotic as during our first transit months before. There were many ships around us, and with our restricted capacity to manoeuvre now, we were on the surface; we had to test our anticipation skills to the full. This is never easy when you can't understand the language and the ship in front (French Navy) wasn't communicating what it was doing anyhow! As we edged towards the entrance to the canal, the ship in front stopped rapidly without warning. We couldn't easily do the same, and although we managed to slow down and stop, we ended up pointing in the wrong direction.

Once the pilot embarked, we corrected and started the approach. When we were in the canal and settled, I had time to talk to the pilots. Each one of the three pilots who led us through the canal that day agreed life was now better for them personally; however, the tourist trade had been hit hard. The improvement in their personal circumstances made me feel happy. Perhaps it would be the same in Libya in a few years' time, and our efforts would have been worth it. While I was initially sceptical about our contribution and motives, it would be good if we had contributed to making a difference for some people. The tragedy, of course, is that three years down the line that would absolutely not be the case. (As I write this, Libya is back in a state of turmoil, with ISIS and jihadism gaining the most from Western intervention. Most ordinary Libyan citizens probably have less control today than when Gaddafi was in power.)

The temperature outside felt exceptionally cool—almost cold. We had become used to the warm weather of the Gulf of Oman and anything less than 24 degrees was now considered cold. We passed through the canal without incident and entertained some Egyptian Army officers, including a battalion commander, during the transit. They really enjoyed being on board, which seemed to endorse my view that, even though we had changed crew again and again, the same *Turbulent* ethos and spirit remained strong.

Now that we were in the Mediterranean, we were in a different theatre of operations. Of course, we had been here before, but it was a long time ago. We needed to treat this environment with the respect it was due and ensure we did not get caught out.

We were truly on the homeward stretch, and I began to struggle with some very mixed emotions. I was filled with relief that we were finally coming home so I could be with my family yet had real sorrow about leaving the team to hand over command to someone else. The closer to home we got, the more I found it difficult to perfect the delicate balance between attempting to distance myself a little so that the transition was painless and taking the most pleasure from the buzz of being at the centre of everything on board. I found solace in the large amount of administration, letters, and reports that needed to be done if I were to do the best by my men. While most of my crew would never realise my personal investment in them, I took great satisfaction from knowing that I had been able to make a difference on their behalf.

Late in the evening, I was shaken awake once again. *This is becoming a habit*, I thought as I came to.

'Sir, it's Dan.'

It was obvious I was about to be told of yet another fault, and I was instantly alert.

'One of the two diesels is no longer working,' he continued.

'What? Not recoverable?'

'No, sir.'

It was all said with no humour, which was not normal from Dan. I could guess at least part of the reason why now. We were all getting worried about actually making it home, and this was another blow.

'OK, Dan, I'll be out in a minute,' I said, sounding as confident as I could. 'I know you'll have this, but let's know the risk.'

Although this was a loss in a system that is only there for emergencies, it was another defect in a growing list. It spelt cumulative risk, and I didn't like cumulative risk. In the last few weeks alone, the radio mast had broken and could no longer be used. There was a small hydraulic leak somewhere in the WSC. One of the air-conditioning plants had failed, and there were a host of other smaller problems. The list was beginning to add up, and I couldn't help but be concerned that we were carrying risk upon risk upon risk on our final leg home. The trouble was, what else could we do? We were so close to the safe haven of Devonport. We had to continue if we were to get home to our families. Our only option was to protect everything, take no more risk than was necessary, and not to push already fragile systems. Turbs was made for war but not the one we'd been immersed in throughout this deployment. We'd been fighting outside the area the boat was designed to operate in for seven months solid, and she was old; it was no wonder that all these things were happening. Unfortunately though, the fight was not going to end until we arrived alongside in Devonport, and we needed to be prepared for that.

Sure enough, that same night I received another call, this time in the early hours. Two air-conditioning plants had failed. Going to the control room, I immediately had a flash back to Sweaty Sunday because the men had already started switching off all non-essential equipment. At least the outside temperature was considerably cooler, so this time their actions would have an effect. Whatever happened now, we could cool people down. If we could cool people down, then we could deal with the other problems that we found. Most importantly, in this temperate climate, we had time. That was something we didn't have on the previous occasion.

I sat down in the wardroom with Gareth, Ben, and Ian. The HODs were already on the case, but I felt tired, really tired.

'Do you all have a plan?' I said.

'Yes, sir, we're on it,' said Ben. 'I'm up until 04.00, so if there are any decisions, I can make them if you're happy.'

'Good plan, team, I'll get out of your hair,' I said, feeling relieved.

I went back to my cabin and pondered what might go wrong next before falling asleep.

When I awoke a couple of hours later, the team had managed to get an air-conditioning plant back online, and we were not far from Souda Bay. We needed to go there briefly to pick up our towed array prior to returning to the UK.

What a great place Souda was. It honestly felt like coming home, much like Fujairah used to feel like East of Suez. The same people, the same tugs! We had an exceptional run ashore, were treated well by the locals (particularly well by those looking after us), ate great food, and met amazing people.

We were not far off the time when we were about to leave, and I went on to the casing to make a phone call. I was interrupted by the coxswain, who began to say something about the men going off to muster because the bus had been left in absolute mess and the Greek authorities were demanding action. I really had no idea what he was talking about and was already trying to work out how I was going to smooth this over, particularly as we had done so well with our relationships in the country.

'Sir, the men are fallen in and ready for you,'Paddy said, sounding quite insistent now.

'I don't really know what happened here, so maybe the XO should do this,'I said.

'That won't cut it, sir,'he replied, motioning that I should follow him.

Fearful of what I might discover next, I followed him over to a large group of my men. They were all there, looking a little sheepish.

'Men . . .'I began, thinking ahead of what I might say as I spoke.

'Sir, we wanted to say goodbye properly,'Dave Smyth interrupted, stepping forward and handing me a package as a huge cheer went up.

The crew had bought me a humidor for my cigars to say goodbye. By now, I was struggling to hold back my emotions. I had been quite emphatic that the changeover of command should be a quiet affair; I fully intended to step off Turbs on arrival in the UK and never come back. The new CO would join the next day without having to go through the experience of having to see the crew say fond goodbyes to the old CO. I still remembered the discomfort I felt when I joined and heard them cheering the old CO. It felt like the challenge was on; I had to make the team mine to overcome the intense relationship they had with my predecessor. All that was out of the window now. My team wanted to say goodbye in their way, and I wasn't going to stop them.

Welling up a little, I said a few words about being part of the best team. It wasn't one of my best speeches, but they knew what I meant and, most importantly, how much they all meant to me.

An hour later, it was time to leave. We began an exceptionally fast transit speed to our next position, a rendezvous with a US maritime patrol aircraft in the middle of the Med. I loved watching my team being so professional, I didn't have to do anything, but they automatically settled back down. It was as though we had never been alongside.

It was early in the morning when suddenly the boat shuddered. There was a loud noise, and everything vibrated. It felt like we had hit something. I rushed to the control room from my cabin. I looked at the coxswain, who was on ship control, and we both knew.

'Emergency stations, emergency stations, loud bang heard, all compartments carry out phase 1 damage control checks and report to DCHQ,' he said over the main broadcast system.

I looked at the brand-new OOW, who seemed a little in shock—training versus experience wasn't yet balanced for him.

'I've got this,' I said. 'I have the submarine. Let me know when we're in control.'

It was like every other emergency we had dealt with. I aimed to be calm and professional, listening to reports, taking my time to think.

'Sir, phase 1s are in, no damage,' Paddy said.

'OK, let DCHQ take control of this, and then we'll get back to our normal state.'

I went to the sound room, hoping my sonar experts would tell me something.

'Sir, something's gone through the propulsor,' said the sonar controller. He was one of my outstanding team of sonar leaders and had kept us ahead of the enemy on every occasion.

'Any idea what?' I said. 'It doesn't sound like a drift net this time.'

We had little choice but to go through the usual routine.

'Officer of the Watch, go ahead and astern no more than fifty revolutions and shake it free,' I said. 'Are you happy?'

Fortunately, it cleared quite quickly this time, and once the situation had been contained, we continued our high-speed transit.

I wondered again when all this was going to stop. There had been challenge after challenge after challenge. We had done nothing to deserve this. Turbs was tired, and we were tired, but we needed to keep going. We needed to muster our reserves of energy, keep on the alert, and complete this final phase safely.

We just mustn't change the way we do things, that's when mistakes will happen, I thought. *We've done really well. There's been no complacency, just consummate professionalism. I'm proud of what they do.*

I didn't need to say anything of this to the men; they all knew it.

Our transit took us across the Mediterranean, past our old hunting grounds off the Libyan coast and towards the Sicilian Channel. The unchallenging channel proved to be a complete non-event in the light of our heady experiences of transiting the Straits of Hormuz and Bab el-Mandeb, but it was dealt with using our customary professionalism and given the respect it deserved.

Once through, our journey to Gibraltar was uneventful. That was fine; we deserved some quiet. We surfaced off Gibraltar to embark a reporter who was going to cover our final journey back and carried on our transit out of the Mediterranean into the Atlantic. Chatting with the reporter, we realised that we had worked together before in 1994 when he came on board a Dutch submarine that I was navigating at the time while on exchange with the Royal Netherlands Navy. We discussed what had changed and what had not.

'It's obvious to me that warfare hasn't changed a bit. Enemies are still out there, submarines are the first line and the last line of defence,' I said. 'Despite the technical nature of submarines, this is a personal and human process.'

This was a distraction from getting home though. We had to prepare ourselves to face one final enemy—the weather. The forecast for the Atlantic and around the UK was awful. Submarines are not built to operate on the surface in the best of times, so factor in bad weather and it would be quite probable the crew wouldn't be in a good state on arriving in Devonport. Indeed, the scheduled arrival might not be possible at all if the bad weather didn't let up. This was, of course, a disaster because much is pre-planned around a homecoming like this, and VIPs, TV crews, and most importantly, families would have had our arrival in their diaries for months. We had never missed a commitment once during this deployment and had always been on time everywhere we were supposed to be. It would be a huge shame if Mother Nature managed to stop us this time. The men had put so much effort into making the boat look really good in preparation for presenting it to the VIPs and our families.

As we proceeded further north through the Atlantic and into the Bay of Biscay, an area notorious for bad weather and feared by most seafarers, we could feel the weather worsen even at depth. We were entering a force 12 storm. While it is possible to have a degree of control over most things or certainly a level of influence, the weather and the sea were both our greatest friend and our worst enemy. The boat rocked at a depth of 150 metres, even at speed, and when we rose to 60 metres and went slower, the submarine lurched alarmingly. It all added up to one thing—PD was going to be awful.

'Gareth, we need to keep going, and we need a plan for how we're going to deal with periscope depth,' I said prior to O group. 'I know we've done it before, but let's brief it. Leave nothing to chance.'

'Sir, the proposed plan is to go as far as possible, north, come up at the last possible moment, broach [the term used to semi-surface], use a quick burst SATCOM transmission to get the broadcast routine [communications], and go deep soonest,' he said. 'We've analysed the risk and assessed that it is worth taking in order to avoid weather damage if we stay at periscope depth. We'll surface, placing the sea on the "quarter" as well.'

'Good plan, let's avoid meal times too—brief the whole team,' I said.

Any doubts about this plan swiftly dissipated when we rose to PD. It was dreadful. The submarine rolled in excess of 30 degrees, and it was impossible to stay on depth. Broaching made sure the SATCOM mast was clear of the water. The ship control team did a valiant job, and we went deep as quickly as we could. I kept telling myself, 'We are on the home straight, and this is simply one of the final challenges. The weather could not beat us this close to home.'

Not far from the south coast of Devon, in those hunting grounds where we used to prepare ourselves for the deployment, we surfaced for the last time and prepared for the short surfaced transit. When the coast of Blighty came into sight—Cornwall to be precise—I stood on the bridge, drinking it all in. I am sure if you never leave a country, you begin to take it for granted. Leave it for a while though, and you'll start to appreciate how wonderful it is. We all like a little grumble now and then, but look at what we have—green fields, a common language, human rights, a fair policing and judiciary system, free healthcare, a free press, freedom of religion and sexuality, a right to express our views, as well as the right to learn, eat what we want, and complain now and again. The list goes on. And of course, there is our wonderful weather! That is what we were protecting, and we had done it well, although most would never know what it was we had done.

Overnight, we continued closing Devonport, and first thing in the morning, we were almost there. I went to the bridge for what was going to be a busy and emotional last day. *Weather guys were right*, I thought as I poked my head into the freezing cold wind that bristled over the bridge. As we closed the breakwater to make our approach to Plymouth, the worst hailstorm I had ever experienced started. I couldn't help but give a wry smile. *What else?* I asked no one in particular. *What else?*

The pressure was on. If we didn't get in now, we didn't get in for a few days. In addition, we were holding up HMS *Trenchant*, who was on her way back too. It was only thanks to some deft assistance from the pilot and gymnastics from the casing party that we managed to get attached to the buoy. We were home. Well, almost.

Almost immediately, we readied to receive the admiral. He was coming on board to congratulate the team and to listen first-hand to our operational success. In addition, the Military Wives Choir was due on board with film crew and reporters.

'Gareth, let's make sure that we deconflict this properly,' I whispered to the XO with a smile. 'I'm not sure I want to hear the admiral sing, and I'm certain he'll not want the wives to receive the operational debrief!'

'It's in hand, sir,' he replied. 'You need to go straight to the casing to meet the choir as soon as you've finished briefing. We'll deal with the rest.'

I had already given the team the brief I was going to give the admiral on the transit home. It was a way of praising them for everything they had done and, more importantly, giving them context for their achievements.

The film crew set up, and we reunited one of the choir members with her husband whom she was seeing for the first time in five months. It was very emotional for all concerned and great TV.

After a few interviews and presenting them with some submarine dolphins, the choir was gone, and we had three hours before we would be on our way up river to face more TV crewmen and, most importantly, our families. Gareth had organised all the families to be there despite some short-notice changes, and everyone was looking forward to it. When that moment came, I could then slide away, and *Turbulent* would carry on under my successor.

Those three hours were precious. I got around as many of the crew as I could, tidied up, and removed my personal stuff from my cabin into bags ready to go. I was surprised at how much stuff I had amassed! Gareth asked me to come down to the senior rates' mess, and they presented me with an original painting of HMS *Turbulent* entering Portsmouth in 2010. I smiled as I saw us there on the bridge. I went back aft, and the marine engineers gave me a model of a reactor that they had been making out of metal over the last three months. It was incredible. Then finally, I went back to the wardroom, where they had set up a final dinner. Our steak meal tasted the sweetest of all by far, and the concluding game of Uckers on board was without a doubt the most hotly contested yet. Gareth and I won, although there were hints it was all staged to send me on my way with a good feeling. I wasn't convinced but didn't argue.

Then after all those months of highs, lows, triumphs and disappointments, it was time to start our final journey together into harbour at night. Our arrival alongside was bittersweet. I was giving up being part of the most amazing team, yet I would now be with my family again, having brought us home safely.

Once we were tied up, I called down from the bridge, 'Finished with main engines and steering. Men, it's been a privilege.'

It was a struggle to hold back tears and contain my emotion as I came down from the bridge for the last time. This was the finale to an amazing a year, but ultimately one where *Turbulent* achieved real success and made a difference. Now it was time to finally give back to those who had sacrificed time while we were away.

The deployment was long, and we saw some dramatic events. Osama bin Laden was killed, Libya revolted, and Gaddafi was killed. The situation in Syria worsened, and Iran and Israel were becoming increasingly belligerent towards each other. We did our duty and went there to do a job for Queen and country, and we made a difference. During our more than 280 days away, we covered more than 40,000 miles and spent over 200 days underwater. We conducted a series of top-secret operations, carried out a series of pathfinder missions that had never been done before, liaised with our allies, and trained many submariners. We won a variety of awards, promoted over fifty people, and qualified seventy-six submariners from other submarines. We lived by the rules, spied well, and never got caught by the enemy. Most of all, we lived our vision, empowered our people, made decisions, understood our enemy, and ensured the will to succeed overpowered the need to avoid failure.

I had been chatting with Ollie Lea, and he summed the major challenge better than I could.

He said, 'It strikes me, sir, that all the way through this, we weren't fighting the enemy. We were fighting her.'

Looking back, he was right. Every issue rarely involved the enemy. We controlled that activity well. Our battle was keeping the Old Girl going.

My command was, at an end, having led 484 personnel over three years on one deployment, six covert intelligence gathering patrols, two periods of operational sea training, and four major NATO exercises. This chapter of my leadership journey was at an end, and I knew then that I would never be able to recreate a similar experience.

I walked up the gangway, shaking hands with people as I left. Just as I had asked, there was no ceremony, nothing. Then, there on the jetty was my family. What a great moment that was—personal yet so public. All the other families were there as well, and so were the TV crew. While everyone was enjoying the moment, I slipped away with Corrinne and the kids and went home. The last part of my time with *Turbulent* was filled with happiness. The military band was playing, families were smiling, and the team was all immersed in feeling the joys of success. All this was achieved at the expense of my family, for which I will owe them forever, but it was worth it because we made a difference.

AFTERWORD

In June 2012, HMS *Turbulent* was decommissioned. A few months before the decommissioning, I went to Faslane to say my own goodbyes. *Turbulent* was visiting the port for a short break. I found it quite difficult. Rather than hanging around with the multitude of officers and guests milling around the vessel, I sought out some of the team that I knew who were still on board. I found them reminiscing about old times, and it was strangely cathartic to join them in this. As always, Sweaty Sunday was the focal topic of the conversation, and we all told the story for the hundredth time, describing how we had recovered from a near disaster. Despite the fact we knew we were nearing the end of an era, there was lots of laughter.

The ceremony to celebrate the decommissioning was a great event in Devonport. The summer sun shone, and all the previous captains and many of their crewmen were there for this auspicious occasion. Everyone wanted to give her the send-off she deserved. As I looked around me, I felt touched to see so many shipmates from every generation who had served on Turbs. They'd all kept in touch and still enjoyed sharing experiences even though some of them had happened so many years before. HMS *Turbulent* had created her own community, and we would always belong to an exclusive club, united by the fact that we had fought our submarine well.

I couldn't help but think back to the last day I spent in command of Turbs on 14 December 2011. That day evoked such a strong mixture of pride, happiness, and real sadness, but no regret. I had spent six months preparing my successor to take over from me and did not need to hang around for a prolonged handover. I left the boat, smiling for the TV cameras, and joined my family. My joy at that long-awaited reunion easily outweighed the sadness about what I was leaving behind. Holding my wife and kids, whom I had only seen for 10 days out of 286, was a very emotional moment. It was easy enough for us to slip away together because everyone else was distracted by their own reunions.

The new captain joined *Turbulent* the following day, and the team began the intense process of leadership change once again. For me though, the first few days at home were very strange. While I basked in every moment with the family, it was hard to get used to having no professional purpose. It was odd not to be constantly asked for my view or decision. I no longer needed to constantly run through the what-if process in my mind, planning ahead, working through challenges, and dealing with bureaucracy. Even the phone didn't ring—I had passed it on to the new captain. It hit me then that I had just been at the zenith of my Royal Navy career; nothing was ever going to better what I had just done. There would be some tough choices ahead.

I had had a very successful *drive* (the term for Royal Navy command), and even before we arrived alongside, I already knew that I had been selected to become commanding officer (or teacher as it is known) of the submarine command course Perisher. The post would be quite a challenge and a real opportunity, and it was an absolute honour. The more I thought about it, the more enthusiastic I became about what I could achieve. Now the rest of the fleet would be able to lever off what my team and I had learned over three years and on that last lengthy deployment. I would play a vital role in enabling others to achieve success, and along the way, I would inevitably see many of my crew again scattered across the submarine community. I had offered everyone my mentorship and was determined to see this through even though I was no longer their captain. It was my duty to help those who had been so selfless to the submarine; they deserved it.

First though, I had big decisions to make—was I going to stay in the Royal Navy? That question had been on my mind from the moment I stepped off HMS *Turbulent*. I knew then I would never be able to replicate the true pleasure that I had while in command despite the forthcoming job and potential promotion. I wanted to leave on a high, having given back everything I knew, owing the submarine service everything but nothing. I now knew I needed to leave sooner rather than later.

Once I had made up my mind, I planned my exit meticulously. It would be a year before I left, and I wanted to play fair and do the right thing. I wanted everyone to learn from my experiences, so I offered my services to talk to anyone about Sweaty Sunday and the challenge. I didn't mean to restrict it to just those in the submarine service either. I wanted others to hear and benefit from the story and immediately extended this offer far and wide. The first to take me up on the offer were teams preparing the 2012 Olympic Games. Virgin Active, BP, Shell, Debenhams, and a number of schools and smaller groups followed. I talked about how amazing my team was on that fateful day, and invariably, every time I got to the part about finding Ben in the wardroom in a terrible state, I almost always choked with the emotion of it all. I was glad to tell the story over and over again though because I could relive my pride at how much the team had achieved.

My intention was to present a new perspective to leadership during these talks. I have read many books on leaders, leadership, warfare, and strategy, and despite the analysis, I am convinced that actually most leaders are far too concerned about perception rather than execution. True leadership is about serving your crew, and the prize (if you really need one) is legacy. You should want to be remembered for having done the right thing and for serving your crew.

This book was part of that process. It is about offering others the opportunity to learn from the experience recounted here.

Before I began teaching Perisher, I took over as ST1 (sea trainer 1), leading a smaller team of experts, providing training to all attack submarines in the fleet. During this time, I was selected by the Royal Navy to do the Windsor Leadership Programme, which is the first part of the strategic leadership journey. It was an incredible experience. I learned lessons from so many other great leaders in a range of different sectors and industries. I was pleased to see that nearly all of them were selfless in their approach. It made me realise that my decision to leave the Royal Navy was right. Indeed, it was, in fact, an enabler. Taking my leadership message to the wider world was the only way to give back to everyone what I knew.

I started as commanding officer of the submarine command course in January 2012. My first course began in Nelson's cabin on

HMS *Victory*. I chose the venue on the grounds of 'Why not, he is the godfather of naval leadership'. While I was alone in the cabin, waiting for the trainees to arrive, I reflected on the great leadership journey I had been on and the fact I was in the closing phase. This was my last chance to share all I knew with the next generation of seafarers. Not for the first time, I felt the weight of responsibility.

I had planned my course meticulously. I didn't intend to teach Perisher as I had been taught. There was nothing wrong with what had gone before—quite the opposite, in fact. It was just with the knowledge I now had, I saw the opportunity to make it more relevant to our times. I wanted to introduce twenty-first century techniques to the course, particularly focusing on teaching skills for leading out of context. I used techniques honed by other experts such as the Royal Marines and the Scottish Police (which I had learned while undertaking the silver commanders' course) to make sure that my trainees would be exposed to a wider range of leadership techniques than just those promoted by the submarine service. I thought a lot about the way I wanted to present my message; I didn't want to tell trainees *how* to lead, rather *the moment* to lead.

There was something else I needed to do too, and I did it almost immediately once all the trainees had arrived. After welcoming them and briefly describing the challenge that lay ahead and my philosophy, I told them I was leaving the Royal Navy. I wanted them to know I was taking this course *only* for them, not for my own career progression. My candid admission set an amazing tone for the course. Everyone got it straight away. I was there for them, and this was purely and simply about their success. The atmosphere in my group was electric.

At the end of the six-month course, I passed most of the student captains and increased the pass rate. I did fail a few too—some who seemed incapable of controlling their emotions and a handful who lacked the necessary decision-making abilities. I assured all the people who didn't pass that, while they would not command a submarine, I was always ready and willing to be their mentor if they wanted help and advice.

At the end of my first command course as teacher, I informed the Royal Navy I was going to leave. Naturally, they were a little surprised, taken aback and unhappy about my decision, but I explained that I wanted to spread my leadership narrative to a far broader audience. I would be unable to fully tell my story if I were still attached to the Royal Navy. (Ironically, because of the nature of the operations I undertook, I still can't paint a full picture.) After I told them more about what I wanted to do, the Royal Navy was supportive of my decision and has remained so.

I left the Royal Navy after I had finished taking my second submarine command course. As ever, I didn't want any fuss. I slipped away quietly, marking the occasion with a quiet dinner with those that had helped me on my leadership journey. My first captain was there, as was Gareth, my final XO. Sadly, two other people who had a great impact on my career couldn't make it. However, John Richardson (now a four-star admiral) and Mike Bernacchi left me touching and inspiring messages. Managing to leave as quietly as I had joined was to me a great finale to a long career and one where I knew I had always done the right thing for my team.

Not long ago, I returned to the Royal Naval College in Dartmouth to attend my class reunion. It was twenty-five years since I had joined the navy, and going back into that environment was surreal experience, particularly being alongside the people I joined up with. In some ways, it felt like I had never been away. In others, it felt like I had never been part of this life at all. One of my old friends who was also there quipped, 'Those that were interesting then are still interesting now, and those who were dull, still are!'

His comment made me laugh. You really can't change who you are. Once again though, I was reflecting about my crew. This was not unusual. I often found myself thinking about our journey together. I guess, however good life is, deep down, there would always be an HMS *Turbulent*–sized piece missing within me. Even now, I still seize upon any opportunity to reminisce with those I met on other submarines and find that we would talk about the great times we had as a team and all the things we did, almost a self-help group called Turbulent Anonymous! I do always feel good though, knowing I have touched a few lives, and particularly for those who have started their journey in leadership and war-fighting, I set the right example.

I fondly remember all the crew as all being great individual characters (even the challenging ones!), and maybe that was what made our journey so great. Hopefully, I gave everyone the opportunity to explore their real ability, and perhaps that is what contributed to our success.

Returning to the reunion, a young midshipman approached me. He'd been waiting beside the bar and was clearly hoping to gain my attention while I was chatting to others.

'Sir,' he began, stepping forward.

'I've left the navy, you don't need to call me sir. Please call me Ryan,' I interrupted, returning his smile and putting out my hand to shake his.

'You won't remember me, but I visited the simulator when you were teaching Perisher last year. You trained me and one of my fellow midshipmen to conduct a visual attack. Afterwards, you told us both that the whole thing about leadership was serving your team and that submarines were the best place to do that. You also told us that we should never worry about what the issue is; it's about how we deal with it that counts. We did that, and we've passed.'

The rest of the evening didn't matter. I had influenced the next generation just as I had hoped I would do. I couldn't ask for more.

Photo's post first ever dived transit of Bab El Mandeb

The real test of strategy (Uckers!)

Trailing another submarine

The hero of 'Sweaty Sunday' POMA Steve Bolton

Officers team building at Royal Marines Lympstone

The officers in Jordan prior to the air display

APPENDIX

AB—able seaman
ABA—attack breathing apparatus
AME—assistant marine engineers
ARL—all-round look
ASW—anti-submarine warfare
BAM—Bab el-Mandeb
BCST—broadcast
CCIR—critical intelligence requirement
CD—counter-detection
CMSA—Cruise Missile Support Agency
CO—commanding officer
COI—contact of interest
COMSEC—communications security
CTF—commander, task force
C2—command and control
C3—command, control, and communications
DCHQ—damage control headquarters (also the wardroom)
DMEO—deputy marine engineering officer
EPM—emergency propulsion motor
FOST—Flag Officer Sea Training
GE—garbage ejector
GPMGs—general-purpose machine guns
HODs—heads of department
HUMINT—human intelligence
INDEX—independent exercise period
ISR—Intelligence, surveillance, and reconnaissance
JO—junior officers
J2—joint intelligence

LO—logistics officer
LRO—leading radio operator (historic term still used)
ME—marine engineer
MEO—marine engineering officer
NM—nautical miles
O Group—Operations Group
OOW—officer of the watch
OPEX—operational exercise
OST—operational sea training
OSINT—open-source intelligence
OUP—Operation Unified Protector
PD—periscope depth
PDA—pre-deployment assessment
PG—planning guidance
ROE—rules of engagement
RFI—request for intelligence
RS—radio supervisor
SATCOM—satellite communications
SIGINT—signals intelligence
SMCC—submarine command course (also known as Perisher)
SOP—standard operating procedure
TASO—tactics and sonar officer
TCL—traffic checklist
TG—turbo generators
TML—twelve-mile limit
TLAM—Tomahawk land-attack missiles
TSO—tactical systems officer
TST—time-sensitive targeting
UKMCC—United Kingdom maritime component commander
WE—weapon engineer
WEO—weapon engineering officer
WPP—weekly practice programme
WSC—weapon storage compartment
WT mast—radio mast
XO—executive officer (second in command)

Annex: Example of the Seven-Question Operational Planning Tool (Operational Sea Training Prior to Deployment against the fictional enemy GING simulated by NATO forces)

Q1. What are the enemy doing and why?

I have decided that GING (Enemy force simulated by NATO units) is the potential enemy, and therefore, the focus of the 7Q is on them.

Strategic Level

GING defence vision states that they intend to:

- encounter threats to the security or interests of the federation
- meet national economy and policy interests
- conduct peacetime military operations
- employ military force.

It is noted that their leadership has stated previously, 'To make GING strong, significant investment will be made in SM forces and espionage.'

Operational Level

- They will respond to an armed invasion into the territory of GING or its allies.
- They intend to have a strategic nuclear force that is well equipped and mobilised.
- They intend to have forces that are well trained, equipped, and ready for either mobilisation or reaction.
- They will conduct partial or full strategic deployment of a nuclear deterrence force.
- They will conduct GING frontier air and underwater protection.
- The military force shall be used to defend the safety of GING.
- They will defend GING against local enemies simultaneously.

Tactical Level (Constrained to the Area I Will Be Tasked to Operate In)

They will continue to build and trial new equipment. At present, OSINT indicates that GING has built one if not two types of new submarine. They are continuing to design and build new missile systems. There has been no investment in new surface units. They do state that they are to:

- constantly upgrade arms and military hardware
- contribute to defence research and defence education
- maintain strategic deterrent capability
- provide for constant readiness troops augmentation
- improve operational and combat training.

CCIRs/RFIs (Trials)

1. What is the status of new submarine units?
2. Where are the historic areas for sea trials of new units?
3. What are the warnings that these units will sail?
4. Are they escorted?
5. How do they communicate?
6. Are they under a different C2 to operational units?
7. What new missile systems are in build?
8. What was the trial process for the most recent missile systems?
9. Where are these missile systems tested?
10. What is the process for testing the systems?
11. Do they establish areas outside of the WPP?
12. How do they inform other units (civilian/military) of firings?
13. How do they range clear, and has that changed in recent years?
14. What indications can I utilise to observe in the correct position?

CCIRs/RFIs (Operations)

1. What is GING doctrine?
2. How does GING translate doctrine to techniques and tactics?
3. What are the GING tactics?
4. Do these tactics ever vary/develop?
5. What is the national C2?
6. What is the local C2?
7. Can I access information within C2?

8. What is the individual unit training process to make units operational?

9. What is the collective training process?

10. What is the individual (person) training process? (Know my potential enemy.)

11. Who is in command of every unit I may encounter? (What is GING experience?)

12. What is their experience in comparison to mine and my teams'?

13. How are exercises scheduled (outside of WPP)?

14. How do GING forces act on detection of an intruder? (Is this changing?)

15. How do GING forces posture?

16. What will be the indication of the mass movement of GING forces?

17. What will be the indication of deployment of individual GING units?

18. Is there an indicator of transition to war?

19. What are the periodicity, indicators, and length of deployment for strategic forces?

20. Is GING strategic force still done alongside?

21. What was the last reaction to CD?

Q2. What have I been told to do and why?

- To conduct tasking in accordance with strategic intelligence gathering (the collection analysis, fusion, and distribution of strategic defence intelligence).

- Within the strategic arena of intelligence gathering on GING, I anticipate that there are in principle three customers who have requirements. The balance will need to be made between these customers.

PG (Off Board)

1. It is important that discussion has been had between the customers.

2. There must be a central point of contact for these customers.

3. There must be an agreed collection priorities list.
4. What degree of risk will be tolerated by external authorities when in comparison to the priority of collection?
5. Which forms of intelligence are unique products gathered by me?

PG (On Board)

1. We must have a structured plan for pre-deployment training.
2. We must have a structured plan for pre-deployment exercising.
3. We must ensure that all equipment is calibrated.
4. We must integrate personnel who have been changed over post-training.
5. We must have a structured plan to enter areas.
6. This plan must involve increasing the time at PD.
7. This plan must allow us to become at one with the environment we will operate.
8. The plan must allow both teams to become confident operating with traffic in the region.
9. My teams must learn to operate within the limits that I provide them.
10. My teams must have integrated the additional riders on board.
11. We must have a withdrawal plan.
12. We must have escape routes. What is the latest guidance on using them?

Q3. What effect do I want to have on the enemy?
I want to ensure that the enemy act as they would without me being there. I want to ensure that, when required, I can exercise offensive operations against GING forces when CTF requires.

Q4. Where can I best accomplish each action?
This will be dependent on the answers provided to my CCIRs/RFIs. I anticipate that primary areas will be the E/F/G with secondary A/B areas.

1. Is it possible to correlate all previous events by latitude and longitude on to an SCXA chart in order to show:

a. where the events were
b. whether they were deliberate or not
c. whether the unit was CD'd (Where have previous CDs been?)
d. the form of intel gathered.

2. What is the guidance with respect to free-floating oceanographic objects and the approach to the permanent area?
3. Any update to the 'other' units: sonar grams, radar fits, op pattern, etc.

Q5. What resource do I need to accomplish each action?

Planning Guidance

N1 (Personnel)
- All personnel must be trained.
- All personnel must have conducted pre-deployment preparations.
- All personnel must inform families of the constraints of our patrol.
- All outside agencies must be informed of communications constraints.
- They must be informed that we cannot land personnel.
- We must have a medical officer on board.
- We must have sufficient medical stores on board.
- All reports must have been landed prior to departure.
- Reports that arise during patrol and landing dates must be agreed with outside agencies.
- We must identify learning and teaching opportunities.

N2 (Intelligence)
- We must have sufficient J2 support.
- The product we receive must match our expectations.
- We must conduct significant analysis prior to arriving in Joint Operations Area.

- We must have sufficient heads-up of potential events.
- I must have continual updating of political trends to understand strategic trends.
- I must have understanding of out-of-the-ordinary C2 decisions.
- All intelligence personnel must be fully integrated.

N3 (Short-Term Operations)

- I need commander's guidance/political authorisation.
- I need commander's constraints on my operations.
- I need to understand the risk my commander is willing to take.

N4 (Logistics)

- Stores for ninety days.
- Sufficient stores to maintain personnel morale.
- CAL in date and on board.
- Patrol stores.
- Specialist stores.
- Maintenance requirements and guidance for preps need to be planned.
- What is the guidance with regard to the use of SCOGs in the event of GMP failure?

N5 (Long-Term Operations)—See N3

N6 (Communications)

- Correct BCST
- BCST support
- Correct news and sport (morale)
- Accurate vetting, minimising repetition and length of information
- Monitoring of GING BCST (SIGINT)
- Monitoring of GING tactical communications (COMINT)

N7 (Doctrine and tactics)—See Question 1

N9 (Legal)
- What is the legal framework I am going to operate in?
- What is the potential ROE?
- Will the ROE change?

Q6. When and where do the actions take place in relation to each other?

My plan must be feasible and acceptable to both the CTF and me and must be exclusive. It must be based on others' successes and must avoid others' failures. Understanding where these actions will take place will not occur until the reception of all intelligence briefings. I need to understand my enemy first before I can determine where I need to position.

Q7. What control measures do I need to impose?

- Main briefings from NATO (provides me with relevant information)
- PDA training plan (allows me to digest info and exercise team)
- Briefing to CTF when ready to execute mission (demonstrates to CTF that I am ready to conduct mission)
- Ship's company briefing (allows team to understand what we are doing)
- Family briefing (allows families to understand the constraints in which we are operating in this time of continual access)
- At sea, my patrol orders must be understood and adhered to
- At sea, O group/command brief process must be robust enough to ensure we are having effect
- Seventy-two-hour check on what we have and what we must achieve
- Weekly summary of what we've achieved achie
- Tactical recognition of CD
- Tactical recognition of tempo shifts
- Tactical recognition of team limitations
- Tactical recognition of my limitations (command rider)

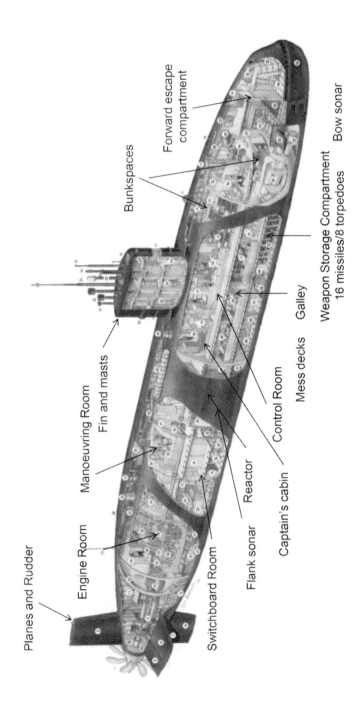

Forward escape compartment

Bow sonar

Bunkspaces

Weapon Storage Compartment
16 missiles/8 torpedoes

Fin and masts

Manoeuvring Room

Galley

Engine Room

Control Room

Mess decks

Planes and Rudder

Reactor

Captain's cabin

Switchboard Room

Flank sonar

INDEX

Lightning Source UK Ltd.
Milton Keynes UK
UKOW02f0622011216
288875UK00003B/43/P